Myths of the Civil War

The Fact, Fiction, and Science behind the Civil War's Most-Told Stories

Scott Hippensteel

STACKPOLE
BOOKS
Guilford, Connecticut

STACKPOLE BOOKS

An imprint of Globe Pequot, the trade division of
The Rowman & Littlefield Publishing Group, Inc.
4501 Forbes Blvd., Ste. 200
Lanham, MD 20706
www.rowman.com

Distributed by NATIONAL BOOK NETWORK

British Library Cataloguing in Publication Information available

Library of Congress Cataloging-in-Publication Data

Names: Hippensteel, Scott, 1969– author.
Title: Myths of the Civil War : the fact, fiction, and science behind the Civil War's
    most-told stories / Scott Hippensteel.
Description: Guilford, Connecticut : Stackpole Books, [2021] | Includes bibliographical references
    and index. | Summary: "In this genre-bending work of history, Scott Hippensteel reexamines
    many long-cherished myths of Civil War history—and ultimately shatters them, based on physics
    and mathematics"— Provided by publisher.
Identifiers: LCCN 2021013639 (print) | LCCN 2021013640 (ebook) | ISBN 9780811739979
    (cloth) | ISBN 9780811769822 (epub)
Subjects: LCSH: United States—History—Civil War, 1861–1865—Historiography. | United
    States—Armed Forces—Firearms—History—19th century. | United States—History—Civil
    War, 1861–1865—Equipment and supplies. | Ballistics—United States—Case studies. | United
    States—History—Civil War, 1861–1865—Miscellanea. | United States—History—Errors,
    inventions, etc.
Classification: LCC E468.5 .H57 2021 (print) | LCC E468.5 (ebook) | DDC
    973.7072—dc23
LC record available at https://lccn.loc.gov/2021013639
LC ebook record available at https://lccn.loc.gov/2021013640

♾™ The paper used in this publication meets the minimum requirements of American National
Standard for Information Sciences to Permanence of Paper for Printed Library Materials, ANSI/
NISO Z39.48-1992.

For Tenley

Contents

1

An Overview of the Tall Tales

Joshua Lawrence Chamberlain found himself, on July 2, 1863, in command of four hundred men from Maine, tasked with securing the extreme-left flank of the federal fishhook line at Gettysburg. Facing him across the ravine between the Round Tops were around one thousand Alabamians, commanded by a twenty-nine-year-old colonel named William Oates.

The Rebels attacked the 20th Maine with such ferocity that after the fight, men from both sides described the bullets as flying through the trees with the intensity of hail in a great storm. The Rebels used their new rifle muskets, which had revolutionized warfare, to decimate the federal command structure on Little Round Top, with several senior officers falling to sniper shots from more than a half mile away.

The fight between Chamberlain's and Oates's men was in much closer quarters than this, of course, with the Rebel charges pushing through the boulders and trees with such ferocity that many of Chamberlain's newer, panic-stricken soldiers began to load their rifles, time after time, without ever discharging a round. This, combined with a need to match the leaden precipitation produced by the boys from Alabama, led to a rapid exhaustion of their ammunition supply. Chamberlain, knowing retreat was not an option, ordered his men to fix bayonets and charge into the oncoming Southerners. This they did, raging down the rock-strewn hillslope, leaving a swath of dead behind so dense that after the fighting ended a person could walk across the field without ever touching the ground.

That combat is precisely what this book is about—this description of Chamberlain's 20th Maine on Little Round Top, made so famous by Michael Shaara's book *The Killer Angels* and Ted Turner's movie *Gettysburg*.[1] Except not at all.

This book is about the dreadful writing, awful clichés, and terrible tropes that found their way into the first three paragraphs of this book and, on an infinitely larger scale, onto the pages of our Civil War books and magazines. This tome tackles all of the tropes from Civil War literature—from bullets falling like hail to rifle muskets revolutionizing warfare to panicked soldiers loading their rifles more than twenty times without firing—and looks at them from a scientific perspective. For example, appraise those first three paragraphs again: Did the men from Maine and Alabama really have enough slow-reloading rifles to produce an incoming fire of minié bullets that would approach the intensity of hail strikes during a severe storm? Many a history book contains this colorful analogy, but could it have actually happened? Were enough men killed in this fight to actually produce a carpet of death across this sector of Little Round Top? And what about the officers killed on the crest of the hill from a thousand or more yards away—could that really have happened? History books and magazines tell us yes, but science is doubtful.

We can test all of these historical tropes using a combination of several different branches of science and some critical reasoning:

- *Meteorology.* Around 1,200 men were present at the start of the Chamberlain-Oates fight. Firing at three rounds a minute would put sixty bullets in the air per second. Seems fairly intense, until you consider these bullets were falling across an area of around two acres (the space the three regiments were covering). So that is thirty bullet strikes per second *per acre*—hardly lead precipitation.

- *Spatial analysis.* Approximately four hundred casualties were suffered during the fight, with most of these being wounded or captured. Even *if* all of these men had died on the battleground, there would only be around two hundred dead men per acre. Even *if* all of these men had perished directly in front of Chamberlain's line, there would still be significant distances between the bodies—a very shabby "carpet of death."

- *Physics.* Given the ballistics of a Civil War–era rifle musket, for a skilled sniper to target and kill a man standing on Little Round Top from one thousand yards away, he would have to estimate the range to his victim to within a dozen yards and then aim another dozen feet above his intended victim. Also, there could be no wind. Simply put, that didn't happen—or at least it did not happen in the way our history books report.

So, in the end we are left with three opening paragraphs that would not stand out in a typical book about the Civil War but that contain at least five references to events that either are highly exaggerated or couldn't possibly have occurred. This book explains why we can be certain, from a scientific perspective, that this is true.

Each chapter of this book selects a different historical exaggeration or analogy and then seeks to find reality by employing scientific testing and evaluation. How was General John Sedgwick actually killed at Spotsylvania? How densely were the corpses spread across the fields after the Battle of Franklin? Why were so many of the guns that were salvaged after the Battle of Gettysburg loaded more than a half-dozen times? And how truly effective were these "game-changing" rifle muskets? Critical reasoning provides answers that our history books have not.

Here is what this book will *not* do: debate history. Many historical controversies cannot be tested, and scientific analysis has little to contribute to the discussion. For example, did Joshua Chamberlain actually give the command to charge at Little Round Top or merely order his soldiers to fix bayonets? Did he actually lead the charge? Were the Alabamians already in full retreat when the charge began? Crompton Burton wrote an entire chapter in *Memory and Myth* investigating this question,[2] and historians on both sides of the argument used first-person accounts for evidence, not science or critical reasoning. *The Killer Angels* and *Gettysburg* tell one story, some historians tell another, and science—and this book—choose not to comment.

William Oates would have agreed with much of what is in this book. He wrote in his memoirs that "No two men can participate in a great battle and see it just alike."[3] Historians can argue endlessly about which of two eyewitnesses to an event was probably more correct in description or interpretation; science, however, can be used to contribute something equally as important and much more definitive: it can tell you what *didn't* happen. That is what this book focuses on: What tales have history books passed down over the years that simply did not happen or that happened in a completely different manner than the way they have been described?

My battle herein is not with the soldiers of the Civil War or their colorful and frightening descriptions of experiences that were captured in their letters home or memorial speeches. Instead, I quibble with historians and interpreters who take these descriptions and turn them into tropes, to be repeated over and over, passed down through generations of books and articles for lay readers, all with no sense of skepticism.

To be especially clear here, no disrespect is intended to the men who first wrote these apocryphal tales. I have never experienced combat and have, as a result, never attempted to describe the experience or the aftermath of battle to others. At the same time, however, I am trained as a natural scientist, and the incredulousness of some historical writing (and lack of any form of critical reasoning) is bothersome.

Many soldiers who participated in the Civil War had a similar historical skepticism. As an example, we can return again to the writings of Colonel Oates, who demonstrated this wariness of the inauthenticity of some after-battle accounts: "All of us, on both sides, who were in such hot places as these were made to exaggerate it in favor of our respective sides, and do it honestly in most cases." Another Southerner echoed these same sentiments: "Some of these accounts are simply silly. Some are false in statement. Some are false in inference. All, in some respects, are untrue."[4]

The target of this book, then, is to use scientific reasoning to identify the silly and the false included in the collective recollections and writings of the soldiers of the era—and, on a grander scale, to identify these tropes in the history books that carry these fallacious fables forth to a new, unskeptical audience every time they are published. Each chapter of the book takes an oft-repeated historical claim—our "trope"—and analyzes it using a three-part methodology:

1. *Introduction and historical claim.* Here the specific historical claim is defined and described in detail. Also included in this section of research is an outline of who has made this claim in the past

and where it has been published, including multiple documented examples of the trope in literature. History books tell us repeatedly, for example, that a skilled Civil War sharpshooter could consistently target and kill a man at more than five hundred yards. The purpose of this subsection of the chapter is to provide examples of this claim and demonstrate how widespread and commonplace this understanding has become.

2. *The science.* In this subsection, the background scientific principles are introduced and explained in a nontechnical manner. For the sharpshooter example, this would include a discussion of the ballistics and trajectories of the Civil War guns employed by riflemen on both sides of the conflict.

3. *Analysis and evaluation.* This subsection brings the historical claim and the science together, studying and discussing the potential reality of the antiquated trope and suggesting alternative and more realistic scenarios. Sometimes the results are definitive (sniper claims), and sometimes they are partially true or more difficult to directly delineate. Occasionally a legendary story from the Civil War—thousands of discarded rifle muskets at Gettysburg were loaded dozens of times by panicked soldiers who never fired them—turns out to have been partially correct, with multiple other, more plausible explanations available, but these alternative scenarios appear to have never been considered, let alone published.

This book is organized so that it begins with subjects where science has the potential to offer the most insights and ends with questions where the science and critical reasoning offer tools for analysis but the findings are more subjective: For example, how realistic is modern artwork that depicts Civil War battle scenes? When viewing a photograph of battlefield carnage from the first half of the 1860s, what is the probability that the image is either fraudulent or manipulated in some significant manner?

Finally, a note about the perspective with which this manuscript was written: This text was produced by a scientist who is especially interested in how science can be used to interpret history. I am a geology professor who prefers to teach historical geology (and paleontology) over physical geology (minerals, rocks, and plate tectonics); anywhere science and history (or ancient history) come together, an interesting story can be found. Also, I grew up near Gettysburg, Pennsylvania, so I've always been exposed to historically important rocks. That being said, the most interesting "fieldwork" of my career involved working on the Confederate submarine *H. L. Hunley*, where I used sediments and microfossils to help reveal the geoarchaelogical history of the boat and to provide insights into the fate of the crew. This book follows that path—science as a tool for interpreting history—not a history of science per se but a book about how scientific principles can be used to reinterpret historical accounts. I personally don't think Robert E. Lee was a particularly good tactician or strategist (see note above about growing up near Gettysburg), but that opinion won't be found in these pages, because I cannot use science to support my arguments. I will leave the history debates to the historians. In short, if a specious or spurious historical claim resists being studied through a natural science lens, it will not be discussed here. Nevertheless, the literature to emerge from the war—the letters, diaries, and official reports—and the books and articles that continue to be published today are full of tropes and exaggerated analogies that can be tested and scientifically evaluated, providing captivating insights into what did happen—and, more often, did not happen—on Civil War battlefields.

2

Sedgwick Was Correct:
The Myth of the Civil War Sniper

INTRODUCTION

GROUNDHOGS ARE A REAL PROBLEM IN CUMBERLAND COUNTY, PENN-sylvania. The burrows and holes created by these varmints are equally capable of breaking a tractor axle or cow leg. When I was a young man, my grandfather would take me hunting for these pests on the rolling limestone fields surrounding his house and barn near Shippensburg, Pennsylvania.[1] He had two guns for hunting: he carried a high-power .222 Remington and let me borrow his more diminutive .22 rimfire, a gun better suited to squirrel hunting. This made all the sense in the world; he was a better offhand shot at range. (For the record, I was better at shooting moving targets, especially in the air; unfortunately, groundhogs rarely took flight.)

The ballistics of our two guns made the selection of targets across the clover and alfalfa fields simple. The low velocity of my .22 meant I would only shoot at whistle-pigs that were closer than seventy-five or a hundred yards. Any target at a greater range was strictly my grandfa-ther's shot, with his high-velocity, flatter-trajectory rifle. It was pointless for me to fire at a groundhog that was two or three hundred yards away with the little .22; I'd need to aim several feet above the hog and hope it didn't move in the moments after I pulled the trigger. With the .222, by contrast, my grandfather only needed to compensate by a few inches to hit a groundhog three football fields away. I watched him kill groundhogs at almost four hundred yards; when I was hunting alone with the .22, if

I spotted a groundhog at that range, I'd have to find a path of approach using the scattered forests and rolling landscape to quarter the distance. Otherwise, I'd only be wasting a five-cent round.

These lessons learned on the farm fields of central Pennsylvania gave me an appreciation for the challenges facing Civil War sharpshooters on the nearby Gettysburg battlefield, especially with respect to ballistic advantages available to modern snipers. The .22 rifle I carried is rather remarkably similar, in terms of bullet shape, accuracy, and muzzle velocity, to a Springfield or British Enfield rifle musket. I used to hunt with Remington hollow-point bullets—the most common round available for a .22. These shells propelled a twenty-nine-grain bullet at 1,095 feet per second. When sighted at fifty yards, the bullet would drop nearly six feet before it hit a target two hundred yards away. Civil War rifle muskets had a muzzle velocity similar to, or slightly lower than, the tiny rimfire. The musket's much more massive bullet would better carry its energy downrange, but the similarity in muzzle velocities and trajectories demonstrates the difficulty in hitting any target with either weapon at a distance beyond two hundred yards.

A modern military or police sniper carries a weapon that is very similar, in terms of muzzle velocity and trajectory, to my grandfather's .222. He fired a streamlined fifty-five-grain soft-point bullet that traveled at 3,095 feet per second. The most common sniper rifle in the modern US military arsenal uses .308 Winchester ammunition, which has a muzzle velocity a little under three thousand feet per second. When sighted to hit a target at one hundred yards, the shooter can expect a bullet drop of less than four inches at two hundred yards, and even at three hundred yards the expected holdover of the target would only be about a foot. In short, the higher the velocity of the bullet, the easier it is to hit a target at longer ranges; varmint hunters and snipers alike choose weapons that fire at velocities exceeding 2,800 feet per second—and preferably above three thousand feet per second.

The problem surrounding so many accounts of long-range shooting during the Civil War is that they describe the sniping as if the marksman were using modern equipment instead of a rifle with the muzzle velocity of a .22-caliber rimfire rifle. Just as it is pointless to attempt to kill a single groundhog at more than two hundred yards with a .22, it was hopeless for a Civil War sharpshooter to aim at and attempt to kill a single specific officer at more than a few hundred yards; the exterior ballistics and accuracy of the available weapons made this task nearly impossible, regardless of the shooting talent of the soldier.

Now to stretch the Civil War/groundhog analogy beyond its useful limits: If you encountered several groundhogs gathered closely together at three hundred yards, you might take an elevated shot, hoping your plunging little bullet might strike one of the critters by chance. This was the vastly probable fate of the high-ranking Civil War officers who were cut down by directed sniper fire during the war; the long-range shot was fired in their *vicinity* but not directly at them individually. It was the misfortune of the victim of the lucky shot that it hit him and not another person nearby. History remembers the propitious shots (General John Sedgwick at Spotsylvania: "They couldn't hit an elephant at this dist—") and not the near misses (the wounded federal surgeon standing next to Abraham Lincoln in Fort Stevens).

This chapter investigates the claim that skilled Civil War snipers were able to fire their rifles accurately enough to kill individually selected targets at ranges over seven hundred yards. Stories of astounding accuracy exist for all major engagements from the war. Some astonishing tales tell of men killed by gunfire at ranges over a mile. My favorite, which I heard from a Gettysburg Battlefield tour guide when I was a child, goes something like this:

> *As the sun was setting at the end of the second day of the battle, two sharpshooters took up position across the Valley of Death from one another. The federal crack shot was hidden among the boulders of Little Round Top, while his foe was in Devil's Den. This sniper-countersniper duel began at several hundred yards, with both men firing and apparently missing. They crept closer, and both fired again, but to no success. For a third time, they approached each other and fired, and, to their surprise, both men again survived. Once again, they stealthily made their way through the boulders to close the range and fired. Perplexed and frustrated, they had both failed again. At this point, both men were bewildered and expressed their disbelief by standing and slowly*

walking in the open toward one another, observing a confused silent truce. It was only when they met that both observed eight bullets, fused nose-to-nose in four pairs, equidistant from where both had started the encounter.

According to this legendary account of shooting—versions of which have been retold in print—these men were so precise with their weapons that each fired four consecutive, perfectly aimed shots at the exact rifle muzzle of the enemy, with exactly the same trajectory, at exactly the same time.[2] Examples of bullets fused nose-to-nose have turned up on the battlefield, although they are testament more to the volume of fire than any degree of expert marksmanship (figure 2.1). While many of the historical descriptions of marksmanship relayed in this chapter are far less ridiculous than this apocryphal tale, they still acquire a note of implausibility after scientific analysis.

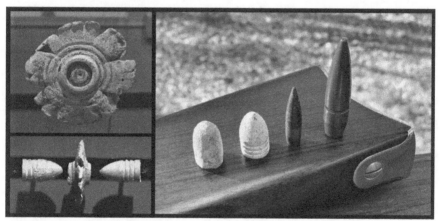

Figure 2.1. Left: Two sets of bullets that collided in midair. The top photograph is of a set of fused bullets on display in the American Civil War Museum (formerly known as the Museum of the Confederacy) in Richmond, Virginia. These bullets were purportedly collected from the Spotsylvania battlefield. The bottom picture shows a set of bullets from Petersburg. Right: On the left are two minié bullets, an Enfield .57 base and a Springfield .58 caliber. In comparison, on the right are a German 7.92-millimeter spitzer bullet from Normandy and an American .50-caliber M2 round. Both calibers were popular for sniper rifles in World War II (7.92 Mauser) and Afghanistan (.50 Browning). These bullets are photographed on the buttstock of a .58 Springfield rifle musket.

THE HISTORICAL CLAIM

On numerous occasions during the war, snipers on both sides individually targeted and killed officers at ranges beyond five hundred yards, and in several cases high-ranking officers were killed by specifically targeted shots at ranges approaching or even exceeding a half mile.

Accounts of officers who were killed at great ranges can be found for battlefields from all theaters of the war, and the frequency of long-range killings appears to have increased as the war progressed. Before the details of these "snipings" can be described and analyzed, a few points of clarity about the role of the sharpshooter during the war should be elucidated.

First, Civil War snipers did not truly exist—or, at least, they weren't called "snipers" by their fellow soldiers. The term had originated around the time of the American Revolution and was used by the British to describe men who were so talented with a rifle that they could bring down snipe, the fast-moving and maneuverable game bird. The term *sniper* did not really find its way across the ocean until well after the American Civil War. In the Union and Confederate ranks, the soldiers responsible for firing at great range were better described as sharpshooters.[3] These men were selected from the regiments or specially recruited based on their talent as marksmen—and specifically their ability to fire reliably and accurately at longer ranges. Union Colonel Hiram Berdan organized the most famous collection of sharpshooters, the 1st and 2nd United States Volunteer Sharpshooter Regiments—the USVSR. Members of this elite group were specially clothed in green uniforms and were required to demonstrate an ability to fire ten consecutive shots at a target two hundred yards away, with the cumulative distance of the shots from the bull's-eye not exceeding fifty inches. In the South, the selection and employment of sharpshooters was more informal and haphazard; normally the best shots in each company were given the most accurate weapons and expected to use them more expeditiously in combat.

Sharpshooters were also not typically used in most major battles in the traditional way we think of modern sniper employment in combat. Instead, they were usually deployed as skirmishers—men who would advance in front of the main battle line and engage the enemy while using any available cover to fire at selected targets during an advance. They were engaged in this manner because they were the best marksmen and were expected to generate more havoc in the enemy ranks than their numbers would suggest when compared with an ordinary infantryman. Nevertheless, the combination of rapid movement and counterfire did nothing to improve the sharpshooters' long-range accuracy. As the war progressed and the value of eliminating the commanding officer from an enemy brigade or regiment was more fully understood, skirmishers began to concentrate their fire at targets that appeared to be of higher value, including officers on horseback and artillery crews.

Perhaps the most famous example of a high-ranking officer having his life suddenly ended by a sharpshooter's bullet was Union major general John Sedgwick. Sedgwick was fifty years old when he was killed at the Battle of Spotsylvania Court House. This is what historian agree were the circumstances of his death: (1) He was directing the placement of his artillery and infantry against the left wing of Lee's line. (2) He was gently scolding his men for taking cover from isolated sharpshooter fire originating from the Confederate line somewhere around one thousand yards distant. (3) A bullet slammed into his head, just below his left eye, resulting in a massive loss of blood and his death soon after.

This is what the historians disagree about with regard to the circumstances of Sedgwick's death:

1. *His last words.* This is a silly argument, but there is a split between those who report the general was complaining to his soldiers, "Why are you dodging like this? They couldn't hit an elephant at this distance," and those who strongly believe that he didn't finish the sentence, being ironically interrupted after the first syllable of the word *distance.*

2. *The general's position when shot.* Nearly all accounts have John Sedgwick walking among his men, but the company officer of the soldier most often credited with taking the kill shot reported that the shooter was firing at a mounted officer.[4]

3. *The range of the shot.* The reported distance for this shot has stretched from five hundred yards to a mile.[5] Nonetheless, most estimates for the range seem to center around eight hundred to one thousand yards.[6]

In summary, then, the most famous case of sniping from the Civil War required a successfully aimed shot at an individual man from around nine hundred yards away. The sniper would have needed to be firing a Whitworth rifle, the story concedes, because an aimed shot with an Enfield or Springfield rifle musket would have been impossible. After-battle accounts from Confederate soldiers make this choice of weapon plausible; there were a few scarce Whitworths scattered among the infantry ranks.

A second famous sniping incident involved another federal major general, John Reynolds (figure 2.2). The range and source of this sharpshooter's bullet is even more controversial than that which brought down Sedgwick. Reynolds was killed on July 1, 1863, during the early fighting on the first day of the Battle of Gettysburg. The general was directing and encouraging the famous Iron Brigade when a projectile struck him in the back of the neck, after which he wavered in the saddle on the back of his horse before falling to the ground, dead. Most traditional accounts of his death attribute the shot to a Rebel sharpshooter armed with either an Enfield or a Whitworth rifle. Benjamin Thorpe of the 55th

Figure 2.2.   Alfred R. Waud's sketch "The Death of Reynolds—Gettysburg" included a supplemental map (not pictured) of the incident that indicates the deadly bullet was fired by one of Archer's men long after his brigade had crossed Willoughby Run. (*Credit:* "The Death of Reynolds—Gettysburg," Library of Congress, LC-DIG-ppmsca-21109, https://www.loc.gov/item/2004660757/.)

North Carolina Regiment claimed that he killed Reynolds at eight hundred yards after firing two ranging shots at 1,100 yards and then nine hundred yards. Other accounts have Reynolds killed at more than four hundred yards by sharpshooters in the McPherson barn or hiding along Willoughby Run.[7] Contrasting accounts of the general's death point to artillery shrapnel, short-range direct fire from Brigadier General James Archer's line, short- and medium-range fire from skirmishers, and even friendly fire.

Renowned sniping and shooting authority John Plaster clearly disagrees with these "nonsharpshooter" hypotheses:

> *That he was the victim of a sharpshooter's bullet is almost universally accepted. . . . Revisionist historians and Civil War buffs attempting to demonstrate their superior knowledge have pecked away at the sharpshooter claim for many years, despite almost all reports at the time attributing the shot to a Rebel sharpshooter. While nearly all these critics lack any familiarity with firearms, and especially with long-range shooting, they're expert enough to insist that this piece of woods or that barn was too distant, the angle of the shot was too sharp, or there were too many trees and so on.[8]*

Of course, generals Sedgwick and Reynolds were not the only high-ranking officers brought down by extreme-range, accurate, individualized, small-arms fire. "Amazing as it may seem," write Pat Farey and Mark Spicer, "deliberately aimed shots at this distance (approximately half a mile)—with a fair share of successful hits—were documented for both Union and Confederate sharpshooters using scoped rifles. With such accurate shooting, and with high-ranking officers still taking to the field in virtually every engagement, it is not surprising that sharpshooters were directly and correctly attributed with the deaths of more than twenty generals, dozens of majors and colonels, and countless lower-ranked officers."[9]

Included in this list of slain officers are Brigadier General Stephen Weed and Lieutenant Charles Hazlett, both cut down on Little Round Top by a Confederate sniper concealed in the massive dark gray boulders of Devil's Den. This remarkable killing involved two consecutive shots, uphill, at more than five hundred yards. "In the fighting for Devil's Den," writes Martin Pelger, "a Confederate sharpshooter killed Brigadier General Stephen H. Weed; Lieutenant Charles E. Hazlett, the commander of a Union artillery battery, ran to Weed's aid and was shot dead by the same man, falling on top of the dead general."[10]

And these weren't the only victims of sharpshooting from the Den. "A hundred yards along the line," Pelger continues, "Union Brigadier General Strong Vincent and Colonel Patrick O'Rourke both fell to sharpshooters' bullets. It was not a good day for Union officers at Gettysburg."[11]

So here we have a detailed account of six federal officers killed at three different sites by snipers who were firing from more than four hundred yards away. There are multiple other accounts of officers being killed while leading infantry counterattacks on horseback or being shot dead at ranges beyond one thousand yards, but the deaths of Sedgwick, Reynolds, Weed, and Hazlett will provide the data for analysis of the plausibility of these killings at range—that these men were selected by a sharpshooter for individualized targeting and brought down by a single, precise, perfectly aimed shot.[12]

THE SCIENCE
Basic Ballistics of Civil War Rifles

The best tool for long-range sniping is a highly accurate rifle that fires a high-velocity, aerodynamic, heavy bullet with a flat trajectory. These were not in existence during the Civil War. Specialty target rifles were certainly accurate, but it wasn't until the development of more advanced, faster-burning, smokeless gunpowder toward the end of the nineteenth century that bullets began to be propelled in excess of two thousand feet per second.

Low muzzle velocity, and the resulting parabolic trajectory of the bullet, was the greatest challenge to precise long-range shooting. The plunging fire at range made exacting estimates of distance critical for a successful hit on a far-off target with a rifle musket; at five hundred yards, the range would need to be successfully estimated to within fifty yards, or else the bullet would strike the ground in front of the target or sail over his head. With an Enfield or Springfield, historian Brent Nosworthy relates, "To fire accurately, it was critical to estimate the range accurately to within ten to twenty yards and then to adjust the backsight accordingly."[13] Of course, for most minié rifles the backsights are only adjustable in one hundred–yard increments, introducing a degree of guessing to the guessing.

The Whitworth rifle was the best sniping weapon available during the Civil War. It provided a muzzle velocity that was around 50 percent greater than the Enfield or Springfield rifled musket's, so it fired with less of a "rainbow" trajectory, and the range of its killing swath was longer.[14] Muzzle-velocity estimates and tests have determined that the Whitworth was capable of propelling a 530-grain hexagonal bullet at between 1,200 and 1,500 feet per second. The weapon also had the advantage of firing a smaller-diameter, elongated .451-caliber bullet, compared to the stubbier .58 Enfield and Springfield bullets. This smaller-radius, streamlined bullet would lose velocity and energy more slowly as it traveled downrange when compared to the minié rifles. Despite these advantages, the Whitworth was slow to load because of its hexagonal bullet and bore, was unpleasant to shoot because of its relatively light weight and heavy recoil, and was somewhat rare on the battlefield: only around 250 guns had been imported from Britain during the war, and only a fraction of these had been fitted with a four-power scope for improved long-range shooting.[15]

When Whitworth rifles were unavailable to Confederate marksmen, sharpshooters typically chose the imported Enfield P1853 rifle musket as a second choice. While this weapon was similar in caliber and ballistics to the more common Springfield rifle musket, the Enfield had demonstrated better performance from six hundred to nine hundred yards.[16] The British rifle fired a .577-caliber, 500- to 530-grain bullet at a velocity between 850 and 1,115 feet per second (with the general consensus falling around nine hundred feet per second). The bullet fired by the Enfield was just slightly more streamlined and aerodynamic than the typical rounds from the Springfield, and this factor—and the superior quality of construction of many of the guns—could account for the better accuracy of the British rifle beyond five hundred yards.

In the North, a completely different type of sharpshooting rifle was preferred, hinting at the primary role of sharpshooters as skirmishers. The breechloading Model 1859 Sharps rifle offered both accuracy and rapid fire—at least compared to rifle muskets. This forty-seven-inch-long weapon incorporated the advantage of having a falling-block action; it did not need to be loaded from the muzzle. This mechanism increased the rate of fire from two or three rounds per minute for a musket to ten aimed shots per minute. It was also as accurate as a Springfield or Enfield, and, important for a skirmisher, it could be quickly reloaded by a soldier who was kneeling or prone. The Sharps fired a 475-grain, .52-caliber round at a velocity of around 1,400 feet per second.

Union sharpshooters used several other types of rifles, including repeaters like the Spencer, Colt, and Henry rifles, but their inferior long-range ballistics emphasized the selection of these weapons for their quantity of fire over quality of fire. The Spencer and Henry were devastating at ranges under 150 yards, but the repeaters were far inferior to the Sharps beyond this range. Nevertheless, as trench warfare became more important in the second half of the war, these weapons became more sought after, especially by skirmishers.

In stark contrast to the Henry or Spencer, some sharpshooters carried heavy-barreled target rifles onto the battlefield. These rifles were usually scoped and were exceptionally accurate, if very slow to load. They were also fragile and weighed between thirty and sixty pounds. Most of these target rifles had a muzzle velocity between eight hundred and 1,400 feet per second, so while they offered an advantage over the Sharps or Springfield with respect to accuracy, they were still limited at range by the trajectory of their bullets.

The most common federal rifles in use during the Civil War were the Model 1855, 1861, and 1863 Springfield rifle muskets, which also found their way into the hands of sharpshooters. These rifles fired a 500-grain minié bullet at between 1,000 and 1,200 feet per second—a shade faster than the Enfield.

Understanding trajectory and accurately estimating the range of the enemy does nothing to improve first-shot strike probability if the shooter does not compensate for the wind. For this estimate, the velocity and direction of the wind must be accounted for along the path the bullet will travel, and this is especially important for extreme-range shots, because the bullet will be in the air for more than a second. Miscalculation of drift can result in the bullet's falling several feet to the left or right of the intended target, despite the range having been accurately assessed. Even for modern, high-velocity rounds, a wind speed of five or ten miles per hour will cause a drift of thirty-two and sixty-four inches for an eight hundred–yard shot; for a Whitworth or Enfield, the drift would be more than double these values.

Finally, an extreme-range shot, in which both range and wind have been accurately determined and compensated for, will be unsuccessful unless the weapon of choice has the precision to hit a human-size target at distance. This complicating factor is not accounting for human error in shooting—only the inherent error introduced by the quality of the rifle. Hiram Berdan's riflemen famously qualified by proving they could consistently hit a five-inch target at two hundred yards.[17] To accomplish this task, the human-induced error (marksmanship) and weapon-induced error (quality of sights, trigger pull, tolerance of rifling and barrel, quality of powder, consistent weight of bullet) could not add up to more than five inches at two hundred yards or 2.5 minutes of angle (MOA).

Two and a half minutes of angle means the shooter should be able to print 2.5-inch groups at one hundred yards, five-inch groups at two hundred yards, and ten-inch groups at four hundred yards. The testing of Civil War rifles, both during the war and more recently, offers some insights into the capabilities of producing minuscule MOA.

In the late 1850s and early 1860s, the British military conducted numerous tests comparing the accuracy of the Enfield and Whitworth rifles. These tests documented that the Whitworth could produce one-MOA groups at one hundred yards but only 7.7-MOA groups at 1,800 yards.[18] At five hundred yards, the Whitworth produced deadly subfive-inch groups. By contrast, the Enfield could not keep the grouping of ten shots under twenty-five inches at this same range.

Testing of Civil War rifles in the 1950s and 1970s by military historian and firearms expert Jac Weller revealed that the Enfield was the most accurate of the common rifle muskets (7.5-inch groups at one hundred yards), and the Springfield (10.25-inch groups) and Austrian Lorenz (thirteen-inch groups) rifles were slightly inferior. When fired over a longer range (four hundred yards) at a larger target (a five-square-foot board), the results were repeated: the Enfield hit the board with thirteen out of fifteen shots, the Springfield hit with seven out of fifteen, and the

Lorenz only hit on three out of fifteen shots. A Whitworth was also fired and hit the target with all fifteen shots but was only able to produce an approximately five-inch group at one hundred yards. Other modern tests compared the two best-sharpshooting rifles from either side of the conflict: the Sharps rifle produced respectable two-inch groups at one hundred yards and twenty-six-inch groups at five hundred yards, while the Whitworth proved superior at eight hundred yards (twelve-inch groups) and one thousand yards (twenty-nine-inch groups).[19]

There are many other, less significant factors that will influence the external ballistics of a bullet as it travels toward the target, but these will have a far smaller effect on the probability of a first-shot hit at long range than a misestimation of the range or wind or the inherent accuracy of the rifle. For example, the parabolic trajectory of the flight path is not symmetrical; the bullet will slow down en route to the target because of aerodynamic drag and strike from a slightly higher angle than it traverses during the first half of the flight path. Bullets from all the weapons discussed so far are also poorly designed with respect to drag coefficient when compared to modern sharp-point, boat-tail rounds (figure 2.1, above). The flat or hollow base of a Whitworth or minié bullet generates a considerable amount of turbulence in its wake, diminishing both the velocity and the stability of the round in flight.

Springfield and Enfield rifles fire at a velocity that never exceeds the speed of sound, so the gunshot would be heard at the same time—or just before—the bullet hits. The Whitworth bullet, by contrast, is traveling faster than the speed of sound when it leaves the barrel (approximately 1,500 feet per second versus 1,126 feet per second for the speed of sound at sea level), so it will strike before the report is heard (but not before the puff of white gun smoke from the shooter can be spotted). For very long-range shots, the Whitworth bullet will be slowed by drag to the point of the sound barrier, and its flight path may become more inconsistent after it becomes subsonic.

For extreme-range shots, still other factors may influence flight performance, such as the Coriolis effect, air pressure, temperature and relative humidity, and change in elevation. Modification of aim for these factors—using iron sights or nonadjustable scopes—is pointless, as the degree of change introduced by these variables is dwarfed by the inherent error introduced by the aiming device (that is, compensating for the rotation of the planet when using a three-power scope is just plain silly).

ANALYSIS AND EVALUATION

Three famous sniping incidents drawn from the historical literature will be analyzed and discussed with respect to strike probability, and possible alternative scenarios for the killings will be evaluated. It should be restated that for each of these famous shots the marksman was purported to be a solitary, highly skilled rifleman who identified and targeted a lone individual victim—a specific Union officer. These shots will be investigated and discussed in the order in which they were introduced—in order of the notoriety of the killing.

The most famous long-range sniper shot from the Civil War was said to have brought down Major General John Sedgwick at Spotsylvania Court House. The distance of this shot has been debated as being between eight hundred yards and a mile, but the weapon of choice is universally said to have been a Whitworth.[20] To re-create the ballistics and trajectory for this shot, the most favorable variables for success will be used for the simulation (i.e., the shot will be assessed using the physical and environmental conditions most favorable for sharpshooting success) (figure 2.3). The parameters chosen for data analysis of this shot fall consistently on the side of the shooter; any modification of the data (e.g., lowering the muzzle velocity of the Whitworth from a maximum estimation of 1,500 feet per second to one closer to the historical consensus—1,200–1,400 feet per second) would increase the difficulty of the shot.

To kill Sedgwick, a sniper would need to fire the 530-grain Whitworth bullet almost a half mile and compensate with a holdover of 166 inches to account for bullet drop. To successfully hit Sedgwick in the skull from eight hundred yards, the sniper would need to aim almost fourteen feet over the general's head, and the officer would need to stand perfectly still—and remain so—for two full seconds.

To add a bit of perspective, imagine that at the instant the sniper fired at Sedgwick a fellow soldier dropped a bullet from shoulder height. Both bullets are falling toward the ground with the same velocity. The dropped

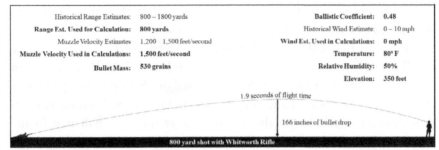

Historical Range Estimates:	800 – 1800 yards		Ballistic Coefficient:	0.48
Range Est. Used for Calculation:	800 yards		Historical Wind Estimate:	0 – 10 mph
Muzzle Velocity Estimates	1,200 1,500 feet/second		Wind Est. Used in Calculations:	0 mph
Muzzle Velocity Used in Calculations:	1,500 feet/second		Temperature:	80° F
Bullet Mass:	530 grains		Relative Humidity:	50%
			Elevation:	350 feet

1.9 seconds of flight time

166 inches of bullet drop

800 yard shot with Whitworth Rifle

Note: If range is increased to 1,000 yards bullet drop rises to 280 inches and flight time is almost 2.5 seconds

Figure 2.3.   Firing parameters and trajectory of the claimed shot that killed John Sedgwick at Spotsylvania.

bullet would strike the ground before the fired bullet had progressed even halfway toward the general. Thus the requirement for a holdover of more

Figure 2.4.   Alfred R. Waud's sketch "Spot Where Genl. Sedgwick Was Killed." Note the trees in the background and the orientation of the cannon, indicating the likely location of the Confederate line. Would it have been possible to see more than a few hundred yards across such terrain? (*Credit:* Ca. May 9, 1864, Library of Congress, LC-DIG-ppmsca-21408, https://www.loc.gov/item/2004660899/.)

than a dozen feet and the prerequisite that Sedgwick remain stationary during the two seconds of flight time (figure 2.4).

The shot that killed John Reynolds at Gettysburg, if fired from the McPherson barn or from along Willoughby Run, might have been even more ambitious than the shot that killed Sedgwick. While Sedgwick was standing among his staff and soldiers, Reynolds was on horseback. Even though the range between shooter and target was only half that in the Sedgwick killing, the sniping of Reynolds would have required hitting a moving target—a mounted officer in the midst of directing and position-ing his infantry.

The consensus among historians is that Reynolds was struck in the neck by a bullet from an Enfield or Springfield rifle musket. The slower velocity of these weapons, and the more parabolic trajectory of the bul-let, makes this an even more challenging shot when compared with the Whitworth volley that purportedly killed Sedgwick.

In some accounts, the precision of the shot that killed John Reynolds is described in such a manner as to be impossible for even a modern-day sniper. Martin Pelger suggests that the hit in the neck was a "typical shot indicating perhaps a slight misjudgment of range on the part of the shooter."[21] John Plaster concurs, adding, "His killing wound, a single shot to the neck, fits the modus operandi of a sharpshooter attempting a head shot or employing a bit too much elevation for a center-mass shot."[22] Analysis of this long-range shot demonstrates the fancifulness of these claims, providing the shooter with an unimaginably grand skill in deter-mining range, calculating holdover, and predicting the future movement of others.

To re-create the ballistics and trajectory for this Enfield- or Springfield-fired shot, the environmental conditions for July 1, 1863, will be used for the northwestern portion of the Gettysburg Battlefield. The range will be set at four hundred yards to test the historical accounts, and, as with the Sedgwick scenario, wind speed will be eliminated from the equation, and all parameters will favor the shooter.

The slow muzzle velocity of the .577 Enfield bullet meant that the Confederate sharpshooter would need to aim 100.6 inches—or more than eight feet—over the general's head. Reconsider the claims that the shooter was attempting a head shot with a "slight misjudgment of range": Under these circumstances, the shooter estimated the holdover at ninety-four inches instead of the correct value of just over one hundred inches? Believing that the Civil War sharpshooter was aiming at Reynolds's head and misjudged the holdover by a mere 5 percent, resulting in a fatal neck shot, also requires belief that either (1) the shooter had a laser rangefinder or (2) the shooter was firing a .308 Winchester rifle. Neither possibility seems particularly likely in 1863.

General Reynolds would also need to have remained stationary for nearly a second and a half as the bullet traversed the quarter mile (figure 2.5). The slow minié bullet would strike Reynolds's neck at around 775 feet per second, having lost more than one hundred feet per second during its journey from the barrel. At this velocity, the bullet is still deadly but falling at an even greater angle than it had risen during the first half of the flight path.

The final long-range, officer-killing scenario to be discussed took place a day after Reynolds was killed, and, if the historical accounts are correct, this shooting may have been the most impressive of the war. A Confederate sharpshooter positioned in Devil's Den shot Brigadier General Stephen Weed, who was standing on Little Round Top around 550 yards away. When Lieutenant Charles Hazlett rushed to the stricken general's side, the same sharpshooter shot and killed him as well. That would be two consecutive shots, uphill, at more than five hundred yards,

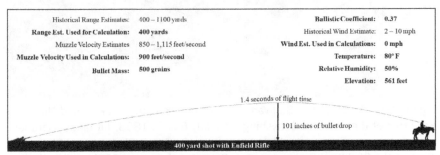

Historical Range Estimates:	400 – 1100 yards		Ballistic Coefficient:	0.37
Range Est. Used for Calculation:	400 yards		Historical Wind Estimate:	2 – 10 mph
Muzzle Velocity Estimates	850 – 1,115 feet/second		Wind Est. Used in Calculations:	0 mph
Muzzle Velocity Used in Calculations:	900 feet/second		Temperature:	80° F
Bullet Mass:	500 grains		Relative Humidity:	50%
			Elevation:	561 feet

1.4 seconds of flight time

101 inches of bullet drop

400 yard shot with Enfield Rifle

Note: With a Whitworth Rifle bullet drop falls to 42 inches and flight time is just over a second.
With a modern .308 Winchester rifle bullet drop is less than a foot and flight time is 0.5 seconds

Figure 2.5. Firing parameters and trajectory of the claimed shot that killed John Reynolds at Gettysburg.

with a rifle musket. This is one of the more famous sniping stories from the Civil War—no doubt in part because of Alexander Gardner's series of photographs from Devil's Den, which helped the shooter nest in our imaginations (figure 2.6).

The simulation of these two long-range shots is slightly complicated by the presence of Little Round Top. For the shots that brought down Sedgwick and Reynolds, the battleground over which the shots were fired are relatively flat. When firing from Devil's Den at a target on Little Round Top, there is a 163-foot change in elevation, so the shooter must aim approximately five degrees uphill.

Figure 2.6.   Timothy H. O'Sullivan took this photograph, "Rocks Could Not Save Him at the Battle of Gettysburg," on July 6 or 7, 1863. Alexander Gardner included this photo as plate 41 in his popular *Gardner's Photographic Sketch Book of the Civil War* (Washington, DC: Philp & Solomons, 1866), adding the caption, "Home of a Rebel Sharpshooter, Gettysburg." (*Credit:* Detail and enhanced, Library of Congress, LC-DIG-ppmsca-35214, https://www.loc.gov/item/2013645929/.)

Although the dead Confederate "sharpshooter" in Gardner and Timothy O'Sullivan's photograph had a Springfield rifle musket, it is more likely that a dedicated sniper on this position of the battlefield would have been carrying an Enfield.[23] Therefore the ballistics and trajectory calculations will be similar to those for the July 1 Reynolds scenario.

To strike General Weed and Lieutenant Hazlett on Little Round Top, the shooter would have needed to aim two hundred inches above the officers to compensate for bullet drop, and Weed—and the kneeling Hazlett—would have needed to remain stationary for two full seconds (figure 2.7).

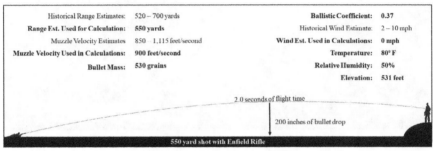

Historical Range Estimates:	520 – 700 yards	Ballistic Coefficient:	0.37
Range Est. Used for Calculation:	550 yards	Historical Wind Estimate:	2 – 10 mph
Muzzle Velocity Estimates	850 – 1,115 feet/second	Wind Est. Used in Calculations:	0 mph
Muzzle Velocity Used in Calculations:	900 feet/second	Temperature:	80° F
Bullet Mass:	530 grains	Relative Humidity:	50%
		Elevation:	531 feet

2.0 seconds of flight time

200 inches of bullet drop

550 yard shot with Enfield Rifle

Note: With Springfield Rifle Musket bullet drop and flight time are essentially unchanged but accuracy is diminished.

Figure 2.7. Firing parameters and trajectory of the claimed consecutive shots that killed Stephen Weed and Charles Hazlett on Little Round Top at Gettysburg.

Several other Union officers were wounded or killed on Little Round Top on July 2, including Brigadier General Gouverneur Warren, "the Savior of Little Round Top." A slightly larger-than-life-size statue of Warren stands on Little Round Top today, and visitors are told of the strategic importance of his recognizing that the hill was a key defensive position that needed to be held.

The view of this statue from the "sniper's den" in the boulders of Devil's Den through a four-power rifle scope provides a sense of the difficulty of range estimation at distances over five hundred yards (figure 2.8). And even from this perspective it must be remembered that this view was captured through a modern, high-quality, light-gathering Leupold riflescope;

Figure 2.8.   Statue of Gouverneur Warren as seen through a four-power riflescope from a shooter's perspective in Devil's Den (left), and enlarged detail (right). The scope is aimed as if it is going to strike the statue with a modern sniper rifle, and the circled "x" marks the spot that the bullet would strike if fired using a Civil War weapon. Note that the Warren statue depicts him as larger than in real life, and this scenario assumes there is no wind present.

imagine the scene with poorer-quality glass or without magnification of any type, using iron sights.

A modern sniper firing at Little Round Top would estimate the range—perhaps with a laser rangefinder—and wind speed before adjusting the windage and elevation of the riflescope for the shot.[24] A modern sniper would also aim slightly low, adjusting for the five-degree rise in elevation. If the riflescope is not set to adjust for bullet drop, a slight holdover would be needed. Figure 2.8 shows the proper holdover for a .338 Lapua Magnum firing a 225-grain bullet. The shooter needs to aim around forty inches high for a torso strike to the bronze "general." If armed with a .577 Enfield, by contrast, the same aiming point would produce a shot that fell sixteen feet below the aiming point and target (marked with a circled "x"). Even if such a shot had been ranged perfectly and aimed correctly, the accuracy of the Enfield only gives a fifty-fifty probability of hitting the target. And all of these calculations assume that the target never moved during the two seconds the bullet is in the air and that there is no wind. To match historical accounts, all of this needs to play out perfectly on two consecutive shots. Even in this impossible scenario, the inherent accuracy of the rifle reduces the probability of success to 25 percent.

This chapter focused on the trajectory of long-range sniper shots with little regard to wind drift. The lack of accurate meteorological records from more than 150 years ago makes estimating the degree of drift difficult across a Civil War landscape, and the difference between a three-mile-per-hour and seven-mile-per-hour crosswind could mean the difference between a headshot and a miss by several feet. As notes Fred Ray, author of *Shock Troops of the Confederacy*, bullet drift is more challenging to a long-range shooter than trajectory; even with the venerable Whitworth, the wind drift can exceed two feet in tests at five hundred yards.

There were, in summary, three key challenges facing a Civil War sharpshooter attempting to make a first-shot killing of an individual, targeted officer at ranges exceeding five hundred yards, and these three factors combine to make the task nearly impossible. The first two include correctly estimating the distance to the target and making the correct adjustment for range when firing a rifle with a muzzle velocity below 1,500 feet per second. The Confederate sharpshooter who found himself in a position to fire at John Sedgwick would have needed to correctly estimate the range of his shot to within a dozen yards of the true distance to obtain a head shot and then also correctly estimate where a 166-inch holdover would be above a target that was almost a half-mile away. The shots taken at Reynolds, Weed, and Hazlett would have required similarly exacting estimates—and most likely without the aid of a magnified riflescope. At five hundred–plus yards, the crudely calibrated adjustable rear sight on the Enfield and Springfield rifles made estimating distances other than three hundred, four hundred, or five hundred yards difficult. Additionally, the front sight of these muzzleloaders was much broader than a human-size target at five hundred yards. Between the required holdover and the width of the front sight, any view of the intended victim of the sharpshooter is completely obscured at this range.

The third primary challenge for each of the famous shots was wind, and this was the most difficult to estimate for both the shooter and the analysis herein, because the meteorological conditions for entire battles are often completely unknown and debated by historians. For calculation of wind drift during a particular shot, the meteorological conditions for one particular part of the battlefield must be known at a specific time during the battle; these records simply do not exist. John Sedgwick was killed around nine o'clock in the morning on May 9, 1864. Heavy rain and torrential thunderstorms would have had a profound effect on the Battle of Spotsylvania, but not until May 12, when Grant launched a massive assault on the muddy Mule Shoe Salient. According to accounts of Sedgwick's death, three days prior to Grant's offensive, the weather was clear, and there were no reports of windy conditions; nevertheless, even the gentlest breeze would have produced many inches of drift for an eight hundred–yard rifle shot.

At Gettysburg the meteorological conditions are easier to crudely quantify because of the work of Professor Michael Jacobs, a mathematics and science instructor at Pennsylvania College.[25] He took multiple simple weather measurements during the three-day battle, and his reports account for a slightly clearer picture of what the wind conditions were like when John Reynolds was killed. For July 1, 1863, the professor reported "A very gently warm southern breeze" he estimated at two miles per hour.[26] This measurement was likely recorded within a mile of where Reynolds fell, suggesting wind drift may not have provided much difficulty for the sharpshooter who killed the general. The deaths of Stephen Weed and Charles Hazlett occurred the next day, when the weather was slightly warmer, but there is scant evidence that the wind had picked up significantly. On July 4, however, the weather deteriorated, and the wind speed and gusts increased to a velocity that would have prohibited accurate long-range fire, had the armies still been engaged.

Multiple other nonsharpshooting scenarios have been proposed for the deaths of John Sedgwick and John Reynolds. These include closer-range fire from sharpshooters acting as skirmishers, a lucky shot from an "ordinary" infantryman, a stray bullet or inadvertent shot, artillery shrapnel, and friendly fire. Many of these explanations have been summarily dismissed by historians for some of the same reasons conspiracy theorists refuse to believe that John Fitzgerald Kennedy was killed by a lone loser gunman making an unremarkable shot; it is disconcerting to think a president or high-ranking general could be killed in unextraordinary circumstances. Instead, it is far more reassuring to think that a highly skilled marksman killed these "great" men at a tremendously great range, selecting them for death precisely because of their rank and value to the enemy.

Instead, it is much more probable that the sharpshooters who targeted Reynolds and Sedgwick never knew who they were shooting at and only targeted the officers because they were, or had recently been, on horseback—an indication of a higher-value target that can be witnessed at range. Based on the difficulty in range estimation and the trajectories of the weapons involved, the overwhelming evidence is that the Confederate sharpshooters were shooting at the approximate area where the generals and their staffs were located. The fact that the sniper hit Reynolds in the neck and Sedgwick under the eye is pure happenstance; doing so would have required that the shooter to estimate the distance of fire to within ten yards—a precision that would be impossible at a distance of over a quarter mile.

Fred Ray explains: "Sharpshooters often employed their Whitworths in an area-fire mode; that is, rather than singling out an individual at long range, they would aim at the center of a larger target, such as a mounted man, an artillery battery and their horses, and a column of troops or wagons."[27] There is ample evidence in the record to support the "area-fire" scenario for the killings described in this chapter. Sedgwick, as a primary example, was scolding his soldiers for dodging incoming sharpshooter fire when he was hit. These scattered shots, falling all around the men, were direct evidence of a sniper—or snipers—firing at a volume of targets, not an individual target. The shooter or shooters were unlucky on their early area-fire attempts, before striking gold (err . . . brass) when a bullet hit Sedgwick in the face. In short, the sharpshooters were aiming in the vicinity of the general and were rewarded with a lucky shot.

Confederate accounts also support the area-firing scenario for the death of Sedgwick. Ben Powell, traditionally the sharpshooter given credit for the extraordinary shot, claimed to be aiming at a group of horsemen he recognized as officers. The attribution of the shot to Powell is dubious, however, as he claimed the bullet from his Whitworth knocked the general from his horse and the remaining officers dismounted to provide aid. All federal accounts of the incident, problematically for the Confederate sniper seeking credit, recount Sedgwick as having been on foot when killed. As Andy Dougan surmises, the sharpshooters "were simply aiming to take out commanders and scored a spectacular success."[28]

As for Reynolds's death at Gettysburg, the case against a specifically aimed, long-range sharpshooter bullet providing the fatal shot is equally strong, despite statements in books from the last decade describing the consensus on the mode of death: a sharpshooter's bullet is "almost universally accepted."[29] In his biography of Reynolds, Edward Nicholas is skeptical of the sharpshooter hypothesis; however, he still describes this mode of death as "widely accepted" and lists six different historical references confirming the long range of the shot.[30]

Despite these arguments, the physics of a discretely aimed sharpshooter shot from Willoughby Run or the McPherson barn killing the general seems highly dubious. Both shots would have required precise range estimates of a moving target and compensation for more than eight feet of bullet drop—and Reynolds would have needed to have stopped moving, or else the shooter would have also needed to have aimed precisely where Reynolds would be a second and a half into the future. Even pro-sniper accounts concede these difficulties: Benjamin Thorpe of the 55th North Carolina regiment is the sharpshooter most commonly given credit for the kill shot, and he claimed to have fired at Reynolds three times, estimating the range first at 1,100 yards, and then adjusting down to nine hundred yards, before finding success at eight hundred yards. Had he even overestimated the range by fifty yards, setting his holdover for 850 yards, he would have missed. For his first two attempts, he overestimated the range by 27 percent and 11 percent and then correctly nailed the range within 3 percent and made the successful shot? If true, the eight-hundred-yard hit was overwhelmingly a matter of luck.

While the scenario of a long-range, targeted shot at Reynolds is extremely unlikely, the mode of death from area fire is also far from certain. For the killing of John Sedgwick, sniper fire was falling all around the officers and staff, and there were no reported Confederate infantry in close proximity; area fire seems reasonable. For John Reynolds, by contrast, multiple other sources of small-arms fire were nearby. Mark Adkin points to skirmishers from Archer's brigade, against whom Reynolds was directing the IX Corps' assault.[31] "A bullet from a Rebel skirmisher in the trees drilled his head behind the right ear," Allen Guelzo concurs.[32] Stephen Sears also points to infantry as the culprit—this time the 7th Tennessee.[33]

So, it seems that over time historians have recognized the difficulty of such a long-range shot at a moving target. The solution could be as simple as refocusing on the definition of the term *sharpshooter*. Early accounts of the killing—from Catton and Tucker—appear to describe the "sharpshooter" in the *sniper* role, where more recent (twenty-first-century) accounts point to the "sharpshooter" in the *skirmisher* role. Long-range ballistics and bullet trajectories strongly concur with the latter explanation for the death of Reynolds.

Of the three sniping scenarios presented in this chapter—Sedgwick at Spotsylvania, Reynolds at Gettysburg, and Webb and Hazlett at Little Round Top—the final targeted shots are the most plausible, and yet they remain nearly impossible. The successful killing of two officers, on consecutive shots, uphill, from more than five hundred yards with an Enfield rifle musket, strains credulity. Instead, there were likely multiple sharpshooters around the base of Little Round Top, in the Slaughter Pen between the Round Tops, and on Houck's Ridge who were firing at federal soldiers on Little Round Top. Any man standing on the barren top of the hill would have made an inviting target, officer or not. The diabase boulders strewn across the crest of the hill would have been illuminated by the late-afternoon sun on July 2, and the surrounding thick forest canopy would have provided a vignette-like setting, focusing the attention on movement between and across the massive boulders and rocky outcrops. The rocks of Devil's Den, Houck's Ridge, and the Slaughter Pen also provide a degree of cover and concealment for a potential sniper, increasing his confidence and providing security while he took careful aim.[34]

To accomplish this shot, the sniper would need a holdover of two hundred inches and to correctly compensate for the five degrees of upward aim (bullets hit higher than expected when firing uphill or downhill). The distance would need to be accurately estimated to within fifty yards, and the wind conditions between Devil's Den and the Round Top would need to be compensated for. This would have been an extremely difficult shot—to correctly aim at, and kill, Stephen Weed. The second shot, which brought down Charles Hazlett, would have been slightly less challenging, because the sniper's first shot had verified the correct range and adjustment for bullet drop, wind, and elevation. The second shot is also slightly more plausible because Hazlett was likely to have been stationary during the two seconds of bullet travel time; he is said to have been kneeling down beside his mortally wounded friend when the minié bullet hit him. All of this assumes, of course, that the sniper could see the success of his first shot. More than likely he would not have been able to: At 550 yards the figures would have been miniscule, and the smoke from his black-powder Enfield would have obscured his vision during the two seconds of travel time. Had the smoke cleared quickly while the bullet was in the air, providing a clear line of sight, the wind responsible for this diffusion would have made the long-range shot even more challenging.

With all this being said, the successful killing of two federal officers with two consecutive shots in this scenario and at this range is almost certainly impossible for one overarching reason: the accuracy of the Enfield rifle musket.[35] At 550 yards, the Enfield was capable of producing thirty-inch groups. For comparison, a modern sniper rifle would be able to shoot groups five or six times smaller than this at that range. This lack of precision for the Enfield meant that even if the sniper in Devil's Den had taken the perfect shot—perfect aim, perfect range estimate, perfect adjustment for wind drift and bullet drop—he still only had a roughly fifty-fifty chance of successfully hitting the torso of his intended victim. A repeat of this successful (read: impossible) shot, on the very next attempt, leaves the shooter with no better than a one in four chance of both shots hitting. All of these probability calculations assume, of course, that the intended victims did not move or that the sniper perfectly predicted where they would move to two seconds in the future.

Tests conducted by Jac Weller in the 1950s and 1970s also demonstrate the utility of the Enfield for the "small-area fire" variety of sharpshooting. He was able to strike five-foot-by-five-foot targets with thirteen out of fifteen shots taken at four hundred yards. At 550 yards on Little Round Top, the Confederate sharpshooter could have landed consecutive shots *near* Webb and Hazlett rather easily, but it would have taken an absurd amount of luck to kill both men with only two consecutive shots.

In summary, then, analysis of the range, trajectory, and accuracy of Civil War rifles suggests these unfortunate federal officers were not brought down by Confederate snipers who had individually targeted them for death, and certainly not by sharpshooters firing headshots at more than four hundred yards. John Reynolds was probably killed by a skirmisher or infantryman firing from less than two hundred yards away. The multiple officers killed on Little Round Top were picked off by lucky long-range shots fired in their general direction—the closest scenario here to match "the myth of the Civil War sniper." John Sedgwick was killed by a sharpshooter who was aiming at the group of men surrounding the general and not specifically at the general himself. In some ways, Sedgwick was largely correct with regard to his final pronouncement: a Confederate sharpshooter, even armed with a scoped Whitworth rifle, would have a great deal of difficulty hitting a lone elephant standing a half-mile away. The final stop—the period—at the end of this sentence appears larger, when held at arm's length, than a pachyderm at one thousand yards. Imagine trying to establish the precise range of that tiny dot for a first-shot hit. Given five or six shots, as the Confederate who killed Sedgwick was allowed, it would be much more possible to hit Dumbo, but a first-shot head shot at this range would have been close to impossible—or at least extremely lucky. Perhaps the best summation of the myth of Civil War sniping and the role of specific, aimed sharpshooter fire killing officers is a restatement of military-sniping and small-arms expert Leigh Neville's comments regarding the death of Sedgwick: "A phenomenal shot with such a rudimentary weapon and optics."[36] Adding one word to this synopsis makes it more scientifically accurate: "A phenomenally *lucky* shot with such a rudimentary weapon and optics."

Successful sniping during the Civil War, from the viewpoint of how we think of sniping in modern combat, was rare at ranges over four hundred yards, and specifically aimed and successful kill shots at eight hundred yards or more did not occur. Webb, Hazlett, Reynolds, and Sedgwick were not brought down by remarkably talented marksmen; they were brought down by remarkably bad luck.

3

The Density of Death

BEFORE CIVIL WAR PHOTOGRAPHERS BEGAN TO BRING SEPIA IMAGES OF the aftermath of battles back to the home front, nearly all citizens of the United States had only eyewitness reports and artists' renderings to help them visualize the carnage left behind on the postcombat landscape. The initial vision of bloated bodies of the heroic dead scattered across the fields must have made for a stunning and horrific sensory experience. The terrible loss of life and the human destruction left behind by the fighting was a vision that writers struggled to convey, and today there is a growing pool of scholarship that focuses on the true nature of the fighting and its aftermath. This chapter respectfully investigates the blurred lines between the actual appearance of a battleground in the hours and days after the fighting had ceased and the eyewitness descriptions of the butchery that have been passed down in the literature during the century and a half since the war ended.

Perhaps no vivid phrase has been more often repeated to describe the intensity of death from a battle than the "carpet of corpses" across the landscape—a variation of "the dead covered the ground so that you could walk across the field and never touch the ground." Accounts of this density of death exist for battlefields from Fredericksburg, Antietam, Gettysburg, Petersburg, Shiloh, Franklin, Perryville, Pickett's Mill, and Nashville.

Bloody descriptions of the landscape are not limited to bodies "paving the earth," as one soldier wrote after the Battle of Williamsburg in 1862. The vivid sobriquet "slaughter pen" was applied to portions of at least five Civil War battlegrounds—most famously at Stones River and Gettysburg, but also at Perrysville and Fredericksburg. The entire battlefield at Cold Harbor was dubbed "Grant's slaughter pen" after his disastrous frontal assaults on June 3, 1864. Grant's losses were horrific, and he regretted ordering the attack in his memoirs, but it was at an earlier battle in his career, at Shiloh, that he, like so many other authors, returned to the "carpet of corpses" trope: "I saw an open field, in our possession on the second day, over which the Confederates had made repeated charges the day before, so covered with dead that it would have been possible to walk across the clearing, in any direction, stepping on dead bodies, without a foot touching the ground."[1]

This chapter is focused on testing the validity of this similitude. For Grant's quotation above, this examination cannot necessarily be adequately completed, as his description of the field provides no testable premise to scrutinize: Grant doesn't tell us the size of the plot of land he is describing; perhaps the "open field" was only a hundred square feet, covered by a dozen bodies. Nevertheless, the repetition of the description for other well-known landscape features, including the infamous Wheatfield at Gettysburg and the equally notorious Cornfield at Antietam, provides both data points necessary for studying the density of the fallen: casualty figures and acreage.

Three battlefields stand out among all others in the literature with respect to the "human-carpet" descriptor. These three fighting grounds, then, will be analyzed with respect to the spatiolateral distribution of the dead: Antietam, Gettysburg, and Franklin. In each case, two variables will be calculated and compared: the number of those killed in action with respect to the surface area of combat. This ratio will allow for a determination of the probability of producing a landscape that could be trod across without touching the earth.

CASUALTIES, KILLED IN ACTION, AND BATTLEGROUND SURFACE AREA

There exists a frustrating confusion among members of the general public with regard to the term *casualties*. Many folks seem to equate the term with men killed in action instead of with the correct amalgamation comprising soldiers killed, wounded, captured, and missing. During the Civil War, a soldier became a casualty whenever he was unable to fight the next day, and many casualties would return to the ranks and fight again, sometimes more than once.

Perhaps the most astonishing swapping of the term *casualties* with *killed* occurred in conjunction with the 1993 release of Turner Pictures' film *Gettysburg*. As Thomas Desjardin explains in his book *These Honored Dead,*

> *Newer Gettysburg myths seem to have no basis in the veterans' stories at all. For example, millions of Americans believe that fifty thousand men died at Gettysburg, a larger loss of American life than in the Vietnam War. In fact, approximately ten thousand men died at Gettysburg, less than one-fifth the number killed in Vietnam. This misapprehension is attributable in part to Ted Turner. In 1994, as part of the television debut of the movie* Gettysburg *(which Turner financed), he broadcast his own commentary on the film and story. He stated that more men died at Gettysburg than in the entire Vietnam War. A television audience of approximately forty million viewers heard this statement. Turner's company perpetuated the misstatement on the packaging for the home video of the film, proclaiming to all who bought or rented the video that "when it was all over, fifty thousand men had paid the ultimate price."*[2]

Denzel Washington—no stranger to Civil War movies—repeated the misconception six years later in *Remember the Titans* when, in an effort to inspire his struggling football team, his character drags his players across the boulders on the battlefield. "Anybody know what this place is?" he asks them. "This is Gettysburg. This is where they fought the Battle of Gettysburg. Fifty thousand men died right here on this field, fighting the same fight that we're still fighting amongst ourselves today."[3]

Other gross misunderstandings of the volume of killed in specific Civil War battles propagated by the popular media are equally easy to find: the independent newspaper *The Guardian* ("fifty thousand men died"), the *Clermont Sun* ("more than fifty thousand Americans had died"), the Travel Channel ("fifty thousand men lay dead or dying"), *The*

History Engine at the University of Richmond ("with a combined 51,112 men killed in the battle over a three day span"), CBS News ("Roughly fifty thousand soldiers died at Gettysburg"), and the International Committee of the Red Cross ("around fifty thousand soldiers from both sides were killed during those three days").[4]

Had more than fifty thousand men been left on the battlefield at Gettysburg, it might be plausible that a twenty-acre patch like the Wheatfield was covered with corpses. With the correct figure of around eight thousand killed in action, however, the vast area encompassed by the combat sheds light on the density of death. The Gettysburg Battlefield is large, and the fighting during the three-day battle covered more than ten square miles. While there were certainly areas where the fighting and casualties were concentrated, the ratio of deaths to surface area indicates that *on average* each acre of the battlefield would have had only a single dead soldier. The analysis in this chapter is aimed at providing insight into just how variable the distribution of the dead on the battlefield needed to be to produce a scenario in which there was human ground cover.

THE HISTORICAL CLAIM

This is the claim to be tested: *The intensity and concentration of fighting was so great that in the immediate aftermath of battle a person could walk across a landscape feature like a farm field while stepping only on corpses, never once touching the ground.*

Postbattle reports including some variation of this claim can be divided into three general categories. Grant's famous quotation about the losses suffered at Shiloh falls into this first category: first-person accounts of the carnage. The second category of claims are made by historians describing the battleground, often including quotations or descriptions from those who witnessed the destruction. The final grouping of quotations includes nonfictional and historical-fictional retellings of the postcombat conditions of the fields (not necessarily based on eyewitness reports). All three are abundant in the Civil War canon.

In some accounts, the carpet of death is described for multiple battlefields. Historian Drew Faust described two such battlefields in *Harvard Magazine:* "Witnesses to battle's butchery often wrote of the impossibility of crossing the field without walking from one end to the other atop the dead. 'They paved the earth,' a soldier wrote after the Battle of Williams-burg in 1862. . . . With grim precision Eugene Blackford described a two-acre area at Fredericksburg containing 1,350 dead Yankees; others estimated stretches of a mile or more at Antietam or Shiloh where every step had to be planted on a dead body."[5]

Other authors are more specific with location, identifying both a battlefield and a particular location on the field for the carpet of death. Antietam's Sunken Road (later "Bloody Lane") is particularly popular in this respect. "One Union soldier later remarked that there were so many bodies that one could walk across them for as far as the eye could see without touching the ground," write Mark Swank and Dreama Swank.[6] Robert McNamara adopts a similar tone: "One soldier, shocked at the carnage, said the bodies in the sunken road were so thick that a man could have walked on them as far as he could see without touching the ground."[7] Frederick Tilberg follows suit for the National Park Service. "The Sunken Road was now Bloody Lane," he writes. "Dead Confederates lay so thick there, wrote one federal soldier, that as far down the road as he could see, a man could have walked upon them without once touching ground."[8]

It should be noted that the Sunken Road has only one small bend along its traverse, meaning that it is simple to see from one end to the other on a clear day. Tom Huntingdon echoes a similar description: "The Union's superiority in numbers eventually forced the Confederates back, leaving Bloody Lane so packed with the dead and dying that it appeared you could walk down it without touching the ground."[9] Peter Carlson describes the gruesome scene with the same "end-to-end" prose: "The Rebels fled, leaving behind so many dead comrades that, as one Union soldier put it, a man could have walked the road from end to end without ever touching ground. The Sunken Road had earned a new nickname: Bloody Lane."[10] So does Michael Sanders, in *More Strange Tales of the Civil War*: "A person could walk from one end of the Bloody Lane to the other without touching the earth but instead stepping on the bodies of the dead and dying."[11] Codie Eash goes a step further, providing a degree of quantification for the dead: "The road—appropriately renamed Bloody

Lane—contains thousands of fallen corpses, so many that 'one could walk along the road without touching the ground.'"[12]

It is now simple to see how this trope became ingrained in children and adults alike. This from Charles Mitchell's *Travels through American History in the Mid-Atlantic: A Guide for All Ages*: "The Union suffered more than three thousand casualties at the Bloody Lane, and veterans would later swear that a man could walk across the corpses without once touching ground."[13] James McPherson is similarly careful to not include a specific distance over which the walk on the dead could be completed: "Once again, as many soldiers testified and photographs proved, one could walk along the road without touching the ground."[14]

The Sunken Road was not the only location in the fields around Sharpsburg so described. Much of the morning phase of the battle took place across the Miller farm, and one twenty-plus-acre field of corn switched hands multiple times (figure 3.1).

Norman Risjord describes the scene: "The cornfield was so littered with bodies that one soldier claimed he could have walked through it

Figure 3.1.   The location of the Cornfield at Antietam. The East Woods are in the background. This is the view from the Confederate position along Stonewall Jackson's line, looking northeast.

without touching the ground."[15] And Richard Clem of the *Washington Times* specifies a direction for the walk: "A witness to the aftermath of the morning encounter recorded, 'One could cross the entire length of Miller's forty-acre cornfield without touching the ground by walking on the dead.'"[16] Terry Kroenung wrote a historical drama describing the field in rather histrionic terms: "Satan's hopscotch. You could have walked across that field without once touching the ground . . . if you don't mind blood and brains on your good Army shoes."[17] Nicholas Peel similarly describes the Cornfield in his work of fiction: "You could walk across that cornfield on gray and blue bodies and not touch the ground."[18]

Returning to works of nonfiction, in *Landscape Turned Red* Stephen Sears provides a firsthand account of the density of the federal dead: "Sergeant William Andrews of the 1st Georgia recalled, 'Where the line stood the ground was covered in blue, and I believe I could have walked on them without putting my feet on the ground.'"[19] James McPherson adds a welcome note of skepticism: "Dawes's regiment fought mainly in a thirty-acre cornfield. So did dozens of other regiments on both sides, back and forth in attacks and counterattacks for several hours, until the field was filled with so many dead and wounded men that, as many soldiers who fought there put it (doubtless with some exaggeration), one could walk through the field without ever stepping on the ground."[20] Similar accountings of the field have ended up online, modified without the skepticism: "'The whole landscape for an instant turned red,' one Northern soldier later wrote. Another veteran recalled, '[The cornfield] was so full of bodies that a man could have walked through it without stepping on the ground.'"[21] And "It's said every corn stalk (the fight was on Sept. 17, 1862) was cut down to inches from the ground and that you could walk from end to end of the multiacre field stepping only on bodies from both sides."[22] Eventually, as might be expected, the apocryphal tale ends up in the classroom (although in this case, perhaps not for the most noble of reasons): From CourseHero.com, a phrase from a sample "term paper" available for purchase: "You could walk from one end of the cornfield to another without touching the earth because there were so many bodies lying around." Apparently, the author of this passage is suggesting the corpses may have something else to do other than lie around. Lazy corpses.

The Battle of Fredericksburg was one of the most lopsided contests from the war, and the battlefield apparently held the record for the greatest distance a person could walk without touching the ground. Massed and deadly federal attacks against Marye's Heights produced delusory descriptions: "It was madness to pit human beings against the odds which nature there provided, and the fact, that after the battle you could walk for three-fourths of a mile on the bodies of the Union dead, without touching the earth, amply attests to the folly of the Union forces engaging in battle there."[23] And "One could have walked up from the river to the heights, it was said, without ever touching earth."[24] And "As the sun set on December 13th, the Union dead and wounded so littered the ground that Confederates wrote in the diaries that they could have walked on bodies for a half mile into town without having their feet touch the ground."[25] And "One observer claimed that a person could walk in front of the stone wall from one end to the other across Union corpses without touching the ground."[26]

Union major general Ambrose E. Burnside sent more than a dozen disastrous charges against the stone wall and Sunken Road below Marye's Heights, costing his army well in excess of five thousand men. As darkness fell on December 13, many hundred shell-shocked and wounded Union soldiers remained on the fields between the city and the stone wall. Most would remain there until the next afternoon, and many would perish in the intervening hours, adding to the number of dead on the field. Nevertheless, the distance between the Heights and the river is almost 1,500 yards; walking this distance only on the dead would require that nearly six hundred corpses be aligned in one long, continuous row and that the bodies be positioned in the same direction as their fateful charge (i.e., that the row of corpses be perpendicular to the Sunken Road and the stone wall).

The Wheatfield at Gettysburg witnessed a degree of fighting that approximated the ferocity found at the Cornfield at Antietam, changing hands multiple times on July 2, 1863. It is not surprising, then, that it would also later be described using "carpet of death" language. Steven Foster summarizes this claim in the literature: "Some historians note that in the Wheatfield alone, there were so many bodies one could walk across the field without touching the ground. Near Devil's Den, there were nearly eight thousand dead after just the first three hours."[27] Even without a detailed spatial analysis, there are clearly problems with this claim: this scenario would require that nearly all the dead from the entire three-day battle would have fallen "near Devil's Den"—and in only three hours of combat. One has to wonder what the armies were doing during the other two days of the battle.

Bradley Gottfried presents a more plausible scene when quoting Captain Hillyer of the 9th Georgia: "He admitted that many of the enemy had taken flight, but in front of them 'there was a long blue line on the ground so close together that anyone could have walked over them as far as their front extended, without touching the earth.'"[28]

Historian James McPherson wrote of the blanket of death at both Antietam sites and added a cautious note when describing eyewitness accounts of the Wheatfield in his book *Hallowed Ground: A Walk at Gettysburg*: "Beyond the woods behind the Rose farm was the Wheatfield, a thirty-two-acre field over which attack and counterattacks surged back and forth, leaving so many dead and wounded that one soldier afterward said (no doubt with some exaggeration) that he could have walked over it without touching the ground."[29]

All the aforementioned corpse-covered fields and mile-long paths of dead were found on battlefields from the eastern theater of the war. In the west there were multiple battlefields, in addition to Shiloh, where this gruesome description was repeated.

At Perryville, Kevin Carroll notes livestock added to the carnage, to increase the surface coverage of the dead: "Dead soldiers, horses, and mules scattered about in some places so thickly covered one could walk over a hundred paces and not touch the ground."[30] At the Pickett's Mill Battlefield outside Atlanta, Marc Wortman combines several postbattle descriptions: "Soldiers observed they could walk the field, body to body, afterwards and not touch ground for hundreds of yards."[31] The same description is used for the Nashville Battlefield by Michael Thomas Smith: "Following the charge, blue-clad bodies littered the hill's slope in such large numbers that it seemed possible to walk across the battlefield on them without touching the ground."[32]

The Battle of Franklin was in many respects the "Fredericksburg of the West," but this time with the Confederates suffering stunning casualty numbers after launching catastrophic assaults against their entrenched enemy. Franklin also had a landscape that was commonly described using the "carpet of death" descriptor. Examples are found across a vast swath of publication types—from National Public Radio programs to local tour books to contemporaneous veteran's accounts to works of fiction.

Initial accounts from Franklin were divided as to where, geographically, the "carpet of death" was found (on the Carter family grounds versus in front of the earthworks on the federal left). William Allen Keesy quotes several participants in the battle: "He tells me, and others confirm it, that he saw that portion of the battle-ground over which I ran, the next morning after the battle, and it was so closely strewn with bodies that he could have walked all over four acres of it on dead men without touching the ground. Of course those four acres should not be understood as the whole battle-ground. While it perhaps was the part where the greatest slaughter was, the entire line was nearly four miles long."[33] H. P. Figuers wrote in the *Confederate Veteran* that "From the Lewisburg Pike on the east, along, in front of, and just south of the federal breastworks as far as the Columbia Pike and west of the pike as far as the locust thicket, the dead and wounded were so thick upon the ground that it might be said without exaggeration that one could walk upon the dead and never touch the ground."[34]

These sentiments were repeated a century later in local guidebooks to the area, often dropping any mention of the wounded. Jackie Sheckler Finch echoes that "There were so many dead that they said you could walk eighty yards across the Carter garden and yard without touching the ground, just stepping on all the dead bodies."[35] And Sally Walker Davies writes that "the bodies were reportedly so thick on the ground, one could barely walk without stepping on one."[36]

Newspapers also added to the claim of massed carnage. In an article for the *Williamson Herald*, Carole Robinson writes, "In the seven-, eight-foot ditches that served as trenches for protection, blood ran in streams. 'The dead were stacked like wheat and scattered like sheathes of grain,' said Confederate General Frank Cheatham. 'You could walk on the field on the bodies without touching the ground.'"[37] Brian Craig

Miller quotes an eyewitness to the battle, writing for the *New York Times*: "A military chaplain declared, 'I could have trodden on a dead man at every step.... The dead were piled up in the trenches almost to the top of the earthworks.'"[38]

The most vivid—and perhaps clichéd—retelling comes from a work of historical fiction, based on a true story. From Robert Hicks's *Widow of the South*: "It was said you could walk across the battlefield upon the bodies of the fallen and not once touch the ground. Others have described the dead as being stacked like cordwood or like sheaves of corn or like sacks of meal. By different accounts the ground ran with rivers of blood, or it was stained with blood, or it was blood."[39]

The most confused understanding of the difference between casualties and killed in action, as well as the "carpet of death" descriptor, comes from Nashville Public Radio. In a blog post, describing the aftermath of battle for the citizens of Franklin, Nina Cardona writes, "In some places, the ground was strewn so thickly with bodies that people couldn't walk through without treading on torsos or limbs." Later the blog post is updated with a correction: "The headline of this story has been changed. A previous headline inferred that there were ten thousand corpses after the battle of Franklin. We meant to say that there were ten thousand 'casualties,' a statistic that includes those killed, injured, or missing." Nevertheless, the correction did not extend to the first sentence of the piece, as it still contained the following reversal of killed and casualties: "On December 1, 1864, the eight hundred or so people living in Franklin found themselves surrounded by ten thousand dead and dying soldiers."[40]

In reality, nearly all historians agree that approximately two thousand men were killed at the Battle of Franklin, with another eight thousand men listed as wounded, missing, or captured. Had the citizens been surrounded by ten thousand dead and dying soldiers when the battle was over, the single day of fighting at Franklin would have been bloodier than the three days at Gettysburg.

In summary, this series of quotations indicates that at least eight battlefields had one or more "carpets of death"—and this list is incomplete (Tupelo, Petersburg, and Second Manassas have also had a portion of their postbattle landscapes discussed in this manner). Three battlefields stand out in the literature as having the trope repeated about them the most times: Antietam (Cornfield and Sunken Road), Gettysburg (Wheatfield), and Franklin (Carter grounds and the region between the Lewisburg and Columbia Pikes); these bloody sites will provide the data necessary for a scientific assessment of the historical claims.

THE SCIENCE

The spatiolateral density of death is not difficult to calculate if two variables are known: the number or corpses on the field and the surface area of the ground over which the men were fighting and fell. The first factor is often more difficult to estimate; casualty statistics are sometimes provided for entire battles or for days of battles (e.g., the second day at Gettysburg) or portions of battles (e.g., the morning phase at Antietam), and frequently the numbers are given as a sum of killed, wounded, and captured or missing, not specifying the fraction of the number specifically killed in action. In general, total casualties are positively correlated with the number of men who were killed in combat: for most battles, around one in every five casualties was killed, with a smaller fraction actually killed on the field (and not mortally wounded).[41]

Nor is the surface area of the fighting field as simple to calculate as it might seem. Even a well-defined farm field like the Miller Cornfield at Antietam or the Rose Wheatfield at Gettysburg had multiple estimates of the size of the ground in the historical literature, and direct measurements on the modern battlefield are complicated by shifting land-use patterns over time and other anthropogenic alterations to the landscape (e.g., new buildings or roads).[42]

For the analysis in this chapter, several guidelines for calculation were followed. First, the casualty figures for a given area were estimated using the 20 percent killed/casualty ratio, unless the value for the entire battle was significantly higher or lower. This value may slightly overestimate the number of dead on the field and, as a result, increase the apparent plausibility that the battlefield resembled a "carpet of death."[43] Second, the surface area for a combat zone (indelicately, the "ground cover" or "human carpet") was calculated using the value that is most often cited in historical accounts—the broad consensus of historians. The only deviations from this selection of square-footage data were made when modern measurements appeared to provide a better estimation or where historical accounts of the surface area were not available or were unmistakably inaccurate.

Finally, the surface area covered by a single dead soldier was estimated at fifty square feet. This value clearly represents an overestimation for the ground covered solely by the corpse, but it must be remembered that the coverage provided by the cadaver is not precisely the earth directly under the body, but rather the surface area coverage that would allow a person to walk from body to body without touching the ground (a foot or so could exist between dead bodies and still allow walking without touching the earth). Several flat stones laid across a stream can provide a footpath even though the stones have a very small surface area relative to the width of the stream. Assuming the average soldier was around five and a half feet tall and lying flat on the ground, there would be a zone of ground around him, separating him from the next-closest corpse, that couldn't be more than a foot or so in length if a person were able to step from body to body. Thus, for the purposes of calculating the grisly "carpet of death" scenario, the body would occupy a conservative area of around seven feet by seven feet: approximately fifty square feet.

Figure 3.2 provides a visual representation of three scenarios, all drawn to scale, with increasing densities of death.

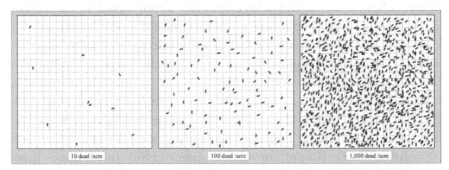

| 10 dead /acre | 100 dead /acre | 1,000 dead /acre |

Figure 3.2. Increasing numbers of fallen soldiers in the same one-acre field. When the entirety of the fighting ground is considered, most Civil War battles had a density of death of around one dead body per acre. *Note:* One acre equals 43,560 square feet such that each side of the boxes above would be 208 feet long; the grid pattern is set a ten-foot increments (all soldiers are approximately five and a half feet tall).

In almost all combat scenarios, the spatial distribution of those killed will not be random. The density of the fallen will be greater where soldiers are positioned behind defensive strongpoints, such as parapets, fencing, or stone walls (or in sunken roads). Soldiers may also be moving and advancing in formation or columns, and those struck down by volley fire or artillery—especially grapeshot or canister—will leave rows of bodies. When infantrymen are assaulting an enemy defensive position, casualties will increase as the distance to the defenders decreases; bodies will be more scattered at farther ranges and grow more densely packed in proximity to the enemy. Defensive positions that are attacked repeatedly will also have more dead on the field, buttressing this distribution of the dead. The federal approach to Marye's Heights at Fredericksburg left fewer men on the field at ranges beyond five hundred yards, but many more men were killed between one hundred to two hundred yards from the infamous stone wall. The Cornfield at Antietam may be the exception to this nonrandom distribution trend for bodies because the fighting there swayed back and forth across the field; historian James McPherson estimates that the patch of ground changed hands as many as fifteen times.[44]

Finally, a general discussion of the volume of death and battleground geographic size, at a larger scale, may provide insight into the distribution of the dead. For the bloodiest major engagements—Gettysburg, Spotsylvania, and Chickamauga—almost exactly one soldier died for every acre of fighting ground (table 3.1). At Gettysburg, for example, somewhere around 7,860 fallen soldiers were scattered across a battle landscape of approximately twelve square miles (excluding the area of the East Cavalry Field). This equates to, *on average*, just over six hundred dead bodies for each square mile of the battlefield. Obviously the number of dead soldiers would have been significantly higher in areas that witnessed the most intense fighting (e.g., the Peach Orchard, Wheatfield, Little Round Top, and Cemetery Hill). In summary, then, a comparison of the number of men killed in action to the size of the battlefield gives an indication of the density of the dead on the battlegrounds, with higher ratios of dead-to-surface area more likely to produce a battleground where one might have walked across a portion of the field without touching the ground.

Table 3.1. Density of death on the largest scale: Number of deaths for large engagements compared with the size of the battlegrounds

Battle	Deaths	Approximate area (square miles)	Bodies per square mile	Acres per body
Gettysburg	7,863	12.5	630	1.0
Spotsylvania	4,192	7.0	599	1.1
Chickamauga	3,969	6.0	661	1.0
Wilderness	3,723	8.0	465	1.4
Antietam	3,650	4.0	913	0.7
Shiloh	3,482	11.0	316	2.0
Chancellorsville	3,271	6.5	503	0.9
Second Manassas	3,205	6.0	534	1.2
Stones River	2,971	6.0	495	1.3
Cold Harbor	2,633	6.5	405	1.6
Gaines' Mill	2,377	1.3	1,828	0.4
Franklin	1,939	2.0	966	0.7
Fredericksburg	1,892	22.0	86	7.4
Second Petersburg	1,888	6.0	314	2.0
Malvern Hill	1,210	1.0	1,210	0.5

Several interesting trends stand out when analyzing the relationships between battle deaths and battleground surface area. Battlefields with terrain that limited large-scale maneuvering had significantly higher spatial densities of dead soldiers. At Malvern Hill, for example, swampy ground and stream-dissected terrain restricted Lee's options once he decided to attack, and the result was twelve hundred dead bodies in a single square mile. At Antietam (913 bodies per square mile), McClellan could not flank Lee's smaller army to the north or south because of sweeping meanders in the Potomac River; the potential battlefield surface area was delimited by the presence of the waterway. In the Wilderness (465 bodies per square mile) and Petersburg (314 bodies per square mile), there were fewer natural restrictions like stream valleys or swampy ground, and large-scale maneuvering in different directions produced a larger surface area and fewer average bodies per square mile.

Tactics also contributed to higher densities of death. Massive frontal assaults resulted in a concentration of the fallen. At Franklin (0.7 acres per corpse) and Gaines' Mill (0.4 acres per corpse), large-scale attacks in the face of a dug-in enemy increased the number of dead per acre. By contrast, battlefields with extended defensive lines (e.g., Fredericksburg) or shifting lines (e.g., Shiloh, Gettysburg, or Stones River) had much larger battlegrounds, spreading out the death and leading to fewer casualties per square mile.

In the next section of this chapter, three battlegrounds are considered with respect to the distribution of the fallen soldiers across the landscape: Antietam, Gettysburg, and Franklin. These battles were selected for discussion because the locations have most often been described in the Civil War literature and popular press as having a portion of the field completely covered in corpses, where a person could walk . . .

ANALYSIS AND EVALUATION

September 17, 1862, was the bloodiest day of the Civil War. The stalemate at Antietam produced more than twenty-two thousand casualties, and 3,650 of these men were killed. The clash around Sharpsburg can be neatly divided into three chronological and geographic phases, the first two of which produced a loss of life that witnesses described in a manner that meets the characteristics of the "carpet of death." Specifically, the two locations on the battlefield that were most often described as having the corpses so closely packed together that you could walk the field without touching the ground were the Cornfield (phase 1) and the Sunken Road ("Bloody Lane"; phase 2).

The Cornfield was located north of the town at the center of the initial federal assaults by Hooker's I Corps (approximately eight thousand men) against the left wing of the Confederate line held by Stonewall Jackson. Hooker's men were pushed back across the Cornfield when John Bell Hood advanced with approximately two thousand men. Lee then pulled D. H. Hill's men from the Sunken Road to the south and added them to the Confederate counterattacks across the Cornfield. The Rebels were in turn pushed back by the arrival of Joseph Mansfield's XII Corps (approximately seven thousand soldiers). Finally, John Sedgwick's division of the

II Corps advanced along the southern border of the Cornfield into the West Woods, where they met disaster in the face of Lafayette McLaws's division. As the federals retreated from the West Woods, the remainder of the II Corps swung south and assaulted the 2,200 Confederates positioned in the Sunken Road.

For three hours the Rebels held the lane under the onslaught of ten thousand federal infantry. When Confederate reinforcements under Richard Anderson failed to reach the defensive line, the combination of confusion among the surviving Confederate field commanders and flanking maneuvers by federal infantry on the eastern edge of the road forced a Rebel retreat.

By early afternoon, the fighting had stopped in the Cornfield and now "Bloody" Lane, and both landscape features were described by soldiers as being completely covered with corpses: a "ghastly flooring." Almost twice as many men fought (and half again as many men died) around the Cornfield than along the Sunken Road, suggesting that the "carpet of death" scenario was more feasible for the farm field than the lane; however, the higher casualty rates are negated by the much larger surface area of the farm field (table 3.2).

So, what is the plausibility that a person could have walked across either the Cornfield or the length of the Sunken Road entirely on the bodies of the fallen, without ever touching the ground? If *all* the men killed in action during the morning phase of the battle fell within the boundaries of the Cornfield—a preposterous assumption—there would still have existed great gaps between the bodies on the field. There were probably portions of the Cornfield where the men fell in close proximity, perhaps from artillery-canister fire, but the claims that a person could walk across the field in any direction are clearly grossly exaggerated. Sixteen hundred men spread over twenty-four acres leaves each body with more than seven hundred square feet to cover. To complete the "carpet of death" at this location, it would be necessary to collect all the killed, wounded, captured, and missing from both armies in the Cornfield and have the men lie prone and evenly distributed across the farm field. The description of the entirety of the Cornfield being blanketed with the fallen is preposterous; even if the men had fallen in a perfectly straight

**Table 3.2. Variables to produce a "carpet of death" at Antietam:
The Cornfield versus the Sunken Road**

	Cornfield	Sunken Road
Range of estimates for surface area	17–30 acres	800–930 yards long, 4 yards wide
Most commonly reported surface area	~24 acres	0.66 acres
Surface area used in calculations (analysis)	25	0.66 acres
Shape of landscape feature	⬭	╲
Casualty estimates for phase of battle	8,000–13,860 (8,000 used)	5,400–5,600 (5,500 used)
Killed in action for phase of battle	~1,600	~1,100
Density of death: All KIA found only in field/road	703 ft²/corpse	26 ft²/corpse
Density of death: Half of KIA found only in field/road	1,406 ft²/corpse	52 ft²/corpse
Number of corpses needed for walking path	107 (width)	342 (length)
Number of corpses needed for "carpet of death"	22,250	576

Note: Density-of-death rows include the number of square feet per corpse, assuming every dead soldier (or half the dead soldiers) from this phase of the battle fell only on or in the Cornfield or the Sunken Road. *KIA* means "killed in action."

line, aligned perfectly across the shortest dimension of the field, it would have required 107 dead to span the width of the Cornfield.

At the Sunken Road, by contrast, the "carpet of death" scenario seems more realistic. The narrowness of the lane produces a much smaller surface area compared to the Cornfield (less than one acre versus twenty-plus acres). As a result, if half the killed in action fell in the lane, each corpse would occupy just over fifty square feet. If evenly distributed, a person could easily cross the *width* of the lane at multiple locations without touching the roadbed, and walking a great portion of the length of the lane solely on bodies might even have been possible.

Two factors suggest that this wasn't the case, however. First, the assumption that half of the casualties or killed in action suffered during this phase of the battle occurred and remained in the Sunken Road is highly dubious; the majority of the Confederate killed may have been in the lane but certainly not the federal fallen. The second problem with the plausibility of the "carpet of death" along the entirety of the Bloody Lane was introduced by Alexander Gardner (figures 3.3, 3.4, and 3.5) in the

Figure 3.3. Alexander Gardner's grisly September 19, 1862, photograph of the Bloody Lane. This is the photograph that most commonly accompanies text discussing the "carpet of death." (*Credit:* Enhanced, Library of Congress, https://www.loc.gov/pictures/collection/civwar/item/2018671456/, "Antietam, Maryland. Dead Soldiers in Ditch on the Right Wing Where Kimball's Brigade Fought So Desperately," 1862, LC-DIG-cwpb-01088.)

Figure 3.4.   A second photograph from Gardner's collection shows large areas of the Sunken Road where bodies are absent. However, at the time of the photograph, burial parties may have already removed some corpses for internment nearby. (*Credit:* Modified, Library of Congress, https://www.loc.gov/pictures/item/2018671463/, "Antietam, Maryland. Confederate Dead in a Ditch on the Right Wing," 1862, LC-DIG-cwpb-01100.)

days immediately after the fighting ceased. Photographic evidence documents the carnage in the lane; yet the bodies are not evenly distributed, and there are large areas in the foreground and background along the lane that are bereft of bodies. It should be noted, however, that the corpses in these photographs may be exclusively Rebels, with the federal burial parties having already removed their comrades.

The 130th Pennsylvania Regiment ("Penn'a Volunteers") was part of the federal attack that captured the Sunken Road. After the battle, these same men were given the gruesome task of removing and burying the dead. According to Civil War photography expert William Frassanito, the unit reported interring a total of 138 Confederate soldiers.[45] If 138 bodies were

Figure 3.5.   A third photograph from Gardner's collection, showing a different part of the lane, farther to the west. The men in the background are probably the Union burial detail, represented in large part by the 130th Pennsylvania Regiment. (*Credit:* Enhanced and cropped, Library of Congress, https://www.loc .gov/pictures/item/2018666241/, "Antietam, Md. Confederate Dead in a Ditch on the Right Wing Used as a Rifle Pit," 1862; LC-DIG-cwpb-00240.)

scattered evenly along the road, the average area for each corpse would be 208 square feet, far too high to have created a blanket of the dead. If the bodies were unevenly distributed—as they appear to be in the Gardner photographs (figures 3.3, 3.4, and 3.5, above)—then approximately one-fourth of the lane could be covered with bodies so closely packed together that you could walk without stepping on the road. For the photographic evidence of scattered corpses presented by Gardner, this seems to be the case.

Soldiers' memories were imperfect. After witnessing the shocking concentration of death in one portion of the lane (figure 3.3, above), a witness may have misremembered the scene, later recalling the dead as having covered the entire course of the roadbed, and perhaps later he—or others—transferred this inaccurate memory to a different, nearby location, like the Cornfield. There are also numerous cases where, in the decades after the battle, soldiers wrote accounts describing a portion of the field covered in dead, and these accounts would later be inflated, with corpses being added over time either to increase the density of the dead or to escalate the size of the field. The letters of Charles D. M. Broomhall, who served in the 124th Pennsylvania Infantry, describe the scene thirty years after he helped bury the Confederate dead: "Near Miller's barn along the fence in the field on the West side of the Pike, opposite the corn, I stood at one end of a row of dead Rebels, and without moving, counted ninety three of them, with their heads to the fence, on whom I could have walked without touching the ground."[46] It is not hard to imagine reading

Figure 3.6. Between sixteen and eighteen dead Confederate soldiers (right) and perhaps one dead federal soldier (far left) along the Hagerstown Turnpike. The Cornfield is located beyond the dead soldiers, across the pike, to the right. (*Credit:* Photograph, Library of Congress, https://www.loc.gov/pictures/ item/2018666239/, "Antietam, Md. Confederate Dead by a Fence on the Hagerstown Road," 1862, LC-DIG-cwpb-01097.)

this saturnine account and later retelling the story with the dead lying in the cornfield, not along a fence opposite the cornfield (figure 3.6). In any event, it is clear that the "carpet of death" scenario is much more plausible for the Sunken Road than for the Cornfield.

At Gettysburg another farm field was described by soldiers and later historians as having been blanketed with the bodies of the mortally wounded and killed. The much-contested Wheatfield was a key landscape feature during the second day of fighting, when late in the afternoon James Longstreet's broad assault on the federal left pushed across the adjacent Peach Orchard, Rose Woods, and patch of wheat, into Devil's Den. The "Bloody Wheatfield" changed hands multiple times as General Hood's and General McLaws's assaults surged toward Houck's Ridge, and, after repeated attacks and counterattacks, around one-third of the twenty thousand men engaged fell as casualties.

The Gettysburg Wheatfield (figure 3.7) was owned by the John Rose family and is similar in size to the farm field that David Miller planted

Figure 3.7. The Wheatfield at Gettysburg. This view is looking directly west, with the Rose farmhouse in the distant center. In general, the Confederates attacked across the field from left to right, and the federal infantry counterattacked in the opposite direction.

with corn outside Sharpsburg (table 3.3). Casualty-figure estimates for the entirety of the fighting on July 2 cluster around sixteen thousand, with perhaps one-third of these men falling in or near the Wheatfield. Historian Jay Jurgensen estimates the total number of casualties in the Wheatfield at 6,135.[47] Assuming 15–20 percent of these men were killed in action, there would have been just over 1,200 bodies scattered across this plot of ground.

Table 3.3. Variables to produce a "carpet of death" at the Wheatfield at Gettysburg

Range of estimates for surface area	19–26 acres
Most commonly reported surface area	~20 acres
Surface area used in calculations (analysis)	19 acres
Shape of landscape feature	▱
Casualty estimates for day 2 at Gettysburg	15,000–16,860
Casualty estimates for Wheatfield	6,000–6,135
Killed in action in or near the Wheatfield	~1,227
Density of death: All KIA found only in Wheatfield	675 ft²/corpse
Number of corpses needed for walking path	143 (width)
Number of corpses needed to create "carpet of death"	16,552

Twelve hundred dead scattered across almost twenty acres gives a density of 675 square feet per body. Had the bodies been lined up to make a footpath through the wheat, 143 corpses would have been needed to cross the shortest dimension of the field. The ridiculousness of the claim of a "carpet of death" for this portion of the battleground becomes obvious when considering this scenario: If all the men killed during the entirety of the three-day battle, including Pickett's Charge, were brought to the Wheatfield and evenly distributed, a person would still not have been able to cross the ground without touching the earth.[48]

The final battlefield to be analyzed with respect to the density of death belongs to the western theater of the war, and this landscape is similar to Antietam in that two separate portions of the battleground have been described as meeting the bloody criteria to match the requirements for a "carpet of death." At Antietam, the history books record the larger Cornfield and smaller, linear Sunken Road as two locations with a blanket of corpses. At the Battle of Franklin, south of Nashville, Tennessee, another rectangular plot, the Carter House and grounds, is similar to the Cornfield from a spatial perspective. The region of the Franklin battlefield in front of the federal earthworks, and between the Lewisburg and Columbia Pikes, is somewhat similar to the Sunken Road, if perhaps a bit broader. Of all of the five scenarios analyzed in this section of the chapter, the surface area for the Franklin battleground was most difficult to estimate.

The Battle of Franklin was an absolute disaster for the Confederate Army of Tennessee and their irrationally aggressive commander Lieutenant General John Bell Hood.[49] The fight witnessed repeated Rebel attacks on a fortified federal line, all of which would eventually prove both unsuccessful and extremely costly. The closest the Confederate infantry came to breaking the Union line came along the Columbia Pike, between the Carter House and cotton gin, located across the road. The Confederates pierced the federal line at this location, but the Union reserve, represented by Emerson Opdycke's brigade, counterattacked along the length of the road, pushing the Confederates south. Fierce hand-to-hand combat surrounded the Carter House and outbuildings until the Union finally sealed the breach, ending the Rebel onslaught.

At the same time that the Union center was in peril, the Confederates were launching multiple attacks against the federal left, which was anchored on the Harpeth River. This line was well supported by artillery sited on both sides of the river and protected by an extensive field of abatis. Only one Southern brigade reached the Union earthworks, and here the men of Brigadier General William Quarles were caught in a tremendous and deadly crossfire.

After the battle, two areas of combat were described as a "carpet of death": the Carter House grounds and the field immediately in front of, and south of, the earthworks on the federal left (figure 3.8). The surface area represented by the Carter House, gardens, and grounds is somewhat difficult to assess in retrospect, although most estimates put the killing ground at around two acres (table 3.4).

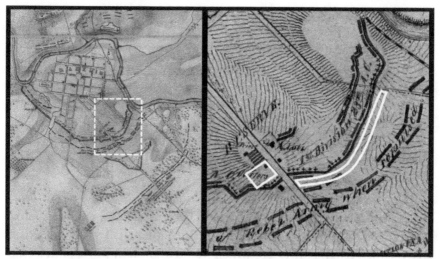

Figure 3.8. Battlefield of Franklin map from 1864 (left); the dashed-line box represents the area with the heaviest fighting, expanded on the map to the right. The two areas purported to being a "carpet of death" postbattle (outlined in white, right) include the rectangular Carter grounds and the area adjacent to the Lewisburg Turnpike. (*Credit:* W. E. Merrill, 1874[?], "Battlefield in Front of Franklin, Tenn., November 30th, 1864," map, retrieved from the Library of Congress, https://www.loc.gov/item/2003630453/.)

Of course, the two-acre estimate for the Carter House grounds includes the footprint of the house and outbuildings, which would have diminished the number of square feet required for the "carpet."[50] Given a surface area of 1.75 acres and a killed-in-action value of 1,939, the only way for the Carter grounds to have been completely covered with fallen soldiers would have been for every single dead soldier, from both armies, to have fallen on the family's property. The same is true for the field in front of the Union left-wing entrenchments: only were every dead soldier from the entire battle killed in this sector—a preposterous assumption—would the density of fallen have been high enough to walk across the battlefield on bodies.

Assuming that only the twenty yards directly in front of the earthworks are considered as a region where all the men had fallen as a carpet (highly doubtful, but still . . .), it would have required that well over half

Table 3.4. Variables to produce a "carpet of death" at Franklin: Carter House grounds versus band of terrain in front of the federal left

	Carter grounds	Federal left
Range of estimates for surface area	1–2 acres	330–420 yards long, ~20 yards wide
Most commonly reported surface area	~2 acres	1–2 acres
Surface area used in calculations (analysis)	1.75 acres	1.6 acres
Shape of landscape feature	▭	⟋
Casualty estimates, battle	9,000–10,000	9,000–10,000
Killed in action for phase of battle	1,939	1,939
Density of death: All KIA found only on grounds/field	39 ft²/corpse	37 ft²/corpse
Density of death: Half of KIA found only on grounds/field	79 ft²/corpse	74 ft²/corpse
Number of corpses needed for walking path	28 (width)	171 (length)
Number of corpses needed for "carpet of death"	1,524	1,473

of all killed during the battle fall on this stretch of ground between the Lewisburg and Columbia Pikes. Obviously the Carter grounds and this area of the battlefield cannot both have been a "carpet of death," and it is highly probable that neither was. What is more likely is that a portion of both combat areas was densely covered with several dozen or so corpses packed closely together and the description of this ghastly scene was conflated to extend across the entirety of the garden or field. Some historical accounts support this hypothesis: Several Carter family members and Confederate soldiers describe a scene where fifty to sixty dead federal soldiers were lying near the Carter House or porch.

In *Hood's Tennessee Campaign: The Desperate Venture of a Desperate Man*, James R. Knight relates the firsthand account of Major General Frank Cheatham, whose infantry were caught up in the swirling fighting around the Carter House: "The dead were piled up like sacks of wheat or scattered about like sheaves of grain. You could have walked all over the field upon dead bodies without stepping upon the ground. . . . Almost under your eye, nearly all the dead, wounded and dying lay. In front of the Carter house, the bodies lay in heaps."[51]

Note that in this description of the "carpet of death" story, the general has added wounded soldiers to the total number of bodies in the field. In doing so, he triples the number of bodies present, whether dead or wounded. He also never specifies which field could be "walked all over" or what specific portion of the battlefield he was describing. It is certainly plausible that one portion of the landscape around the Carter property was densely packed with dead and wounded soldiers of both sides, but it is much less reasonable to believe the totality of the Carter grounds, or the ground in front of the federal left, was blanketed with dead soldiers.

Two eyewitness accounts—one from a Confederate infantryman and one from a Yankee—are included in Jack Lepa's book *Breaking the Confederacy: The Georgia and Tennessee Campaigns of 1864*, and both accounts provide critical parameters for the surface area over which a person could have walked without touching the ground. Federal William G. Bently, describing the carnage on the Union left: "The ditch was literally piled with dead and wounded and for rods you could scarcely walk without stepping on a body." A rod is 5.5 yards long, so this scenario seems entirely possible. Confederate John M. Copley, speaking of the same sector of the field: "Streams of blood ran here and there over the entire battle ground, in little branches, and one could have walked upon the dead and wounded men from one end of the column to the other."[52]

Combine these accounts, and you have a scenario where the description is plausible: dead and wounded soldiers cover a few hundred square feet so densely that you would need to step on bodies to cross the terrain in this particular area. When contrasted with other reports of multiacre fields completely covered with the dead alone, the source of the exaggeration becomes clearer.

In summary, then, it appears that accounts of a Civil War landscape so covered in dead soldiers that one could walk the entirety of the field without touching the ground represents a conflagration of the density of death in the minds of the eyewitnesses and veterans' memories, and this conclusion is not drawn solely from the spatial analysis contain herein. Thomas Desjardin, in his excellent treatise on the Battle of Gettysburg and the later modification of the battle history, provides two contemporaneously skeptical quotations from the men who did the fighting. From a Vermont veteran: "I discover not only an unwarrantable spirit of exaggeration on the part of some officers, but a disposition to detract from others what rightfully belongs to them, so I shall not be surprised if you are led into errors." And from another witness from the fighting: "Much has been written on the subject of this battle, much of which have contained exaggerated statements and distorted facts for the ostensible purpose of making heroes of their favorites and giving the world the wrong impression of the true history of these eventful times."[53] The middle of the nineteenth century was a time when language was greatly embellished, and it is not hard to imagine a veteran adding a bit to his prose after retelling a story for twenty years, slowly adding to the size of the carpet.[54]

Of all the claims of corpse-covered fields, from Antietam to Franklin, several seem easiest to dismiss outright. Accounts that claim a person could walk on the dead for more than a mile or "as far as the eye could see" were clearly exaggerated. Other claims about the Cornfield or Wheatfield that include the qualifier "in any direction" for the route of traverse are also clearly erroneous. The surface area of these farm fields was simply too great for a cross-country hike on the dead.

One claim about the density of death was so preposterous that it was not included in the earlier long list of quotations: At least one account places the "carpet of death" at the site of Pickett's Charge. In a sermon from *The Homiletic Review*, the fields of the disastrous Confederate onslaught are said to have been so densely covered that a person could walk the field "without touching foot to the ground."[55] In reality, the field over which Pettigrew, Pickett, and Trimble led their famous charge could probably have been covered with all the killed in action *from the entire war*, and still it would not approach this concentration.[56]

For the five claims examined herein, the Sunken Lane at Antietam seems most plausibly to have seen a "carpet of death" after the fighting. At that location, a static defensive line, intense and sustained fighting, and a small relative surface area combined to provide many corpses in close proximity. Other fields of combat at Antietam—like the Cornfield—or other battlegrounds were simply too large with respect to the acreage over which the combat took place to have been heavily covered with the killed. Perhaps in future accounts of the fighting, authors, park rangers and guides, and other storytellers should adopt the note of caution provided (repeatedly) by distinguished historian James McPherson—that the description of the blanket of death was being passed on "doubtless with some exaggeration" or that the eyewitness claim was recorded "no doubt with some exaggeration." His modifying caveats to the bloody narratives respect the interpretations of the witnesses to the carnage on the battlefield while at the same time recognizing the repulsion-induced embellishment of the descriptions.

Lead Precipitation

Introduction

The Miller Cornfield at Antietam witnessed some of the fiercest combat of the entire war, with the forty-acre plot changing hands more than a dozen times. The combat in the cornfield was also undoubtedly one of the single greatest inspirations for Civil War tropes: The men marched through "a perfect hail-storm" of bullets,[1] where they fell "like wheat before the scythe,"[2] and after the battle the field was transformed: "every stalk of corn" had been "cut as closely as could have been done with a knife,"[3] and the field "was so full of bodies that a man could have walked through it without stepping on the ground."[4]

The previous chapter of this book investigated the final body-density exaggeration, demonstrating the origin of the legend and the degree of dramatization. This chapter continues this exploration of spatial relationships, focusing on the intensity of hail and the distribution of hailstone strikes on the battleground. I am a geoscientist—not a farmer, like my grandfather—so this chapter will focus on leaden hailstones instead of wheat, cornstalks, and scythes.

In their after-battle recollections and letters home, soldiers and officers often compared the intensity of incoming gunfire to various forms of precipitation. The specificity of these comparisons of ordnance and weather simplifies the comprehension of the analog: one specific type of small-arms or artillery fire ... fell like ... one particular type of precipitation. "Minié balls fell like rain"[5] or "solid shot rained like hail,"[6] or, occasionally, a poetic (if less specific) synthesis, "rained their leaden hail upon us."[7]

This simplicity is why the descriptions are effective: while almost no one in the audience of the writer or speaker had ever experienced the terror of being shot at, everyone had been caught in the rain or witnessed a hailstorm. This chapter will also be specific, analyzing the most common of the "lead-precipitation" scenarios. Bruce Catton vividly described the eyewitness reports from the bloody Antietam Cornfield: "Men said afterwards that bullets seemed to be thick as hail in a great storm."[8]

The Historical Claim

After a great fight, the volume and intensity of small-arms or artillery fire can be difficult to accurately describe. The National Park Service has elected to use vivid numerical imageries to express the magnitude of gunfire at many historical interpretive centers. At Fredericksburg, for example, visitors are shown a large cylinder that contains "more than ten thousand bullets, the number fired in one minute of combat." Just down the road, a second display informs readers that at Chancellorsville "17,500 men fell—one man shot every second for five hours." Continuing the visit, a few additional miles to the south bring battlefield tourists to Spotsylvania Court House, where "On May 12 men of both sides fired as many as two million rounds of ammunition."

During the Civil War, however, witnesses to the intensity of gunfire in combat had no adequate means of clearly quantifying the volume of shot and shell. Instead, they often choose to compare the incoming gunfire to everyday occurrences, like precipitation.

Leaden precipitation was reported by witnesses from nearly every battle of the Civil War; hail was likely chosen for the analogy over snow, or even rain, because of the stones' shape—reminiscent of a musket ball in both size and sphericity—and velocity. It probably didn't diminish the analogy that large hailstone strikes can actually injure a person.

Bullets, shot, and shell fell with the intensity of hail at all of the following battles, listed in roughly the order of storm frequency: Gettysburg, First Manassas, Shiloh, Second Manassas, Antietam, Malvern Hill, Balls Bluff, Chancellorsville, South Mountain, Fredericksburg, Stones River (fittingly), Atlanta, and Port Hudson. And this list doesn't even include references to "a hail of bullets"—only specific references to small-arms or artillery fire incoming with the intensity of strikes as hailstones in a severe storm.

All phases of the Battle of Gettysburg apparently had deadly leaden hail. Private Reuben Ruch of the 153rd Pennsylvania Infantry remembered the Rebel bullets "whistling about like hail" as he retreated from Blocher's Knoll.[9] A nearly identical observation was made a half mile to the west, where Major George Harvey of the 147th New York said the bullets "whistled around their heads like hail."[10] The infamous railroad cut didn't escape the analogy either; Francis Pease described the gunfire: "Rebel balls whistled over the ravine like hail."[11] At one point of the battle, "Minie balls pounded the town like hail."[12]

On July 2 the metal precipitation was just as intense, especially on the southern sector of the battleground. Richard Robins—11th US Infantry—remembered "a perfect hailstorm of bullets" in the Rose Woods, and below Little Round Top federal "minié balls were falling through the leaves like hail in a thunderstorm" (Private William Ward, 4th Alabama). John Stevens, of Hood's Brigade, observed that "the balls were whizzing so thick around us that it looks like a man could hold out his hat and catch it full . . . the balls were flying thick as hail." Confederates returned fire with an equal intensity (a lead isopleth, in meteorological-speak?), with bullets "flying" and "falling" like hail.[13]

At the same time, and on the other end of the federal fishhook, both sides exchanged stones: "The balls could be heard to strike the breastworks like hailstones upon [the rooftops]," wrote Major William Goldsborough of the 1st Maryland. A private of the 20th Georgia remarked that "the balls were striking the trees like hail all around us."[14]

The final day of the great battle was dominated by Pickett's Charge— and it was also, unsurprisingly, not shielded from bad metallic weather. First, Confederate artillery produced the thermal uplifts capable of forming the hail, before Union-combined small-arms fire and artillery began their own storm of lead. Evander Law, a major general in the Confederate Army, described the artillery barrage: "Three hundred guns, about equally divided between the two ridges, vomited their iron hail upon each other." Clinton McDougall (117th New York) pronounced the Rebel ordnance as "sending shot and shell whirling into our midst like hail in a midsummer storm." As the Confederate infantry advanced, it met a similar intensity of shot and shell, as well as rifle bullets: "And now there burst upon our ranks in front and on the flank, like sheeted hail, a new storm of missiles" (Adjutant James Crocker). And, finally, as at the Cornfield at Antietam, the results of the hailstorm resembled the product of a farm implement: "Bullets were coming like hailstones, and whittling our boys like grain before the sickle" (Sergeant Alfred Carpenter, 1st Minnesota Volunteers).

Note that in each of the previous descriptions of hail from Gettysburg the term specifically refers to hailstorms and the intensity of hailstones in the air or striking the ground. *Hail* was an especially common word in the latter half of the nineteenth century, used as a transitive verb (To hail a ship), intransitive verb (He hails from Harrisburg . . . Shells were hailing down), interjection (Hail to the chief), and noun (A hail of gunfire . . . They greeted the general with a hail . . . Precipitation in the form of concentric layers of ice). This chapter deals with only the final use of the word as a noun: the comparison of bullets and shells to balls or lumps of ice. Letters, reports, and speeches are full of all of these uses of *hail*, but the analysis herein only considers the analogy between incoming ordnance and hailstones that meet these two criteria:

1. Hail or hailstones are specifically mentioned in a meteorological context.

2. The intensity and frequency of impacts is the point of the reference or comparison.

Two unsurprising trends surface in the literature when searching for the "hail" trope. First, major battles—and specifically the bloodiest portions of larger battles—are more frequently cited as having hail-bullet storms: Pope's assaults against Jackson's line behind the unfinished railroad grade at Second Manassas, Burnside's inane and repeated attacks against Marye's Heights at Fredericksburg, the entirety of the Battle of Malvern Hill.

The second trend is more unexpected but still not surprising in retrospect: the hail/bullet storm analogy was most commonly used by soldiers who were experiencing combat for the first time. If the size and scale of the battle is considered, the frequency of the descriptions of bullets falling like hail at First Manassas and Balls Bluff rival Antietam or Gettysburg.

The analysis of the hail trope will focus primarily on the degree of exaggeration between the intensity of (actual) bullet-sized hailstone strikes and that possible with minié bullets and musket balls. The description of solid shot and shell falling like hail is also common in the literature. James Longstreet, writing about Fredericksburg: "Solid shot rained like hail."[15] The *New York Herald* describing the gunfire at Shiloh: "Cannonballs were falling like hail."[16] William Simmers and Paul Bachschmid of the 157th Pennsylvania Regiment noted of their experience at Gettysburg, "Shells were now showering upon us 'thick as hail.'"[17] While bullets might conceivably strike in the proximity of a soldier with the frequency of large hail, artillery shells could not; the big guns were simply too slow to reload and fire, and their limited population on most battlefields renders such a comparison completely implausible—and not really worth testing. For example, suppose you had the full artillery firepower available to the Army of the Potomac at Antietam or Gettysburg, and you concentrated the entirety of this cannonade at a single company of Rebel infantry. Three hundred guns, firing three rounds per minute per piece, equates to nine hundred rounds per minute—certainly a deadly scenario. But if this shellfire is spread over sixty seconds and across an entire company of one hundred men, the absurdity of the comparison between shells and hailstones becomes obvious (only fifteen hailstones per second would be spread across an entire company of men). Unless the entire company were collected into the same thirty-foot-diameter circle (target), the entire assembled artillery of the federal army couldn't begin to simulate the intensity of hail in a storm. As a result, this chapter concentrates on small-arms fire: tens of thousands of rifles firing, instead of (potentially) hundreds of cannons, reduces the degree of exaggeration for the hailstorm/bullet scenario by several orders of magnitude.

Finally, special praise is in order for Samuel Smucker, who in his 1865 *History of the Civil War in the United States* really hammers home the hailstorm trope. His manuscript contains nearly every conceivable form of description for the lead precipitation, including "hailstorm of balls," "fiery and destructive hail [ladening] the air," "leaden hail of musketry," "hailstorm of shot," "torn by the iron hail," "thick falling leaden hail," "tempest of iron hail," "the air [seemingly] filled with sulphurous hail," and "contemptuous hail-storm of shot and shell."[18] And this list is far from complete. Left unanswered is whether the author knew how to use a sickle or scythe.

THE SCIENCE

Severe thunderstorms have updrafts that carry raindrops vertically into extremely cold air, where the liquid precipitation freezes. As additional raindrops collide with the frozen drops, hailstones form and grow in size. When the stones grow larger in size, the updrafts are no longer able to keep the stones aloft, and they fall to earth.

The velocity and direction in which hail falls is dependent on the winds associated with the storm and the size of the stones. Small hailstones descend as slowly as ten miles per hour, while one- to two-inch stones may reach fifty miles per hour and fall almost horizontally. Very large hailstones, the size of a cannonball, may reach or even exceed one hundred miles per hour.

The central United States has the most hailstorms; Colorado, Nebraska, and Wyoming all average eight hail days per year. Many Civil War battle sites experience hail on a yearly basis (table 4.1).

Clearly, hail fell more frequently across the western theater of the war compared to the battlefields in the east. Soldiers occasionally mentioned noncombat (meteorological) hail in their diaries and reports. New York artist George Perkins commented on hailstones as large as "English walnuts" on the Virginia Peninsula.[19] Other reports of terrific hailstorms exist for Tennessee (Shiloh), Virginia (Fredericksburg, Hampton Roads), and Mississippi (Okolona). Hail and severe weather continue to menace the battlefields today; as recently as 2019, tornadoes and hail made landfall on the Grand Gulf battleground (figure 4.1).

Spatially, hail falls in paths known as *swaths*.[20] Depending on the velocity of the storm, these linear paths can be a few miles wide but a hundred miles long. The intensity and potential hazard from the hail in these swaths is a function of the size of the stones. Pea-size hail causes little (if any) damage. Minié ball–size hail may damage crops.

Table 4.1. Civil War battlefields that have experienced the most hailstorms (data compiled from NOAA/NWS/NCEP/Storm Prediction Center, Norman, Oklahoma)

Two hundred–plus hail reports between 1955 and 2002
Atlanta, GA
Bentonville, NC
Chickamauga, GA
Pea Ridge, AR
Vicksburg, MS
Wilson's Creek, MO

150–199 hail reports between 1955 and 2002
Chattanooga, TN
Corinth, MS
Franklin, TN
Memphis, TN
Nashville, TN
Shiloh, TN
Stones River, TN

Figure 4.1.   Evidence of a tornado touchdown on the Grand Gulf battleground. This photograph was taken approximately two hundred yards south of Fort Cobun on the Mississippi River floodplain.

Grapeshot-size hail can break glass and damage automobiles. Although rare, cannonball-size hail can damage brick and cause serious injuries or even death.

Most studies of hail intensity, frequency, and damage are produced by, understandably, insurance companies. Crop-related hail losses are a particular concern in the Midwest. From 1950 to 1990, the financial loss from hail-induced crop failure was greater than that of other nonagricultural property damage (cars, roofs). This ratio flipped in the 1990s, with several storms creating more than 400 million dollars' worth of damage across the United States (Wichita, Denver, Orlando).

Hail intensity is a function of the size of the stones and their velocity (kinetic energy), plus the frequency of impact and number of stones (volume of ice).[21] Larger hailstones fall at a higher velocity, and it is not surprising that they can injure a human; a typical three-inch-diameter stone falls with the same kinetic energy as a .22 long-rifle rimfire round.

Hail pads can be used to measure the size distribution and mass of hailstones after a storm passes. These data-collection devices are fairly simple—a panel of plastic foam covered with aluminum foil or white paint. The number and size of the poststorm dents quantifies the size and intensity of the storm. A used hail pad looks like the surface of the moon, with larger dents (craters) representing larger hailstone strikes. These devices do not tell the observer, however, the frequency of the strikes or the number of impacts per minute. As a result, some analysis is in order to predict the survivability of a leaden hailstorm in combat.

ANALYSIS AND EVALUATION

To test the notion that bullets truly "fell as thick as hailstones" during a fight, it is necessary to know the frequency of hail strikes per unit area. And if men were actually "cut down like hail cuts the grain and grass," the duration of both the hailstorm and the episode of combat must be established. This subsection of the chapter concentrates on answering these two questions:

1. How long could a soldier last in a leaden hailstorm before becoming a casualty from the precipitation?

2. What volume of fire—theoretical number of riflemen—would be needed to create an actual hailstorm of lead on any sector of a battlefield?

To answer these questions, two sets of parameters must first be quantified—one meteorological and one military. For the typical damage-inducing hailstorm, we must know:

1. The minimum size of the hailstones
2. The frequency of impact across the land surface
3. The spatiolateral extent of the hail strikes
4. The duration of the storm

The military component of the calculations is much more easily computed: How many weapons were available, and what was the maximum rate of fire for each gun?

It is impossible to know what size hailstones the Civil War witnesses were describing in their hail/gunfire analogy—certainly something larger than pea-size stones. The Illinois State Weather Service states that hail begins to cause damage when it approaches three-quarters of an inch in diameter; so, if soldiers were comparing hail to bullets, we can use this convenient (if slightly arbitrary) bullet size as our cutoff for the minimum diameter of stones in this analysis: 0.58 inches.

The most difficult criterion to quantify in this analysis is the frequency of impacts of hailstones per unit area (square feet). Almost all of the research in this area concentrates on how many stones fell per square foot or square meter in a given storm (density of strikes), but no rate of impact was measured. An insurance company only cares that a roof is damaged or a cornfield destroyed, not how quickly the destruction occurred. There are two potential avenues of approach to add a time component to the hailstone frequency/intensity evaluation: divide the density of strikes by the duration of the storm, or use observational data. Both approaches are used and compared here.

Density and Duration
After a hailstorm, the density and distribution of stones varies on a range of spatial scales, varying from strikes across a single swath or swaths across

several states. In general, Western states have larger hailstones, and larger stones fall in a more scattered pattern. For example, a study of solar-panel vulnerability by the Jet Propulsion Laboratory at NASA found that, on average, 9.2 half-inch stones fell per square foot in an average storm, while 1.5 stones three-quarters inch in diameter fell over the same area. Only one one-inch stone fell for every two square feet. Palencia et al. report that their hail-pad study revealed a higher density of strikes but a similar trend: 0.6-inch-diameter stones—162 strikes per square foot; 0.8-inch stones—fifty-eight strikes per square foot.[22]

A study from Decatur, Illinois, found similar densities of impacts: five to forty strikes per square foot. A review of several other meteorological journal publications indicates an average of around one hundred strikes per square foot for three-quarter-inch hail and twenty-five strikes per square foot for one-inch hail. In summary, then, during an average hailstorm, around fifty to one hundred minié/musket ball–sized stones will fall per square foot of ground.

This density is useful for envisioning the fall of stones, but a better picture of the intensity is established if the duration of the storm is included in the factoring. According to NASA, NOAA, and the Illinois State Weather Survey, the average hailstorm lasts for between three and fifteen minutes. The majority of storms last between 6.5 and 9.5 minutes in the Central and Eastern United States. Research reports from insurance companies agree with these durations, with an average length of storms averaging 7.5 minutes.

Now, with the density and duration estimates approximated, the frequency of strikes per minute is simple to calculate. For hailstones larger than 0.58 inches in diameter, around fifty to one hundred stones will fall per square foot every seven to nine minutes. This gives a minimum frequency of strikes of 5.5 square feet per minute for larger stones in longer storms and 14.2 stone strikes per square foot per minute for slightly smaller stones in shorter storms. All in all, the average hailstorm produces an intensity of around ten bullet-size stones per square foot per minute.

Observational data—watching high-resolution, slow-speed video of hailstorms—provided estimated strike frequencies in the following ranges (see table 4.2).

Table 4.2. Observational data of hailstone strikes per square foot per minute

Hailstone diameter (inches)	Range of strikes/ft^2/ minute	Average strikes/ft^2/ minute
1.0	2.0–18.0	10.0
1.5	2.5–12.0	7.3
2.0	5.0–17.0	11.0
2.5	3.0–5.0	4.0
Average	*3.0–16.0*	*7.0*

Seven observable strikes per minute is in general agreement with the data published in, and calculated from, the meteorological literature, and the observed rate of strikes is for slightly larger stones (and watching and quantifying impacts is difficult and prone to undercounting).

The average surface area for men between the ages of eighteen and forty is twenty-two square feet.[23] Of course, not all of this surface would be exposed to falling hail—or even hail that is being blown sideways. Instead, hail usually has one vertical vector (gravity) and another, usually smaller, horizontal direction (wind), so it falls at an angle dependent on the size of the stone and the strength of the gusts. A soldier standing upright during a hailstorm would be primarily struck on the top of his head and shoulders, and perhaps his feet, if the hail is falling perpendicularly to the ground. This would produce the smallest-conceivable target for the hail—around two to three square feet of surface area. A prone soldier would present the largest cross section during a storm, with almost ten square feet of surface area that might be struck from above.

If we use a value between two and ten square feet for the target soldier—say, a conservative four square feet—this means that a man standing in a typical hailstorm would be struck at a minimum more than twenty times per minute, or once every few seconds (figure 4.2). Even in the best survival case for the unfortunate man, where he is standing completely upright with his arms at his sides and the hail is falling with no side wind, he could expect to be hit in the head and shoulders in less than ten seconds after the storm began.[24] All of these scientific calculations and

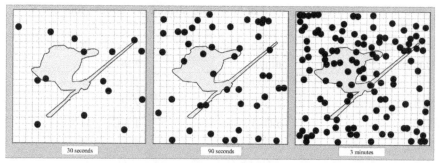

Figure 4.2. The outline in the three figures above is of a Civil War soldier, carrying a musket, when viewed from above. A random-numbers generator was used to calculate the location of hailstone strikes on and around the man for half a minute, a minute and a half, and three minutes. If bullets had fallen like hail, this soldier would have been hit by seventeen minié balls in the first three minutes of combat. It seems unlikely that he would have survived to write about his experience.

observations can be further verified with empirical evidence by going to YouTube and searching for "idiot runs around shirtless in hailstorm."

What volume of small-arms firepower would be required to create a hailstorm of lead on the battlefield? Most references to hailstorms by the fighting men mention comrades in arms—"The hail was falling on *us*." The "us" typically refers to the soldier's company or regiment, or at least the group of men in close proximity to him. If we assume he is referring to a company of men in combat (fifty to one hundred men), the group would occupy, very roughly, a space of approximately 1,250 square feet.[25]

To create the metal hailstorm, these men would need to have been fired upon at a rate of 8,750 rounds per minute. A Civil War rifle musket takes between twenty and thirty seconds to reload and aim quickly, so even at rapid fire, a minimum of more than twenty-five thousand soldiers would need to concentrate their fire at this unfortunate group of men to create the appearance of a leaden hailstorm.

So, for the hailstone/bullet scenario to be plausible, every infantry-man from several entire divisions would have to concentrate their fire at one particular small group of men. At Antietam, for example, a Union regiment entering the Cornfield might have experienced a hailstorm of lead had Jackson's *entire corps* fired solely and relentlessly at that tiny sector, and only that tiny sector, of the federal line.[26] On Little Round Top, Company D of the 20th Maine might have experienced lead precipitation if Brigadier General Evander M. Law's two Alabama regiments had concentrated their fire in only their direction and if Law's men had been supplemented by all the guns of Major General John Bell Hood's and Major General Lafayette McLaws's *entire divisions*. And even if this preposterous situation could have developed, every man in Company D ~~would have been cut down like grain before the scythe~~ would have been killed in a matter of minutes, leaving no witness to report on the hailstorm. The trope, like the soldiers, would have died on the hillslope.

5

Ready, Aim, Reload

INTRODUCTION

NATHAN BEDFORD FORREST UNDERSTOOD WELL THE NATURE OF PSY-chological warfare: "Get 'em skeered, and keep the skeer on 'em."[1] And there is no better way to skeer a common soldier than to drop them into combat, on open terrain, with little cover.

The Civil War rifle musket is a terrifically difficult weapon to operate efficiently when frightened. With an M1 Garand, M14, or even M16, a citizen-soldier needs only to flip off the gun's safety and pull the trigger. Reloading after eight or thirty rounds are expended is slightly more complicated, involving replacing an empty magazine with one that is loaded. With a Civil War musket, a soldier could take only one shot before he needed to conduct the arduous, time-consuming task of reloading. Only then could he fire another solitary shot. To be efficient in this process, he also needed to be standing.

As fear increases in a soldier, combat effectiveness decreases. This relationship is magnified by the use of a single-shot rifle. To load the gun, a soldier needed to follow all of the following steps, most of which needed to be performed in the proper sequence: (1) Tear open a paper cartridge that contained a bullet and powder. (2) Dump the powder down the barrel. (3) Place the bullet at the top of the muzzle of the gun, facing the proper direction. (4) Use a three- to four-foot-long ramrod to force the bullet down the barrel on top of the powder. (5) Cock the hammer to reveal the nipple of the weapon. And (6) place a small percussion cap on this nipple. After this twenty- to thirty-second procedure, the weapon was ready to fire. Once.

Several of these rifle-loading steps require a degree of dexterity that is difficult to achieve when minié balls are flying around, striking those around you, or when you are exhausted. Failure to complete any of the steps—and in the correct order—will cause the musket to misfire. If the bullet is placed in the barrel before the powder, the gun will not fire. If the powder is wet, the gun will not fire. If the percussion cap is defective or falls off, or is simply forgotten, the gun will not fire. If residue from previous shots has blocked the vent—the tube connecting the nipple to the chamber—the gun will not fire. If the bullet is not properly seated on the powder in the breech, the gun might not fire, or it might explode. Now consider a poorly trained soldier, with little experience with firearms, standing in the open, trying to conduct these procedures while being screamed at by an officer and deafened by gunfire—all while being shot at. He would be skeered.

This chapter explores the interrelationship between combat psychology and weapon efficiency: How often did rifles fail because of operator error, and how often did they fail simply because of the nature and design of the long arm? The evidence of this failure was collected from battlefields across the country after armies left the battlegrounds—the astonishing number of salvaged guns that were misloaded and discarded (figure 5.1).

This controversial subject is a bit more of a debate than a trope—or, at least, the trope is more subtle in the retelling. The basic idea to be considered, analyzed, and tested here is why the rifles recovered after major battles were so frequently loaded with multiple rounds. The traditional and most popular explanation, relayed over the years by historians and interpreters, is that the terror of battle led some soldiers to reload without firing, often more than once. More recently, a professor of military science, Dave Grossman, offered a different explanation for the overloaded rifles. He argued that the guns were loaded over and over (and over) by soldiers who were resisting killing the enemy by only pretending to participate in the fight.[2] Some other historians point to the weapons more than the men: The guns, they say, simply failed to fire for whatever reason and were

Figure 5.1. Federal rifles stacked at Petersburg, Virginia, near the end of the war. These appear to be a mix of very well-kept varieties of Springfield rifles: M1861s, M1863s, and M1864s. (*Credit:* "Petersburg, Va. Row of Stacked Federal Rifles; Houses Beyond," detail of photograph, April 3, 1865, Library of Congress, LC-DIG-cwpb-02647, https://www.loc.gov/resource/cwpb.02647/.)

discarded. No one had time to unload a rifle musket in combat, especially when other (seemingly) operable weapons were lying around nearby. Before these three scenarios can be properly considered, it would be best to delineate the exact historical claim concerning the misloaded guns.

THE HISTORICAL CLAIM

The origins of the proof-of-panic story evidenced by the severely overloaded guns—with three, five, ten, or even more than twenty bullets crammed down the barrel—can be traced back to 1865. Major T. T. S. Laidley, of the US Ordnance Department, described the weapons that were collected from the Gettysburg Battlefield after the armies moved south: "Of the twenty-seven thousand five hundred seventy-four muskets collected after the battle, it was found that twenty-four thousand were loaded: Twelve thousand contained each two loads and six thousand (over twenty per cent.), were charged with from three to ten loads each. One musket had in it twenty-three loads."[3]

Over the years, these statistics have been used by battle historians/ psychologists as proof positive that men were too stricken with terror during the chaos of battle to either fire their weapons or register that their gun had not discharged after they'd pulled the trigger. In the simplest scenario, one soldier unknowingly loads the same rifle, over and over and over again, never realizing that not a single bullet has left the barrel—even as his ramrod continues to stop higher and higher in the muzzle after each "shot." Proponents of this scenario for the misloaded guns never consider the mechanical workings of the firearms or the rate of fouling and misfires.

To be clear, the historical claim to be tested is that *the vast majority of the discarded weapons misloaded with multiple rounds were direct evidence of individual soldiers, under unimaginable stress, reloading already-loaded guns.* This certainly did happen repeatedly in the din of combat; nevertheless, is it realistic that all, or at least the vast majority, of these misfired guns were the result of petrified-operator error? Are there any other explanations for the guns that should be considered before passing along the "hysterical infantryman" scenario?

This "panic-induced-reloading" explanation consistently carries two descriptions that provide the grounds for testing and evaluation: an individual soldier is responsible for reloading the loaded weapon many times, and his failure is the result of "hysteria," "anxiety," or being "overly excited."

Here are a few examples of these descriptors from the Civil War literature: In *What They Didn't Teach You about the Civil War*, Mike Wright attributes the mass loadings to insufficient training: "One poor soldier had managed to stuff nearly two dozen minié balls down his rifle, and then probably wondered why it didn't fire. He was lucky the damn thing didn't blow up in his face."[4] In *Fighting Means Killing*, Jonathan Steplyk summarizes the psychological aspect of the constant reloading, as told by his historical predecessors: "Civil War historians traditionally attribute these improperly loaded weapons to lack of training and nervousness among soldiers."[5] Charles Chapel attributes the misloaded weapons and the twenty-three-bullet gun to "near-hysteria and excitement prevailing during the battle."[6] Ian Harvey explains *Why the Guns at Gettysburg Were Found Loaded*: "Apparently, one poor soldier had reloaded his weapon twenty-three times, but the weird thing is that he never fired a single shot. Read that again: he reloaded his weapon, but didn't shoot at all, and he wasn't the only one to do this."[7] This quotation contains both criteria outlined above for the "hysterical infantryman" explanation: He (singular) was in a "poor" state. And he wasn't the only one reloading but not firing.

In summary, then, we are left with three general explanations for why between 32 and 43 percent of recovered rifles from the Gettysburg battle-ground were loaded with more than one bullet:

1. The panicked and hysterical soldiers reloaded many times but never fired their weapons.

2. Men who were averse to killing were mimicking the loading and firing of the weapons in an effort to obscure the fact that they were not actually shooting.

3. Weapons failed to fire for multiple reasons, only to be discarded and picked up later by another soldier, who then reloaded the misfired musket.

This chapter will analyze and critique scenarios one and three, with a particular emphasis on quantifying the probability of a competent soldier finding his weapon inoperable through no fault of his own. Scenario two, where the infantrymen are loading their weapons but only pretending to fire, makes little sense. When Dave Grossman introduced this idea in *On Killing*, it garnered much attention and some degree of ridicule. Grossmann's general contention can be summarized thus: "Most soldiers have an inner resistance to firing their weapons in combat . . . and this resistance is the reason for many (if not most) of these multiply loaded weapons."[8]

Jonathan Steplyk's response to this notion is blunt: "This particular explanation strains credibility," and "this hardly would have been the most practical way of abstaining from killing in battle."[9] Additionally, despite his military experience, Grossman presents a slightly confused understanding of how a rifle musket operates: "Some may argue that these multiple loads were simply mistakes, and that these weapons were discarded because they were misloaded. But if in the fog of war, despite all these endless hours of training, you do accidentally double-load a musket, you shoot it anyway, and the first load simply pushes out the second load."[10]

This double-firing might work under extremely limited circumstances, where the gun was accidentally misloaded in a specific way—one round was properly seated but the percussion cap was forgotten. If a second round were placed directly on top of the first and the bullets were not tight-fitting in the rifling, a double shot *might* be possible. Nevertheless, in almost all circumstances, a rifle musket cannot simply be reloaded and fired with two rounds exiting the barrel. Say, for example, the soldier had placed the minié ball down the barrel before the powder—a completely plausible mistake in combat. The ignition from the percussion cap travels down the vent, but it never reaches the powder, because it is blocked by lead. Misfire. Reloading another round properly will do nothing to alleviate the problem, and it will only make it more difficult to clear the misload.

Had the misfire been caused by another source of failure (faulty percussion cap or temporarily blocked vent, for example), reloading for a second time renders the weapon extremely dangerous for the user and prone to explode; it won't allow the first bullet to simply "push out the second load."

In almost all cases, when a muzzleloading rifle fails to fire—and the reason isn't immediately evident (e.g., percussion cap fell off or hammer not cocked)—the misloaded round will need to be cleared from the barrel using the ramrod and a small tool called a screw (or worm). This device attaches to the ramrod so that, when it is pushed down the barrel and rotated, it will pierce the soft lead of the bullet, after which the round can be "pulled" from the barrel (figure 5.2). This process will take longer than the traditional loading routine, leaving a soldier feeling especially vulnerable in combat, because even after successfully pulling the bullet out, he will still be left with an unloaded rifle in need of proper reloading.

For all of these reasons, the "pretending soldiers" scenario will be discarded. After all, if twelve thousand men were simulating shooting, wouldn't someone notice the lack of gun smoke around certain men—and

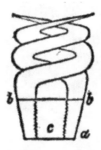 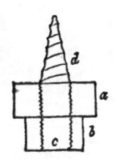 

Figure 5.2.   The illustrations on the left and center are from the US Ordnance Department's handbook for the Springfield Model 1855 rifle musket. In the center is a screw, which attached to the end of the threaded ramrod at point "c." The device to the left is a worm (or bore wiper), which was used to clean the barrel using dry cloth or tow. It could also, with some difficulty, be used to pull out a bullet. The .69-caliber bullet on the right was pulled from a musket, showing scaring from a worm around the ogive.

the fact that their ramrods kept extending farther and farther out of their guns? After a long fight, wouldn't it be strange if a few of the men in a company had no black-powder residue on their faces or hands? Or had to spend a half hour or so unloading their rifles? As a result of these considerations, the analysis in the next subsection will focus on the probability of the first and third explanations for the thousands of excessively misloaded guns: hysteria versus misfire.

THE SCIENCE

The most famous ground over which discarded weapons were collected and counted was located around Gettysburg, Pennsylvania, but this battlefield was not unique with respect to the potential firepower that was left behind on the field. Historian Earl Hess mentions multiple other battlefields that offered proportional bounty for the army left in possession of the landscape. The Confederates picked up almost twenty-five thousand much-needed guns at Chickamauga and another six thousand at Stones River. In the east, Chancellorsville yielded 29,500 guns, and Fredericksburg provided another eleven thousand (figure 5.3).[11] Entire regiments were known to upgrade their weapons after a major fight; both the 47th

Figure 5.3.   Confederate dead behind the stone wall in front of Marye's Heights after the Second Battle of Fredericksburg during the Chancellorsville Campaign, in May 1863. Careful examination of this photograph reveals at least nine rifle muskets, apparently extracted from the debris and dead bodies, and arranged for rapid salvage. (*Credit:* "Confederate Dead behind Stone Wall. The 6th. Maine Inf. Penetrated the Confederate Lines at This Point. Fredericksburg, Va.," Andrew J. Russell, National Archives, ref. no. 524930, https://catalog.archives.gov/id/524930.)

Tennessee and the 31st Illinois traded flintlocks and muskets for Enfields and Springfields after Shiloh.[12] Unfortunately, details of how many of these guns were in a loaded state have been lost to history, with the exception of Laidley's report to the Ordnance Department after Gettysburg.

The guns from Gettysburg had a wide variety of misloads: bullets were loaded backward, loaded without power, loaded before powder, and sometimes entire unopened cartridges had been pushed down the barrel. Many guns were discarded because the ramrod had been lost. This was a common problem on battlefields; soldiers from many fights described hearing the distinctive hissing of a rod as it flew through the air. And, of course, a muzzleloader without a ramrod is no more useful than a club.

Civil War rifle muskets were also prone to rapid fouling. Around half the chemical products of black-powder deflagration are solid, according to Mark Denny, author of the ballistics text *Their Arrows Will Darken the Sun*. Fouling occurs when powder residue collects inside the barrel, reducing the diameter of the lands and grooves of the rifling. With prolonged shooting, the residue makes it more and more difficult to ram a bullet down the barrel.[13] The definition of "prolonged" here is a matter of some debate. Postbattle diary entries and reports are full of descriptions by soldiers of dirty guns that couldn't be reloaded or of situations where a soldier needed to pound the ramrod against a tree or rock to force a bullet down the barrel of his gun.[14] However, while these descriptions are all from soldiers who were in a heavy fight or prolonged combat, only rarely do the men mention how many rounds they had discharged since last cleaning their weapon. When a quantity can be gleaned from these historical reports, the number of shots prior to fouling seems to fall around twenty-five. Historians and shooting experts provide estimates from half to double this number (table 5.1).

Table 5.1.   Estimated number of shots prior to fouling (or difficulty ramming home a round)

Expert	Estimated number of rounds
Andrew H. Addoms III	12–15
David Butler	~20
D. Scott Hartwig	20–25, until difficulty ramming
Earl Hess	20–25, until requiring attention
Sir Howard Douglas	10–15
Consensus of tests/reports, 1855–1865	20–40
Average	*~20*

Value of a Discarded Weapon

If armed with a weapon that is inoperable, for whatever reason, a soldier may choose to throw it aside in favor of another gun taken from a fallen fellow combatant. In *Company Aytch*, Sam Watkins described facing exactly this situation during the Battle of Kennesaw Mountain: "My gun became so hot that frequently the powder would flash before I could ram home a ball, and I had frequently to exchange my gun for that of a dead comrade."[15] As a fight continues, more and more guns are newly available for acquisition, and, at the same time, the existing guns in the fight are becoming more and more susceptible to fouling and misfiring. This creates a situation where men are becoming exhausted (and more prone to misloading a rifle), guns are becoming damaged or fouled, ramrods are being lost, and the quantity of available substitute weaponry is growing (from the wounded or dead or simply discarded because of malfunction).

When acquiring a "new" gun, how difficult would it have been for a soldier to determine whether it was already loaded? For a revolver, the answer is simple: a quick inspection of the gun will reveal whether it is loaded with rounds in the chambers and primed to be fired. A breech-loading rifle or carbine is nearly as easy: just open the breech to inspect the chamber. With rifled muskets, the answer as to whether the gun is loaded is much more difficult and deceptive. With muzzleloaders, there is no simple or easy way to inspect the chamber of the gun. If a rifle musket is in fact loaded with a single bullet, it can be surprisingly difficult to tell. Even with several rounds jammed down the barrel, a rifle may appear—and feel—like it is unloaded.

The following three tables and figures were constructed to demonstrate this point. Table 5.2 compares several common rifle muskets that were used at Gettysburg. Note how similar the rifles are in terms of their weights and barrel lengths. Figure 5.4 compares the various types of bullets associated with each weapon from table 5.2. These measurements were taken from fifteen bullets of each type (and from bullets showing little evidence of oxidation—that is, nearly pristine bullets with little lead oxide). The data are presented as a crosshair for each bullet type, with the maximum and minimum values at either end of the bars, and the average value found where the vertical and horizontal bars cross. Note that in this chart, the Williams Cleaner–type bullets, which had been introduced prior to Gettysburg, had the lowest variance in both weight and length (shortest bars), probably because they were manufactured by fewer ammunition suppliers. Table 5.3 is the most important for this discussion, as it compares the Springfield Model 1861 and Enfield Pattern 1853 in various stages of misloading. For each gun, the changes in weight and apparent barrel length (determined using the ramrod) are listed after one, two, three, five, ten, and twenty-three rounds are added to the unloaded weapon.

Table 5.2. Characteristics of common rifle muskets from 1863

Rifle musket	Caliber	Weight (pounds)	Rifle length (inches)	Barrel length (inches)
Enfield Pattern 1853	.577 and .58	9.5	55.0	39.0
Springfield Model 1855	.58	9.5	58.5	40.0
Springfield Model 1861	.58	9.0	56.0	40.0
Austrian Lorenz	.54	9.4	52.6	37.5

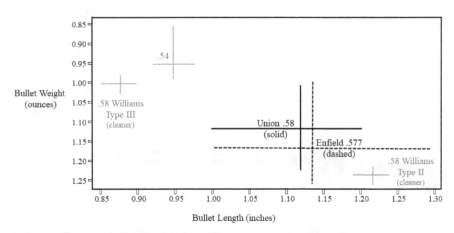

Figure 5.4. Bullet weight versus length for five types of bullets fired from popular weapons from 1863.

Table 5.3. Comparison of the Springfield M1861 and Enfield P1853 rifle muskets in various stages of misloading

	Springfield M1861				
	Number of rounds	**Weight (pounds)**	**Change in weight (percentage)**	**Apparent barrel length (inches)**	**Change in barrel length (percentage)**
	Unloaded	9.05	0	56.0	0
(see below)	1	9.12	1	54.9	2
	2	9.20	2	53.8	4
(see below)	3	9.28	2	52.6	6
	5	9.41	4	50.4	10
	10	9.71	8	44.8	20
(see below)	23	10.73	15	30.2	46

	Enfield P1853				
	Number of rounds	**Weight (pounds)**	**Change in weight (percentage)**	**Apparent barrel length (inches)**	**Change in barrel length (percentage)**
	Unloaded	9.46	0	55.1	0
	1	9.53	1	54.0	2
	2	9.61	2	52.8	4
	3	9.68	2	51.7	6
	5	9.82	4	49.5	10
	10	10.19	7	43.8	21
	23	11.13	15	29.1	53

Note: Data for the Springfield M1855 would be similar.

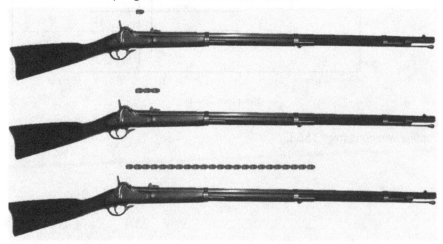

So what does all of this indicate about the cause of the misloadings? First, it is clear that it is impossible to tell whether a rifle musket is loaded based solely on weight, even if the gun barrel contains several loads. A Springfield with five miniés in the barrel weighs only 4 percent more than an unloaded gun; variations in the construction of the rifle or the contractor for the gun, or even the density of the stock, could account for a few percentages of difference between "identical" rifles. Also note that a soldier who discards a malfunctioning Enfield and picks up a Springfield that has been misloaded with five rounds would be trading for a *lighter* gun. Discriminating loaded and unloaded weapons in the field based on heft alone is impossible—unless the gun had been loaded more than twenty times!

If a soldier was very familiar with his gun (and many were not), and if he was picking up a discarded rifle identical to the one he had been using, he might have been able to tell whether it were loaded by using his ramrod. With an M1855 Springfield, the ramrod would extend out of the barrel by a little more than an inch in a loaded gun when compared with an unloaded piece. If the gun contained more than one round, it would stick out 2.5 inches (4 percent more). This assumes, of course, that the new gun has barrel length and ramrod dimensions identical to those of the rifle the soldier had discarded. Note, however, that if the soldier replaces a Springfield with an Enfield (or vice versa), the differences in barrel length, ramrod length, and bullet length introduce complications. If, for example, a soldier discards an Enfield and picks up a loaded Springfield, the difference in barrel length (one inch) means that the Enfield's ramrod will travel almost exactly the same distance down the barrel of both guns— 55.1 inches in an unloaded Enfield, 54.9 inches in the loaded Springfield. Even the savviest of veterans wouldn't have been able to discern this error in the field and would have proceeded to reload the loaded gun.

With a gun loaded more than ten times, of course, this complication disappears. And if the gun had been loaded more than twenty times, the ramrod would only have plunged around halfway down the barrel at most before hitting the top of the latest mistakenly loaded round. This would have been a fairly certain indicator that there was a problem with this musket, and the soldier might have moved on to another cast-off weapon.

At the same time, however, he would have just added another bullet to the already drastically overloaded gun.

ANALYSIS AND EVALUATION

While the report of twenty-three rounds loaded in a single rifle by a hysterical soldier are found in many history books and in every online list of "fascinating facts" about the Civil War, some military experts sound a refreshing note of skepticism in their writing. Paddy Griffith notes, "It is open to doubt whether twenty-three full cartridges could in fact be physically squeezed into the barrel of a Civil War rifle."[16] The statistics compiled in the previous subsection indicate that twenty-three minié balls would occupy approximately half of the length of the barrel of a Springfield or Enfield, but most reports of the twenty-three-round rifle indicate—and as Griffith mentions—that many of these rounds were loaded as entire cartridges, not just bullet or bullet and powder. Depending on the ratio of minié balls to full cartridges, this would come close to doubling the volume of the load, filling the entirety of the barrel; Griffith's doubt is justified.

So if the twenty-three-round claim is set aside as a bit of a fluke, with one unsupervised and clearly bewildered man reloading repeatedly in a panicked state, what are we to do with the other thousands of cases of guns loaded with three or more rounds? Was this also evidence of hysteria? Or was it evidence of the difficulty of keeping a rifle musket operational—or even of determining whether the gun was functional to begin with?

Most men carried somewhere around forty to sixty rounds of ammunition into combat. Given the high rate of fouling, many of their guns would become difficult to load even before this ammunition could be expended. Some historians, including Jeffrey Hall, suggest that many after-battle reports that reference soldiers running low on or out of ammunition should also be read as indications that their guns also needed to be cleaned.[17] It would certainly sound better in the official record that men had exhausted their supplies of ammunition through tenacious fighting rather than that men had stopped fighting because their guns had needed maintenance.

This problem was only exacerbated by the variation in bullets, in terms of both diameter and weight (figure 5.4, above). There were an inordinately high number of complaints about the quality of ammunition after the Battle of Gettysburg, especially in the fighting around Little Round Top.[18] These men were firing a mix of Enfields and Springfields.

This problem with fouling and subsequent resistance to loading was deemed worthy of an official investigation by the acting chief ordnance officer of the Army of the Potomac, Lieutenant Jonathan Edie. After interviewing participants in the fight and summarizing after-battle reports, he determined that "the Rebels had better ammunition," with more consistent powder and more reliable bullet dimensions.

Combining historical and empirical data about the misloaded rifle muskets leaves a set of conclusions for further evaluation:

1. Rifle muskets have a high rate of misfire, approaching or even exceeding 5 percent.

2. Ammunition characteristics and bullet sizes were inconsistent, especially for .58-caliber minié balls and Enfield bullets (figure 5.4, above). Only Williams Cleaner bullets were manufactured to higher tolerances.

3. Rifle muskets were tedious to reload, especially under the stress of combat.

4. Loaded and unloaded rifles are impossible to differentiate based on weight or "feel," and using a ramrod to determine the status of a weapon can be misleading (table 5.3, above).

5. Most poorly loaded rifles (e.g., bullet before the powder) will require the use of a screw to pull the round from the barrel.

6. Many, if not most, soldiers were terrified in combat—even at Gettysburg, where the majority of the participants were veterans of previous battles.

7. The bullets *did not* fall with the intensity of hail.

Two explanations, then, seem most plausible with regard to the quantity of misloaded rifles containing between two and ten rounds. First, many men in the heat of combat may have made an error in loading, rendering their guns temporarily useless. Jonathan Steplyk conjures up realistic example: "If a weapon clogs somewhere in the vent between the gun's breech and the cone where the percussion cap fit, a soldier might cap his musket and still fail to discharge his round. If the soldier could not tell that his weapon failed to fire amid the smoke and noise of his comrades firing around him, then he could unintentionally continue to load multiple rounds down the barrel."[19] In this scenario, it matters little whether the soldier is panicked. Eventually, however, one would think the man might notice that his gun was not kicking or that his ramrod was now stopping three-fourths of the way down the barrel.

A gun in the hands of a collected veteran might become fouled and impossible to reload through absolutely no fault of his own. He would then be faced with two choices: somehow obtaining hot water and beginning to scrub out the barrel with cleaning tools, or just grabbing another gun. Again, it matters little whether he is a calm, experienced soldier.

Third scenario: Terrified soldier drops the bullet in before the powder. He's ~~screwed~~ going to need a screw to extract the bullet before reloading. It probably doesn't help his nerves to pull out a bullet while everyone else is firing, so he just finds another gun.

All of these scenarios leave one (temporarily) inoperable gun on the field and a soldier picking up another discarded weapon. What is the first thing a soldier does with his "new" gun? Either test it to see whether it is loaded or reload a presumably unloaded gun. Checking to see whether it is loaded would likely include replacing the percussion cap and pulling the trigger. The only other possible check would involve using the ramrod to measure the barrel length—already a difficult test. If the gun were loaded and misfired, the ramrod test would still likely be invalid; a blocked vent, bullet without powder, multiple loads—all would still prohibit the gun from firing. So he reloads the loaded gun, adding another round to the futility.

If the soldier picks up a discarded gun and does not "test" it, assuming it is unloaded, he is likely loading an inoperable weapon. At this point, he is also loading a previously loaded gun.

Both processes can be repeated over and over again, increasing the number of bullets in the barrel, regardless of the state of fear in the fighting men.

When historians and interpreters point to the multiply misloaded guns of Gettysburg as definitive proof of panic, they must remember just how common a rifle musket misfire is and how easy it is for a gun to become inoperable. Once this occurs, it is extremely difficult to determine both the functionality of the gun and whether it is loaded, especially when under fire. This was exactly the point that Major T. T. S. Laidley was making when reporting the repeatedly reloaded rifles of Gettysburg to the Ordnance Department. Laidley was using the misloaded guns as evidence in favor of adopting a weapon that avoided the difficulty of determining whether it was loaded: the breechloader.[20]

In retrospect, then, it seems clear that there were multiple causes for the overloaded guns of Gettysburg. Certainly having a skeer-induced operational error led some men to reload repeatedly, but the nature of the weapon, not the steadfastness of the soldier, was responsible for the majority of the multiply misloaded muskets of Gettysburg.

6

The Rifle Musket Revolution

INTRODUCTION

When I was in grade school, I had a favorite book, one that I pored over time after time. *The American Heritage Picture History of the Civil War* was a beast of a volume, with 630 pages full of hundreds of photographs and, best of all, beautifully colored three-dimensional battle maps that sprawled across two full pages, displaying tiny soldiers locked in combat. It was in these pages that the most famous narrative historian of the Civil War, Bruce Catton, first educated me about how the rifle musket had revolutionized warfare.[1]

The rifling in the barrel, I learned, allowed the rifle musket to drop a man "at a distance of a half mile," far greater than the one hundred–yard effective range of the Revolutionary War's smoothbore. Catton told me that the increase in bloodshed at places like Antietam and Gettysburg should be credited to this weapon: "The hideous casualty lists of Civil War battles owed much of their size to the fact that soldiers were fighting with rifles but were using tactics suited to smoothbores."[2]

This notion really stuck with me: technology changed, but tactics had not, and men suffered greatly as a result. Later I repeated this rifle-revolution story many times, walking groups of friends and family across the fields of Pickett's Charge during informal tours of the battlefield, blathering on and on about rifles and smoothbores and comparable effective ranges. I'd have my unfortunate audience imagine they were Lee and Longstreet's men, marching from Seminary to Cemetery Ridge. . . . If the

Yankees had smoothbores, you were safe until you get to that road, way over there near the Copse of Trees and stone wall, and at that point you could make a bayonet charge. But, in reality, the federals on the hill had rifle muskets, so they're killing your men way out here, hundreds of yards from their defensive line . . . and they'll continue to kill and maim as you try to cross all of this open ground . . .

Twenty years after reading my first book by Catton, I was in graduate school, studying geology, when I discovered an account of my long-deceased ancestor's experience in the Battle of Antietam. He had fought with the 130th Pennsylvania Regiment, which had been tasked, in part, with attacking the center of Lee's line along the infamous Sunken Road. Curious to find out more, and lured by a chance to explore the limestone around Sharpsburg, I drove south to visit the battleground and retrace my great-great-great-uncle's footsteps. I wanted to follow the 130th's path across the rolling Maryland terrain to gain perspective as to what the men might have seen and experienced. I didn't carry a rifle with me that day, but I did bring the "rifle-revolution" trope.

The Sunken Road—later renamed the "Bloody Lane"—lies atop a rock unit called the Elbrook Formation. This unit is a combination of harder dolostones and softer limestones, and it weathers to produce a rolling landscape; erosion-resistant dolostones make ridges, and weaker, less durable limestones weather into swales or valleys.[3] The 130th stayed in these depressions as they approached the Confederates in the lane, always hidden from view by dolostone ridges, until they climbed the final hill in front of the Rebel line. From here, eighty-five yards from the enemy, they opened fire.

It occurred to me, standing at that particular spot, that it mattered little whether the men of the 130th Pennsylvania had been armed with smoothbores or a rifled gun; there wasn't anything to shoot at until the men were within the effective range of both guns. I had this same thought when visiting Burnside's Bridge, which is also located above the rolling Elbrook Formation, and again later when touring the wooded terrain of Stones River Battlefield: There really weren't that many places where I could see anywhere near to four hundred yards in any direction. And what with the profound impact black-powder smoke had on battlefield visibility, the true value of the rifle musket becomes as obscure as the enemy during an intense firefight.

Around the time that I took my first university teaching position, I discovered two books that really arrested my attention; they combined critical thinking and reasoning with Civil War history. Paddy Griffith's *Battle Tactics of the Civil War* and Earl Hess's *Rifle Musket in Civil War Combat: Reality and Myth* collected *evidence* for how battles were fought and how much of an impact the combination of rifling and the minié ball actually had on the men in combat. Their arguments, more than anything else, reformed my thinking about the value of a Springfield or Enfield in battle. Had I, perhaps, spent a bit too much time at rifle ranges shooting guns with smokeless powder or on battlegrounds where the rifled guns had shown their greatest potential during Pickett's Charge at Gettysburg, the Cornfield at Antietam, Marye's Heights at Fredericksburg? Everything I had ever read had told me of the revolution of the rifle musket, but the data collected by Griffith and Hess was especially compelling to a skeptical scientist.

This chapter is aimed, so to speak, at providing insights into the traditional "rifle revolution/first modern war" argument that is being disputed by contemporary historians, including Earl Hess and Allen Guelzo. Was the rifle musket a warfare-changing weapon or a minor improvement on the weapons that had come before? Here we are not dealing with the rifle's *potential* in combat but with its actual battle effectiveness in the hands of Civil War citizen-soldiers.

THE HISTORICAL CLAIM

Simply stated, the myth of the rifle musket can be broken down into two components: *(1) The new gun revolutionized warfare, changing forever how battles were fought,* and *(2) it was so deadly that it maximized casualties on the battlefield and, at the same time, rendered the outcome of battles less decisive.* The rifle was touted as the perfect combination of the guns that had come before it—being as fast to load as a Brown Bess but as deadly accurate as a Kentucky rifle. All previous long arms had been flawed in one of two critical ways: if they were "fast" to load, they were invariably inaccurate, and if they were rifled and highly accurate, they were painfully slow to reload. The rifle musket, combined with the new minié bullet, had neither of these deficiencies. Or so the military experts and arms procurers of the 1850s believed.

No single person in American military history was more responsible for the switch from smoothbore guns to rifles than Jefferson Davis. During the Mexican-American War, Davis had been appointed colonel of a volunteer regiment from Mississippi. Davis requested that his new unit be equipped with rifled guns instead of the traditional muskets, but his commanding officer, Winfield Scott, refused, arguing that the only available rifles were the Springfield Model 1841—a weapon that hadn't yet been adequately tested on the range or battlefield. Colonel Davis eventually took his request to the commander in chief, who acted quickly, overriding Scott's decision and giving the Southerners their rifles. It was this hasty action, with the president being no slow-Polk, that transformed the Model 1841 into the "Mississippi rifle."

By 1853, Jefferson Davis had risen to the position of secretary of war. During his tenure, he sought to improve the fighting capabilities of the country's fifteen-thousand-man army by giving them a better weapon than the M1842 smoothbore musket. Not surprisingly, he chose a rifle—the newly developed Springfield M1855 rifle musket. From that adoption until today, the magnitude of improvement between the old smoothbore and the new rifle musket has been debated. Certainly the rifle showed the *potential* to end Napoleonic battle tactics forever. Even in practice the M1855 demonstrated its prowess: target practice is conducted on a *rifle* range, after all, and not a musket range.

Even before the Civil War began, military experts and authors of infantry manuals had been predicting the rifle musket revolution would come. After witnessing well-trained soldiers hitting human-sized targets at two hundred or even four hundred yards' distance, the military tacticians warned against conducting battle in the manner of the previous generation of warfare. First, it was argued, the days of massed frontal assaults, finished with a bayonet charge, were gone forever. The range of the new rifle and minié made it a force multiplier at distance, with the assault waves beginning to suffer casualties a quarter mile from the defenders. Attacking rows of infantry were certain to be cut to pieces long before they even had a chance to think about using their bayonets.

The tactical use of artillery would also need to change. In previous wars, fought with the smoothbore, cannons could be employed on the offensive, rolled to within a few hundred yards of the enemy to fire canister and grapeshot; the cannon crew would be safe, well out of range of the musket-armed defenders. With the new rifle, however, the entire gun crew could be killed quickly at such range. And cavalry charges, as a shock tactic, were now obsolete as well. During Napoleon's time, mounted men could charge across the battlefield while receiving only a volley or two of incoming fire. With the dawn of this new era of rifle technology, they could expect to begin to take losses while still an extremely long way from the enemy line. And as the range of engagement increased, casualties would follow. In short, it was thought, the new rifle musket would change how a battle would be fought, and this shift would be away from offensive tactics and toward the defensive.

During and soon after the close of the Civil War, this revolutionary thinking was confirmed by military writers of the day. Commanding officers were blamed for ignoring the supposed superiority of the rifle musket, and casualty lists from Pickett's Charge, Malvern Hill, and Cold Harbor were considered proof of their failure to tactically adapt. Stories of seemingly impossible long-range sharpshooter kills with Springfields and Enfields only buttressed the myth, as did the ubiquitous construction of sophisticated fieldworks by 1864.

The first hundred years after the Civil War did little to diminish the rifle musket–revolution axiom. Bruce Catton published two important trilogies during this time that helped solidify the prevailing opinion of the superiority of the rifle musket.[4] In the first of these books, readers were repeatedly told of the killing power of the new weapon: "Like the machine gun in 1914, here was a weapon which upset all old theories," and "it would kill at half a mile or more," and "the advancing line came under killing fire four or five times as far off as used to be the case," and "compared with a modern Garand the rifle was laughable; but compared with the smoothbore which had been the standard weapon in all previous wars, it was terrific."[5]

In *A Stillness at Appomattox,* Catton writes, "the range at which charging men began to be killed was at least five times as great as it used to be, which meant that about five times as many of the assailants were likely to be hit."[6] In later works, Catton would continue in this vein: the rifle musket "completely changed the conditions under which men fought," he wrote, and "the killing power of the weapon was brought to a brand-new peak of efficiency."[7]

Reflections on the Civil War was edited from tapes Catton had recorded before his death in 1978, in which he outlines the educational concepts of the war he considered the most important, among which was the point that "One would come under fire at a distance of seven hundred or eight hundred yards, instead of one hundred yards, and the attacking army couldn't possibly run all that distance."[8]

Other important historians later continued the adulation of the rifle musket. John Keegan on the weapon: "They were more accurate, carried a greater range, and, being ignited by a percussion cap, rarely misfired."[9] James McPherson: "The transition from smoothbore to rifle had two main effects: it multiplied casualties, and it strengthened the tactical defensive," and "with an effective range of three or four hundred yards, defenders firing rifles decimated these ranks."[10] Stephen Sears: "What was new, or 'modern' was the instant slaughter these rifles inflicted."[11]

Examples of the rifle musket dictum in publication continued well into the 2000s. Take, for example, Pat Leonard writing for the *New York Times*:

> *Historians began to study the factors that contributed to so much bloodshed . . . and concluded that the introduction of the rifle musket was the primary cause of the staggering rates . . . its long, grooved barrel gave it an effective range up to four times that of a smoothbore . . . It was the rifle musket, researchers determined, that made the bayonet obsolete and drastically transformed the roles of cavalry and field artillery.*
> *Statistics appear to bear out this theory.*[12]

Some have even gone so far as to call the rifle musket the first modern battle rifle.

The science, analysis, and evaluation in this chapter will concentrate on two themes of the rifle musket myth: (1) that the introduction of the rifle and minié bullet was a great leap forward in firearms technology that revolutionized warfare and (2) that the number of casualties resulting from this great gun were proof of its combat efficacy. Stated another way, the rifle and minié represented a tactical game changer on the battlefield, and the staggering bloodshed of the war demonstrated that the gun offered more than just a *potential* revolution.

Critical thinking and analysis help answer historical conundrums about the tactical importance of the rifle musket: Who, for example, would gain more from trading up to a new gun—a soldier armed with a smoothbore who acquires a rifle musket or one with a rifle musket trading for a breechloader? How many men would the Army of Northern Virginia have lost at Pickett's Charge if the Union had been armed entirely with smoothbore muskets? Might the assault have succeeded if there had been no rifle muskets on the field? What if the federal defenders had carried Sharps—or even Spencer or Henry repeating rifles? The rifle musket–revolution trope suggests that this final change in weaponry would have offered little in the way of increased firepower because of the muzzleloading long gun's range and accuracy.

The question of whether the Civil War was especially bloody because of the introduction of rifled weapons (it wasn't) has already been well investigated by other historical "truthers," including Earl Hess and Paddy Griffith, so this chapter will concentrate primarily on the effectiveness of the Springfield and Enfield in combat as fighting weapons. Did these guns, as our history books tell us, truly turn common infantrymen into efficient and deadly long-range killing machines?

THE SCIENCE

The US Ordnance Department has always been conservative when upgrading and adopting new small-arms weapons technology. Before selecting a new potential weapon, the gun must be evaluated based on multiple criteria. In the nineteenth century (and most of the twentieth), these included all of the following: The weapon would need to provide superior, or at least similar, firepower when compared with the weapon currently in use. It would also need to be reliable and robust and resistant to mechanical failure introduced by sand or mud. The new gun should be "soldier-proof"—simple for a moderately well-trained person to be able to load and fire when stressed (and perhaps even to clear and clean). In addition, the newly adopted gun needed to be accurate and, if possible, have a longer range than the service weapon it was to replace. As a government purchase in great volume, the weapon should be as inexpensive as possible. Finally, and somewhat counterintuitively, the new gun should have a *low* maximum rate of fire. The US Army Ordnance Corps was always distrustful of the men they were arming, lacking confidence that the officers in charge could keep the men from firing through all their ammunition indiscriminately.[13] Given a weapon that could shoot, say, ten rounds a minute, a typical soldier would exhaust their ammunition supply extremely quickly, rendering the fighting unit dysfunctional for immediate further operations (figure 6.1). Or so it was reasoned.

Before adopting the Springfield M1855 to replace the in-service smoothbore musket, Jefferson Davis considered several breechloading rifles. When the criteria for adoption are considered for each type of gun— for example, an M1855 and a Sharps rifle (1852 or 1859 model)—the rifle musket becomes the obvious choice. Both guns are robust, reliable, and accurate rifles on the evaluation range. The Sharps may be slightly easier to operate, but it is also a few pounds heavier and not quite as powerful at short(er) ranges. When it comes to cost and (lower) rate of fire, the Springfield wins both contests easily: The breechloader is almost twice as expensive and offers a soldier the opportunity to waste ammunition with undisciplined fire. A repeater like the Spencer or Henry would be even more expensive and potentially wasteful. Reasoning like this explains why George Armstrong Custer's men were better armed for a firefight at Gettysburg (where many had procured their own Spencers) than at the Little Bighorn thirteen years later.

All this mid-nineteenth-century logic falls apart on the actual battlefield (as the 7th Cavalry would grimly testify): The low rate of fire of a rifle musket, thought to be a benefit because of poorly disciplined and shaky troops, is a terrific disadvantage.[14] Add to this the complex and awkward loading procedure and the tendency of the rifle to quickly foul,

Figure 6.1.   Ordnance officers worried that arming men with breechloading rifles, like this cavalryman, might encourage them to waste valuable and limited ammunition. This soldier's degree of training might rightfully be questioned, based on the orientation of his cocked revolver. (*Credit:* Photograph, Library of Congress, https://www.loc.gov/item/2019646735/, "Unidentified Soldier in Union Uniform with Sharps Carbine Rifle, Colt Navy Revolver, and Cavalry Saber," 1861, LC-DIG-ppmsca-67671.)

and the breechloader becomes the obviously superior weapon. And if the breechloader misfires, it can be brought rapidly back into service because the exposed breech is easy to access and, comparably, much easier to clear.

Rate-of-Fire Reality

Arguably the most important criterion for a service rifle is how much lead it can throw at the enemy, in a fairly accurate manner, during a firefight—in other words, how much energy in the form of bullets could be directed toward the enemy in an engagement at a typical battle range of between fifty and 150 yards. This volume of fire can be calculated for the fighting men and their service rifles for each generation of weapons from 1775 to the present day. To calculate the downrange firepower (i.e., lead thrown at enemy at high velocity), we need to find the muzzle energy delivered per unit of time.[15] Muzzle energy—or, roughly speaking, hitting power—is a function of the speed of the bullet when exiting the barrel and the mass of the projectile.[16] To be an effective combat weapon, a gun should deliver a muzzle energy of at least one thousand foot-pounds. In World War II, for example, the M1 Garand delivered 2,400 foot-pounds of energy, which was thought to be more than enough to drop a man, but the M1 carbine fired a smaller bullet at lower velocity, transferring a barely adequate 975 foot-pounds of energy.

The other component in the calculation of downrange striking power is the rate of fire to how many bullets can be thrown at the enemy per unit of time. When compared with the carbine, the Garand delivers a harder-hitting bullet; nevertheless, with a much larger clip and a lower recoil, the carbine could actually deliver more bullets downrange in a firefight. Of course, the Browning Automatic Rifle would combine the benefits of both weapons, firing the Garand's more powerful round at a high rate of fire.

Figure 6.2 illustrates the change in hitting power for each service rifle from 1770 to the twenty-first century. The general trend, as one might expect, exhibits an increase in firepower through time. There is, however, a decrease in downrange muzzle energy during the middle of the nineteenth century, when the army adopted first the Springfield M1841 percussion rifle and then the Springfield M1855 rifle musket of Civil War fame. When the army adopted the rifle musket, the hitting power of the US infantryman hit an all-time low. This seems strange for a weapon that was about to "revolutionize" warfare.

The primary reason the rifle musket shows so poorly in these calculations lies in its slowness to load and reload and slow bullet velocity.

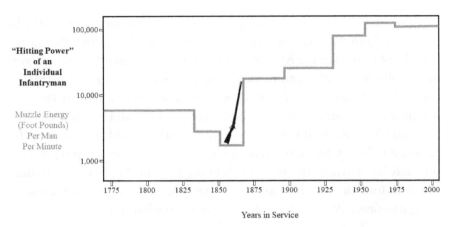

Figure 6.2. Muzzle energy delivered to the enemy (per unit time) for US service weapons, from 1770 to 2005. The highest knockdown energy was during the 1960s, with the fully automatic M14 firing a .308-caliber cartridge; the lowest energy is from 1855 to 1865, with the .58-caliber rifle musket. Note that this estimate of "firepower" neglects any component for consideration of accuracy; a fully automatic M14 delivers terrific muzzle energy downrange but would be difficult to fire accurately.

Compared with its predecessor, the smoothbore musket, the rifle musket is 15–25 percent slower to load and has a muzzle velocity of only 950–1,050 feet per second, compared with the 1,400–1,500 feet per second for the smoothbore. Of course, the rifle musket is more accurate—but for ranges that are not often needed in combat.

There are two great leaps in hitting power for service rifles reflected in figure 6.2 (above). The first occurred in the years after the Civil War, when breechloading guns firing metallic cartridges replaced the rifle muskets. Muzzle velocity increased by around 50 percent, as did muzzle energy, and the rate of fire quadrupled. The other large increase in firepower occurred in the mid-1930s when semiautomatic weapons like the Garand replaced bolt-action rifles as the primary infantry arm. The cartridge remained the same, but the rate of fire with the clip- and magazine-fed semiautomatics made a significant difference in how much lead could be thrown at the enemy.

The all-time high in hitting power in the 1960s and early 1970s, as discerned from the chart, is a bit misleading. The adoption of the short-lived M14 to replace the M1 rifle meant that individual infantrymen now had a fully automatic option, increasing the potential rate of fire. However, this fully automatic fire was more symbolic than useful, as the gun was nearly impossible to fire accurately in this mode, and in actual combat it would likely overheat before hundreds of rounds could be dispensed. In reality, the line in figure 6.2 relating hitting power through time should probably be relatively flat from 1936 to the present day, hovering around one hundred thousand foot-pounds per weapon—more than enough energy to prove devastating to the enemy on the battlefield.

The Parabolic Problem

Properly loading and firing a rifle musket requires at least some minimal degree of training for a soldier. Correctly aiming the weapon at a distant target requires a much greater degree of expertise—especially if the gun is firing a bullet at a measly one thousand feet per second.

On most Civil War battlefields, nearly all rifle fire took place at ranges of under two hundred yards; nevertheless, even if the enemy were visible at more distant ranges, the rifle musket would make hitting him difficult, despite the weapon's terrific accuracy. Low muzzle velocity equates to a rapid drop for a minié bullet as it flies toward the enemy (figure 6.3). This means that hitting a target beyond 250 yards would require adjusting for the growing parabolic path of the bullet. Increasing range to the target, then, requires a more precise estimation of the range of the intended victim.

When a soldier sighted his rifle at two hundred yards and was aiming at the center of mass (stomach) of a man who was one hundred yards away, his bullet would strike any man standing along the flight of the bullet between zero and 155 yards distant (thus the 155-yard killing zone in figure 6.3 for a bullet hit at one hundred yards' distance). If the enemy soldier is estimated to be two hundred yards away, he will still be struck if he is actually only 150 yards away (head strike) or 250 yards away (hit in the foot). But if the man is actually at one hundred or three hundred yards' distance, the minié will either pass over his head or fall short. At

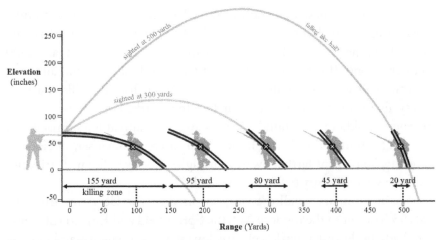

Figure 6.3. The farther the target, the more a shooter must compensate because of the growing parabolic arc of the slow-moving minié. As the range grows, the killing zone of the falling bullet decreases, so when the range extends to five hundred yards, the exact position of the target (within twenty yards) must be either known or precisely estimated. Vertical exaggeration for this figure is around thirty times.

four hundred yards, the shooter would need to estimate the correct range to within around twenty-five yards to ensure a hit, because the killing zone has decreased to only about forty-five yards due to the arc of the bullet. At five hundred yards, the shot becomes almost impossible without a laser rangefinder (these were hard to come by during the Civil War); if the enemy were approaching at this range, the correct distance would need to be estimated to within about twenty-five *feet*, and if the man were moving quickly, the time the bullet would spend in the air (1.5 seconds) would need to be factored into the combat calculation. Otherwise, the enemy soldier would actually run under the bullet as it passed overhead. With a modern semiautomatic weapon, the shooter might be able to find the precise range by "walking in" his fire: spotting where the bullet missed and adjusting accordingly. Not so with a gun that takes twenty to thirty seconds to reload, because with each subsequent shot, the target location and range has completely changed.

Also, with a modern firearm, the difference in ballistics and bullet trajectories makes killing at two hundred to four hundred yards much easier. Imagine figure 6.3 for a gun firing a bullet at more than 2,500 feet per second. If the rifle is sighted at two hundred yards and aimed at the center of mass, the killing zone is extended from the rifle musket's ninety-five yards to more than four hundred yards. If you estimate that the enemy soldier is two hundred yards away and aim at his stomach, you will still hit him in the chest if he is actually 50 percent closer, and if he is, in reality, 50 percent farther away, your high-velocity bullet will strike, uh ... somewhere slightly below his stomach.[17]

So, in summary, of all the weapons used by the US Army from the M1795 Musket to the modern M4, the Springfield and Enfield rifle muskets had the lowest muzzle velocity, lowest muzzle energy, and slowest rate of fire. Was the rifle musket's great advantage in rifling and potential range over the smoothbore enough to merit the accolades these weapons gained during the century after the war ended? And is there any rationale for considering the rifle musket to be the first modern battle rifle (in the first modern war)?

ANALYSIS AND EVALUATION

When compared with the gun it replaced, the M1842 smoothbore musket, the rifle musket had a much longer potential range; however, this came at the cost of being slightly slower to reload and a diminished muzzle velocity. When the black powder explodes, the expanding gases force the cone-shaped depression at the base of the minié bullet to expand and catch the grooves in the barrel (figure 6.4). Thus the rings on the lower half of the bullet push against the rifling in the barrel, spinning the minié. This rapid rotating is not possible without a great degree of friction between bullet and barrel, and friction depletes energy and velocity. As a result, the shooter is left with a stabilized bullet in flight that is more accurate at range but has a higher rate of drop.

The key question, then, is what the value of this trade-off was between increased stabilization and decreased velocity on the battlefields of the Civil War. Rifling certainly made the rifle more precise in its shooting, but aiming and firing it accurately at longer ranges was difficult because

Figure 6.4. Two bullets showing evidence of being fired through rifled barrels—parallel groves that are slightly angled to the long axis of the bullets. These ridges were pressed by the lands of the rifling. The bullet on the left is from a .44-caliber pistol, and the bullet on the right is a .58 minié. Note the conical base of the minié.

of the parabolic bullet path. In other words, it does little good to be able to print ten-inch bullet groups at three hundred yards when your shots are falling ten feet short of the target.[18]

Scientists are careful to differentiate the terms *accurate* and *precise* when discussing data or experiment results. Rifle muskets were much more precise in their shooting compared with muskets; they could produce smaller groups, because their rifling guided all the bullets to a more localized space downrange. However, this precision did not necessarily make the rifle musket accurate in reality; the tight grouping might have been falling short or long of the intended target because of the difficulty introduced by the parabolic flight path of the bullets (figure 6.5).

So the smoothbore and rifle musket were similar in combat taking place at under seventy-five yards, and poorly trained soldiers to with no practice in range estimation would likely have been wasting minié balls when firing at ranges over 250 yards. This leaves a range of 75 to 250 yards where the rifle musket *may* have been more effective. However, battlefield terrain and gun smoke may have completely negated this potential advantage.

Consider, for example, the 75- to 250-yard accuracy improvement of the rifle musket with respect to the Battle of Antietam. During the morning phase of the battle, Hooker's corps was attacking across relatively flat

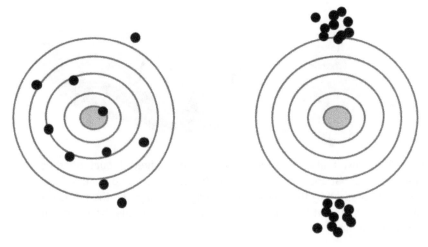

Figure 6.5. The difference between accuracy and precision for rifle muskets. On the left, the rifle has been more accurate but not very precise (thus the grouping is wider). On the right, the rifle was more precise, and yet it missed the target because each of the ten-shot groups was fired without a proper estimation of the range. A precision weapon is only useful in combat if it is also accurate, and low muzzle velocity makes accuracy a challenge.

or undulating terrain, and the added range of the rifle might have been useful before gun smoke obscured the battlefield. During the afternoon and early evening phases of the battle, however, rolling terrain minimized this range advantage. Many Rebels defending the Sunken Road could only observe the oncoming federal infantry during the final one hundred yards of approach because of the hard-rock ridge in front of their position. On the southern part of the battlefield, where Burnside attacked the right of Lee's line, the rolling hills meant defenders could only see the enemy at two hundred or more yards away before they disappeared in a swale, only to later crest the hill in their immediate front.[19]

This landscape phenomenon is well illustrated by an account provided by Private Alexander Hunter of the 17th Virginia: "Each man sighted his rifle about two feet above the crest, and then, with his finger on the trigger, waited until the advancing form came between the bead and the clear sky behind. The first thing we saw appear was the gilt eagle that surmounted the pole, then the top of the flag, next the flutter of the Stars and Stripes; then their hats came in sight; still rising, the faces emerged; next a range of curious eyes appeared, then such a hurrah as only the Yankee troops could give broke the stillness, and they surged towards us." The 17th Virginia waited until the approaching Yankee line was within fifty yards of their position before opening volley fire at short range.[20]

Similar examples of how nature limited the rifle musket–range advantage on other battlegrounds are numerous—including the brush and immature trees of the Wilderness, the combination of cedar glades and undulating terrain at Stones River, and the ravines, gullies, and cane-brakes of Vicksburg.

So the rifle musket had a limited advantage over the smoothbore on some battlegrounds, in some circumstances; it was, for example, a better gun for skirmishers. How does the "revolutionary" rifle compare with the gun that replaced it? In terms of skirmishing, the breechloader is a much better weapon, capable of being more quickly loaded while crouching or prone. The M1855 lasted in service about as long as the M1842; was the improvement from smoothbore to rifle musket as great as that from rifle musket to breechloader?

Smoothbore versus Rifle Musket versus Breechloader

The fate of the muzzleloading rifle was clear by the end of the Civil War. By 1865, the federal arsenal held almost one million rifles. Five thousand of these guns were converted to breechloaders—the first "Trapdoor" Springfields. The top of the old rifle was cut away and replaced by a breechblock and locking latch, and the nipple and vent were replaced by a modified hammer and firing pin to fire a .58-caliber metallic cartridge. This transformation was accomplished using a conversion designed by Erskine Allin from the Springfield Armory, and thus the Model 1865 rifle was called the "First Allin" Conversion. At the end of the process the army was left with a gun that had a fourfold increase in potential rate of fire, at a cost of about five dollars per gun.

The first standard breechloading rifle adopted by the US Army arrived less than ten years later. The Springfield M1873 fired a .45-caliber bullet at a 35 percent higher velocity compared with the older .58 rifle musket, and a well-trained soldier could fire a shot every five seconds.[21]

The Trapdoor Springfield continued in service for twenty years, until it was replaced by the Springfield Model 1892, essentially a Norwegian-designed bolt-action rifle called the Krag-Jørgensen. When the lifespan of different operating styles for weapons is considered (i.e., how the rifle is loaded and how the cartridge is fired), the true impact of the rifle musket becomes apparent (figure 6.6). The lifespan of service weapons selected by the US Army is largely indicative of their significance with respect to changing technology and combat; the most important guns lasted for many decades; the flintlock and semiauto/selective-fire weapons lasted for fifty years. The rifle musket was in service for less than a decade.

Technological improvements to weapons that are important and battle-changing tend to be robust in duration and not often replaced quickly. The M1903 Springfield rifle fought in two world wars. The M1 Garand and the M14 (a slightly improved Garand) provided excellent service in World War II, Korea, and Vietnam. Sniper versions of the later gun were even used in the Gulf War. The rifle musket, by contrast, was simply too slow to load and fire and so challenged by ballistics that it lasted only a short time on the world's battlefields.

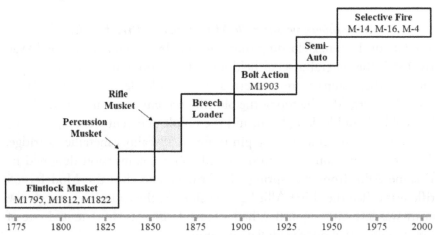

Figure 6.6. For a weapon that "revolutionized" warfare, the rifle musket had a remarkably short lifespan as a service weapon. This was true for the US Army and around the world.

This subsection is focused on assessment, so let's revisit some of the rifle musket's (supposed) attributes as outlined in the traditional Civil War literature: first, the received wisdom that the rifle musket changed how cavalry could be used on the battlefield. The glorious cavalry charges against lines of infantry were a thing of the past because of the range of the rifle, and mounted soldiers began to adopt infantry tactics, switching from fighting on horseback to fighting on foot.

Consider an attack by a cavalry unit across a half mile of open terrain against infantry armed with Springfields and Enfields. The rifle musket legend predicts disaster for the horsemen. However, when exactly would the infantry begin to shoot at the cavalrymen? At five hundred or more yards, any hope of a hit would need a precise estimate of where the cavalryman would be when the minié eventually finished its arced path back to Earth. At two hundred yards, the shot was more feasible, but the long reloading time meant the approaching cavalry would soon reach the defenders' line. With a smoothbore, you could only open fire during the final approach (less than one hundred yards). So the advantage of the rifle musket over the smoothbore is reduced to the opportunity for a single volley at a fast-moving target more than two hundred yards away (although it is a rather large target).

A second battlefield "game-changing" scenario introduced by the rifle musket involves artillery: No longer could cannons be brought forward in an offensive application to support infantry assaults; the gun crews would be cut to pieces if they approached defenders to fire canister or grapeshot. From 1862 until the end of the war, the rifle musket restricted artillery to the defensive, firing from ranges of beyond one thousand yards because of the deadly accurate spinning miniés. This claim is not borne out in the statistics: casualties among artillery crewmembers were lower than infantrymen, and the reason seems clear. The low muzzle velocity of the Springfield or Enfield bullet makes hitting an individual crewmember extremely difficult beyond four hundred yards because of the plunging flight path of the bullet. Estimating the range to a gun battery that is a quarter mile away is very difficult, and hitting an individual soldier at this range would require an accurate estimate of distance to within 5–10 percent. I have actually tried this while hiking across the Antietam and

Gettysburg battlefields while equipped with a precision laser rangefinder that was accurate to one thousand yards. First I would guess the range, and then I would measure it. At three hundred yards or less, I could usually estimate the distance to a cannon within fifty yards, but at ranges beyond this point only a few lucky estimates put me under 10 percent. And while my guesses at three hundred yards and closer in improved with practice, they did not for ranges over five hundred yards. It should also be noted for this comparison that I've ~~wasted~~ spent much more time practicing range estimation (and on rifle ranges with one hundred–, two hundred–, and four hundred–yard distances carefully measured and marked) than any Civil War citizen-soldier.

Finally, there is the combined claim that Civil War rifle muskets made massed infantry attacks a thing of the past, ending the era of Napoleonic tactics with stunningly great battle losses. Bruce Catton and other tradition-alists laid out a threefold argument: First, the rifle's accuracy and increased effective range meant that firing would begin earlier at the approaching enemy. Second, because the firing started at a longer range, more time was available to reload and fire again, increasing the chances to kill. Third, the accuracy of the rifle ensured that casualties would be inflicted at a roughly similar proportion at great distance all across the battleground. In short, do not use smoothbore tactics against an enemy with a rifle.[22]

Let's compare several different-sized groups of soldiers, firing different weapons that all deliver the *same firepower* at fifty to one hundred yards' distance. A Civil War *corps* (thirty-six thousand men) firing Springfield M1861 rifle muskets, where each man fired once every twenty seconds, would deliver 108,000 rounds per minute. This weapon fires a minié bullet with a muzzle energy of around a thousand foot-pounds, so the corps is delivering around one hundred million foot-pounds of energy per minute at the enemy.

A *brigade* of men from World War I (four thousand men) firing M1903 Springfield rifles at a realistic rate of ten rounds per minute delivers forty thousand rounds per minute. The .30-06 bullet has a muzzle energy of around 2,500 foot-pounds, so the brigade is delivering around one hundred million foot-pounds of energy to the enemy; the World War I brigade matches the Civil War corps with respect to firepower.

A *regiment* of World War II soldiers (one thousand men) armed with semiautomatic M1 Garand rifles could deliver forty thousand rounds per minute—forty shots per man per minute, or four times the rate of fire of a bolt-action rifle. The Garand fires the same cartridge as the M1903, so the firepower of a World War II regiment is roughly the same as a World War I brigade and a Civil War corps.

A large *company* of Vietnam-era infantry (four platoons of fifty men each) firing M16 rifles could fire around eighty thousand rounds per minute (four hundred rounds per minute per man, not the maximum capability of the M16, of around eight hundred rounds per minute). The muzzle energy of the .223 round is similar or slightly above that of the minié bullet, so the Vietnam company could also match the firepower of a Civil War corps.

Note that none of these analogies includes the use of machine guns or artillery, because the point of the exercise is to compare long arms. One can only imagine what would have happened on a Civil War battlefield if one side had even a single M60 or M249 SAW. Also note that all scenarios post–Civil War would be firing smokeless powder, so visibility across the landscape would be much less of a problem than with the rifle musket—a significant advantage starting with the bolt-action rifles.

This leaves us with the broadest of the claims about the rifle musket—that it revolutionized warfare and was the primary agent responsible for the "first modern war." Some authors even describe the rifle musket as the first modern battle rifle and say that this new gun led to an increase in bloodshed. Take, for example, this quotation from Pat Leonard's piece for the *New York Times*: "Historians began to study the factors that contributed to so much bloodshed . . . and concluded that the introduction of the rifle musket was the primary cost of the staggering casualty lists."[23] Brett Gibbons, in *The Destroying Angel: The Rifle Musket as the First Modern Infantry Weapon*, leaves no doubt of his opinion of the rifle in his book's subordinate title or text: "The rifle musket forever changed the way battles were fought." His criteria for determining what is a "modern weapon" center around which of the service guns best match the rifles currently in use (M16s and M4s). Because the Springfield M1855 was a rifle, he concludes, it is the first modern infantry weapon (the M4 is also rifled).

Metallic cartridges, clips and magazines, semiautomatic firing capability, and select fire are all simply conveniences; they only mechanically make it easier to load the gun, he reasons.[24] In other words, a smoothbore M16 would be useless in combat. Far at the other end of the "revolutionary rifle" spectrum falls Paddy Griffith: "We have to admit that the arrival of the rifle musket actually made very little practical difference—whatever may have been its theoretical potential to revolutionize the battlefield," and "It remains doubtful that a genuine revolution in firepower had actually occurred."[25] And Earl Hess: "In short, those who believe that the rifle had a revolutionary impact on combat strive to account for every characteristic they see in Civil War battles by referencing the use of the new weapon," and "The rifle musket had only a brief showing in world history. Within five years of Appomattox, opponents in the Franco-Prussian war fought with breechloading rifles far superior to the rifle musket of the Civil War."[26] And Allen Guelzo: "Whatever the gains bestowed by the technology of the rifle musket or rifle artillery, those improvements were only apparent under ideal conditions (which is to say, not in the middle of a firefight)."[27] David Ward sums up this evolving school of revisionist thinking well in *The 96th Pennsylvania Volunteers in the Civil War*: "The rifle musket did not revolutionize Civil War operations because the weapon was not used at long range, the principle technological advancement over a smoothbore musket."[28]

To add some numbers to this discussion and debate, let us conduct another (somewhat contrived) firepower scenario through time with different weapons, including the smoothbore musket. The federal army repulsed Pickett's Charge of 12,500 men with around half that number of men defending Cemetery Ridge. Almost all of these defenders were armed with Springfield or Enfield rifle muskets, so that provides a downrange firepower of around twenty million foot-pounds per minute. Had the Yankees had the faster-firing bolt-action rifle of World War I, the same assault could have been defeated with only a brigade of eight hundred men, or two companies (two hundred men) armed with the Garand of World War II. Even one squad of men from Vietnam—fifty men—could have ended Pickett's Charge with a proper supply of ammunition. And in all of these twentieth-century scenarios, firing would have commenced beyond four hundred yards; no need to worry about gun smoke obscuring the enemy far across the battlefield.

Of course, the federal army also used artillery to great effect during the assault. But this fact doesn't really impact the comparison of the small arms, because later technological advances—faster-firing artillery, mortars, machine guns—would only end Pickett's Charge sooner.

Could the Union Army have turned back Pickett, Pettigrew, and Trimble's grand assault if the infantry had been armed with smoothbore muskets? This is a slightly more complicated scenario, dependent on the number of Confederate casualties that actually occurred near the Emmitsburg Road. This position on the battlefield is well within rifle range for the federal defensive line but just outside of accurate smoothbore range. Nevertheless, the slightly higher rate of fire of the smoothbore would have been a benefit. As for the Confederates participating in the charge, it probably would matter little whether they were armed with rifles or smoothbores.

Had the federals not had a single rifled weapon at Gettysburg, Pickett's Charge would likely have been defeated—but in a different way. The Union defenders would have waited longer to open fire or else deployed some units closer to the fences along the Emmitsburg Road to fire at the Confederates while they were slowed by the picket-rail fence obstacle. When they did open fire at one hundred yards, their striking power would have exceeded that of men armed with rifled muskets; the slightly higher rate of fire combined with close-range buck and ball would have been a deadly combination. However, federal losses would have certainly been higher in this scenario, because more Rebels would have made it to Cemetery Ridge and the proximity of the Copse of Trees. The only way Pickett's Charge could have been successful for the Army of Northern Virginia is if the men who had *not* been cut down between one hundred and two hundred yards away from the federal line (by rifle musket fire, in reality) would have added enough strength to tip the momentum of the attack and pierce the Union line. If so, the battle might have played out more like Gaines' Mill instead of Malvern Hill.

Had the federal infantry been armed with breechloading rifles, which were available at the time, Pickett's Charge would have been an even greater disaster for Lee and his army. The increase in the rate of fire from three rounds per minute to eight or ten would have stopped the charge at Emmitsburg Road, not The Angle. Had Doubleday, Gibbon, Hays, and Robinson's men had Spencer rifles—also available at the time (but not in sufficient quantities)—they could have waited to open fire until the Confederates were within smoothbore range and then emptied their seven-shot magazines with such a firepower fury that it would certainly have stopped the assault.[29]

As one final experiment of the imagination, consider fighting in and around the boulders of the Slaughter Pens at Gettysburg or Stones River. There is an enemy soldier, or three, around every rock or tree. How would you have behaved differently in combat if you had been armed with an M1842 smoothbore musket or an M1861 rifle musket? Would it have mattered which gun you carried? After you discharge a round, you stand upright for around half a minute, trying to reload, hoping no one close by notices that you are (essentially) temporarily unarmed. What if you had been handed a Spencer or Henry before the fight? Take a shot, take cover, take another shot. Over and over and over, and even when you need to reload, it can be done from a crouching position and more quickly than the single-shot muzzleloader. In combat, follow-up shots can be critical, and this factor is just as important as the long-range effectiveness of the weapon, if not more so.

Thus the conclusion here is that, under ideal conditions for the advantages of the rifle muskets (Pickett's Charge—open, slightly undulating terrain, long-range sight lines), the gun is probably slightly more effective than a smoothbore and vastly inferior to a breechloader or repeater. This hardly seems like strong evidence that the rifle musket revolutionized much of any of the aspects of mid-nineteenth-century warfare (figure 6.7).[30] The rifle musket has one advantage over its predecessor: precision. But this benefit could rarely be used in combat and was far outweighed by the gun's lengthy reloading process and poor muzzle velocity. The guns that would follow were harder hitting and faster to fire, as well as easier to properly aim at long range. They were also more reliable and easier to clear after a misfire. The addition of rifling to a musket and the introduction of the minié bullet made for a better weapon, but

Figure 6.7.   If the rifle musket revolutionized warfare, one might wonder why this Union soldier felt the need to arm himself with five supplemental weapons. (*Credit:* Photograph, Library of Congress, https://www.loc.gov/pictures/item/2011645432/, "Unidentified Soldier in Union Uniform with Three Remington Revolvers, Two Bowie Knives, and a Springfield Rifle Musket," taken between 1861 and 1865, LC-DIG-ppmsca-31123.)

it was the introduction of the breechblock, the metallic cartridge, and improved smokeless powder that made a larger difference in how battles were fought and won.

7

Eye of History or Photographic Fraud?

INTRODUCTION

MISCONCEPTIONS ABOUND REGARDING THE NATURE AND LEGACY OF Civil War photography. Photographs from the battlefront were *not* first captured during the American Civil War; Roger Fenton took well over three hundred photographs during the Crimean War, a decade before America's great struggle. And photographs exist from the Mexican-American War, which took place a decade before the conflict on the Crimean Peninsula, although the artist responsible for the images remains unknown.

Another major misconception involves the most famous of the photographers to emerge during the Civil War, Mathew Brady. Most casual history enthusiasts erroneously credit him with taking the majority of the pictures that have been published from the period spanning 1861–1865. Instead, Brady personally captured very few battlefield images, relying on his assistants to actually operate the camera and develop the negatives. Evidence for this arrangement can be found in the very photographs themselves: Even though the majority of Brady's photographs are marked "Brady & Co.," it is clearly the "Co." who took the shots, as Brady himself is in the photographs.

These two misconceptions—about the origins of battlefield photography and the role of Mathew Brady—share something else in common that may come as a surprise: both Fenton and Brady are known to have doctored their battlefield scenes, manipulating the images that were being brought home to the civilian population. Fenton's most famous work, "The Valley of the Shadow of Death," exists in two forms (figure

Figure 7.1.   Roger Fenton's most famous work, from 1855, "The Valley of the Shadow of Death." In an alternate version of this image, taken from the identical viewpoint, the road is completely clear of ordnance. (*Credit:* Photograph, Library of Congress, https://www.loc.gov/item/2001698869/, "The Valley of the Shadow of Death," 1855, LC-DIG-ppmsca-35546.)

7.1). One negative shows a dirt road paralleled by a ditch full of cannonballs. A second, more compelling view pictures the same road from the same perspective, only this time the road is covered with scattered artillery rounds.

Brady's manipulation of a battlefield scene is even more egregious. He did not limit himself to adding or moving ammunition; he had his assistants (and other living soldiers) pose as fallen soldiers, supposedly cut down in the heat of combat. From these two examples it becomes clear that early photojournalism had some problems: both the first person to be recognized as a battlefield photographer and the most famous photographer from the Civil War had a difficult time drawing the line between journalism and artistry.

The key attribute that sets photojournalism aside from other forms of photography is its promise of objectivity. A journalist might be accused of presenting a biased story; a photojournalist, by contrast, can offer photographic evidence to tell a story, and, if the photojournalist follows the basic tenets of the profession, the image provides compelling proof of what factually occurred. This is the very definition of "picture proof," and the audience/consumer of the photograph has a heightened sense of trust in the photojournalist's impartiality. A reporter might have what we today call "implicit bias," but a camera cannot.

Photojournalism differs from documentary photography in a subtle way. Documentary photography usually deals with more complex stories that unfold over longer time periods; photojournalism has more of a sense of immediacy. When Alexander Gardner photographed the dead at Sharpsburg and Mathew Brady displayed the images a few weeks later in his gallery, they were operating as photojournalists, reporting home to the general populace of the North what the battlefield had really looked like after the killing had ceased. The *New York Times* recognized this new type of journalism: "Mr. Brady has done something to bring home to us the terrible reality and earnestness of war. If he has not brought bodies and laid them in our dooryards and along the streets, he has done something very like it."[1] The key phrase used by the *Times* correspondent is "the terrible reality and earnestness," and this turn of words is what this chapter will focus (so to speak) on. Gardner's images at Antietam aren't thought to have been manipulated in any way, but others taken by the prolific photographer certainly were. So, the question that then develops is black and white: journalist or artist? Questions abound about the work of the darkroom documentarians and the historical value of their final product: How many of the iconic photographs from the Civil War could be accurately described as both real and earnest? Were Brady, Gardner, Timothy O'Sullivan, and the like interested in being photojournalists—which they repeatedly claimed to be—or just out to sell photographs? Can careful analysis of the images, combined with critical reasoning, demonstrate the documentarian and historical value of these pictures and to what degree alteration of the subject matter occurred before being recorded for posterity?

Civil War Photography: Technical Challenges and Consequences

During the Civil War, field photographers created their negatives using the laborious wet-plate process. First, the photographer and assistant prepare the future negative—a perfectly clean plate of glass—in a darkened, dust-free cart or wagon. This is accomplished by pouring a syrupy solution called collodion across the plate, covering the entire surface uniformly. The next step requires a good bit of practice: The plate needs to be tilted so as to uniformly spread the collodion, at which point it is allowed to dry until just tacky. After this preliminary step is finished, the technician dips the slide in a silver-nitrate solution (emulsion) that renders the plate light-sensitive. This results in a single frame of film ready for exposure.

The next photographic steps are especially time- (and light-) critical. The wet plate is transferred via a lightproof box from the darkroom wagon to the camera. Because enlargers weren't commonly used during the 1860s, the slide of glass would have needed to be the same size as the paper prints that would later be created via direct contact with the negative; eight inches by ten inches was a common choice.

Once the glass plate is safely in the camera, the photographer needs to take the picture in a short period of time, because the film cannot be allowed to dry. As a result, the entire composition of the future image has been predetermined prior to negative preparation: the tripod-mounted camera has been positioned exactly where the image is to be captured. The tripod is critical for holding the camera perfectly still during the exposure process.

At this point, the plate can be exposed to light by carefully removing the camera lens cover. Wet-plate negatives are orders of magnitude less light-sensitive than modern film or digital-camera sensors. While a twenty-first-century Nikon captures light for a miniscule amount of time—perhaps 1/125th or 1/500th of a second—cameras from the 1860s require a much longer exposure. With a Civil War box camera, a typical exposure takes between five and twenty seconds, depending on the amount of ambient light.

After the negative is exposed, the wet (and drying) plate is returned to the lightproof box and transferred back to the portable darkroom wagon. Here it is developed, washed in water, fixed so the image will resist fading, and washed again. The negative is then allowed to dry and unusually coated with a protective varnish.

After all of these procedures, the Civil War–era photographer would need to transport the fragile glass negatives across the poor roads to the photographer's home gallery, where paper prints could be created from the negative.

Several important aspects of this arduous process need to be considered when determining the authenticity of the final printed product. First, and importantly, the geologically slow exposure interval meant that all movements by people, animals, wind, or water would lead to a blurring of the image or the presence of "ghosts"—people who appear transparent because they changed position midexposure (a ghost appears on the left side of figure 5.1 on page 81).

This situation meant that all photographs needed to be composed of completely motionless subjects, and the impossibility of "action" shots ensured that no true combat photography could occur—only still post-combat images of the somber aftermath. Additionally, candid shots were difficult at best: all subjects in the picture needed to know they were being photographed in order to pose, or at least remain stationary. Any photograph from this time period that suggested a battle scene must be considered a fake from the outset, simply because of the prohibitively slow "shutter speed" available to the photographers.

Another problem for the technicians in the field was that the negatives needed to be exposed while they were still damp. This meant that the picture needed to be planned well in advance—framed and focused long before exposure. Instant or intuitive shots were impossible. Consider, as a short tangent, what Robert Capa's photographs at D-Day would have looked like had he been armed with a Civil War–era camera. He would never have attempted a picture during the actual beach landing, and even after successfully reaching dry land he would have struggled to photograph the dead on the beach because of the movement of the waves (and poor weather).

The wet plate's sensitivity to light also changes with meteorological conditions. The best photographs, in terms of clarity, depth of field, and lighting, were taken during fair weather with little cloud cover—always between 10 a.m. and 4 p.m. Dramatic late-afternoon shadows or early-morning mists were impossible to capture on film because of the reduced amount of solar radiation available for a potential exposure.

All of this means that a photographic team, arriving on a battleground after a fight, had to work efficiently to minimize the disadvantages of a shortened workday and the tedious wet-plate process. William Frassanito, noted expert on Civil War photography, estimates that a good photographer and team might have been able to capture one negative every ten minutes or so once their darkroom and camera were set up.[2]

Gardner's photographs of the dead at Antietam appealed to the public's morbid fascination with gruesome after-battle scenes. To capture future "combat" images, the photographers were left with this chronological challenge to producing similar views:

1. Travel to the battlefield quickly enough that you arrive before all the bodies have been interred (and, if possible, even before the bodies have been gathered prior to burial). This was usually only a few days. After Gettysburg, for example, Alexander Gardner and his team critically had a shorter travel time from the nation's capital than did Mathew Brady from Manhattan. Also note, importantly: The army in possession of the field after the battle must look favorably on what you are doing (i.e., Northern photographers could only work on the battlefields of Union victories). And because the army that wins a battle usually buries their own first, the photographer will primarily be photographing the dead of the enemy.

2. Find the corpses on the field, and take as many negatives as possible before 4 or at the latest 5 p.m.

3. Hope the weather cooperates, or wait for better conditions; bodies cannot be photographed in the rain, but they can be buried. Again, at Gettysburg this was more of a challenge for Gardner, who had arrived after the storms of July 4, than for Brady, who had arrived on the field more than a week later. Gardner had to photograph the dead even if the weather was not ideal (racing burial crews), while Brady could wait for ideal conditions to capture his landscape shots.

Given all of these challenges to photographing the fallen in the field, then, it seems remarkable that around one hundred photographs survive from the Civil War that objectively portray the dead on the field.[3] Together, these images and their captions provide an authentic and invaluable resource for citizens and historians about how the bodies appeared during the battles and where and how the soldiers died. Or do they?

THE HISTORICAL CLAIM

One of the key reasons the battlefield photographs from the Civil War were so important and popular from a journalistic and financial perspective was that they were purported to be unbiased and impartial—a claim repeated by the photographers themselves (as well as by contemporary traditional journalists). These assertions continue to be written, in some degree or another, to the present day. For example, although no definitive citation exists for the quotation, Mathew Brady is often credited with first saying that "the camera is the eye of history." Brady and his employee-colleague Alexander Gardner both presented their work as having a unique claim on objectivity. Brady stated, "My greatest aim has been to advance the art and make it what I think I have, a great and truthful medium of history."[4] Journalistic bias ran rampant during the war. Nearly all newspapers of the time were thought to have an agenda, political or otherwise. "The correspondents of the rebel newspapers are sheer falsifiers, the correspondents of the northern journals are not to be depended on, and the correspondents of the English press are altogether worse than either," wrote *Humphrey's Journal* early in the war. By contrast, the journal noted, "Brady never misrepresents."[5]

Alexander Gardner, in particular, wrote long, detailed captions for his photographs and presented his work as authentic exhibitions of what had really happened: "A sharpshooter, lying as he fell . . . his cap and gun were evidently thrown behind him by the violence of the shock."[6]

These photographs and their captions were repeatedly published for more than one hundred years without anyone ever doubting their authenticity. Even today, this claim to objectivity is still bandied about and repeated in print: "The Civil War was the first great media event in American history and the first war to be thoroughly documented using the emerging medium of photography."[7] Or "For the first time in history, citizens on the home front could view the actual carnage of the far away battlefields."[8] The historical claim to be studied in this chapter is relatively straightforward: *The photographs of the Civil War made great contributions to the emergence of the field of photojournalism; their work of science, not interpretive art, brought home the true, ghastly nature of battle in an unadulterated manner.* The two quotations above state it well: claiming that the images "thoroughly documented" the "actual carnage" leaves little need for elucidation. Working as the honest journalists and purveyors of the truth they claimed to be, these photographers captured images free of political or financial motivation. As such, manipulation of subject matter in any form—adding props, repositioning subjects, providing misleading captions—was strictly forbidden to preserve the photograph's scientific significance, lest it become no more objective than a sketch or painting.

So, while this historical claim is simple, it is also significant. As an illustration: Terrific scorn was dealt to Pulitzer Prize–winning freelance photojournalist Narciso Contreras after it was revealed that he had digitally altered a photograph taken of a Syrian rebel fighter in 2013; Contreras had digitally removed a colleague's video equipment from the background of his picture because he'd felt it might "distract" the viewer and thus lessen the composition. When this modification was discovered, the Associated Press severed all ties with the photographer, citing the modification as a violation of ethical standards required of all photojournalists.

Any manipulation of the subject matter, either during the photographic process or afterward, through darkroom or digital alteration, creates distrust in the entire medium. John Paul Filo won a 1971 Pulitzer Prize for the photograph he took on the Kent State campus—an anguished teenage girl kneels over the fallen body of Jeffrey Miller, a shooting victim of the Ohio National Guard. This photograph was reprinted repeatedly by media outlets, including *Time* and *Life*, before anyone realized it had been altered in the darkroom (a mildly distracting fence post had been airbrushed from directly behind the kneeling girl's head, leaving her agonized face as the undisputed focal point of the image). Twenty years later, the original, unaltered photograph appeared, causing a major eruption online, requiring a response from *Life*.

This point leads us to the historical claim to be tested: Were Civil War photographs scientifically objective, unbiased conveyors of historical events as they actually happened, or might the photographs be better viewed as another form of documentary art, more similar to the work produced by sketch artist and correspondent Alfred Waud (figure 7.2)? After all, he was working for newspapers as a journalist, sending back images of events as he portrayed them—with his unbiased eye.

In order to properly scrutinize this claim, the degree to which Civil War photographs have been manipulated must first be determined. The alteration of subject matter runs the gamut from the photojournalism

Figure 7.2.   Many of Alfred Waud's sketches include a great deal of detail, and compared with contemporary photographs, they had the advantage of being able to capture moving objects. Note the bayonet stuck in the sandbags at the top of the parapet. (*Credit:* "Sharpshooters 18th Corps," slightly altered [sharpened/cropped], July 1864, Library of Congress, LC-DIG-ppmsca-21251, https://www.loc.gov/pictures/item/2004660289/.)

ideal—wherein the subject is photographed as found, with absolutely no changes made to the image as it was discovered in the field—to complete fabrication of the composition. In between these extremes are a few degrees of alteration, including the addition of props (e.g., a rifle musket) or the repositioning a key component of the image (e.g., moving a corpse). This chapter investigates where Civil War photographers tended to fall on this continuum and whether it is correct to continue to refer to their work product as objective, impartial observations of history.

THE SCIENCE

When exploring the authenticity of Civil War photographs, three different scientific specialties come together: chemistry, geology, and forensics. The first of these, chemistry, refers to the chemical processes that are used to create a negative and the inherent limitations these procedures generate for the photographer. Examples of employing chemical constraints to analyze photographs include critically reviewing the relationship between the light sensitivity of a glass plate, the resulting long "shutter speed" or exposure duration, and any movement by the photograph's subject. Civil War–era pictures showing action scenes, for example, immediately draw suspicion with respect to realism, as the chemistry of the photographic process of the day would have prohibited an unposed image from ever having been created.

Also falling under chemistry would be any alteration of images after they have been captured in the field. Darkroom techniques—or "photoshopping," in today's parlance—involve using light and chemistry to airbrush or artificially add material to a picture through dishonest exposure. This wasn't as common a practice as some other types of manipulation in the nineteenth century, but darkroom alterations can create complete fabrications of what would otherwise appear to be "historical" images, creating false photographic proof of something that never actually happened.

William Frassanito is the most important figure in the history of Civil War photographic forensics. In his groundbreaking book *Gettysburg: A Journey in Time*, he describes using forensic photographic analysis to expose the inauthenticity of the captions that had been provided by the photographers for their images of the dead. In doing so, Frassanito effectively demonstrated that many of the descriptions of the scenes were wildly inaccurate and that the photographs often portrayed the same group of dead men, sometimes labeled as Rebels, sometimes as Union soldiers, and often lying on far different parts of the battleground from one image to the next. His most important techniques included using high-resolution and greatly magnified photographs to study and compare the details of clothing from different photographs as well as the positions and orientations of the bodies. In doing so, he demonstrated that Alexander Gardner and his team often repositioned the camera to take multiple images of the same groups of fallen soldiers and then labeled each image as if it were a photograph of different men on a different part of the landscape. This misdirection by the photographer and developer was then compounded by later historians, who added more details, assuming the original captions were entirely correct and truthful.

One complication that made Frassanito's work more difficult was the ever-changing terrain of Civil War battlegrounds. He could demonstrate that the photographers were showing the same group of dead soldiers from different angles, but he couldn't always say where, geographically, this had occurred on the battlefield. Hillslopes, vegetation, fences, and roads all changed between the 1860s and the 1970s; only one thing remained essentially consistent during this time span—the rocks. Most aspects of the landscape change over historical eras; rocks change over geological ones.

The boulders at Gettysburg that created the Slaughter Pen and Devil's Den and cover the Round Tops are composed of the igneous rock diabase. These rocks crystallized from molten magma around two hundred million years ago as the great supercontinent of Pangea was rifting apart and the infant Atlantic Ocean basin was beginning to spread, pushing North America away from Africa and Europe. Over thousands of millennia, the diabase intrusions were slowly revealed at the Earth's surface by erosion. With two hundred million years of weathering, the overburden sitting above the diabase was removed, and great amounts of pressure were dissipated, allowing the rocks to expand. When they did, they began to shed layers of rock, like the skin of an onion, producing a phenomenon known as *spheroidal weathering*. This produced the strangely rounded boulder fields that the soldiers discovered on July 2, 1863—and that Alexander Gardner and Timothy O'Sullivan photographed several days later.

Because diabase is a durable igneous rock, it can act as a natural photographic tracer, providing clues about the location where Civil War negatives had been captured. Frassanito used the distinct geomorphological features of many of the boulders at Gettysburg to identify the position of the fallen on the southern portion of the battlefield. These weathering characteristics included the unusual rounded shapes of boulders and distinct fractures.

Combining forensic and geological analysis, Frassanito made a discovery that garnered significant attention: the moving of the dead sharpshooter from Devil's Den. First, Frassanito used details of the

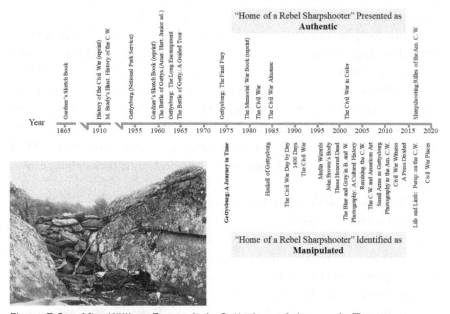

Figure 7.3. After William Frassanito's *Gettysburg: A Journey in Time* was published in 1975, it became much less common for Gardner's photograph to be published without at least a cursory mention of its manipulated origin. (*Credit:* "Gettysburg, Pennsylvania. Body of Confederate Sharpshooter," July 1863, Library of Congress, LC-DIG-cwpb-00874, https://www.loc.gov/pictures/collection/cwp/item/2018670788/.)

dead Confederate's corpse to show that Alexander Gardner and his assistants had been photographing the same man from different angles. He bolstered his claim by using the geology of the Devil's Den region to find the location of the photographs, demonstrating that the body remained stationary while the boulder background was changing. When he repeated the process at a different location, about seventy yards to the east, it was clear that the three bodies were all the same man, though each photograph's title and caption had claimed he was a different fallen soldier. What became clear was that Gardner and his team had first photographed the man from multiple viewpoints before carrying the corpse to a new, more photogenic location. Their final product was, arguably, the most famous "historical" image to emerge from the war; it was also inarguably fraudulent (figure 7.3).

For purposes of the scientific analysis of the authenticity of Civil War photographs, the contribution of each field of science can be summarized in the following manner:

1. Chemistry
    - Any photograph that includes any degree of movement or that portrays soldiers in battle (or on the "day of the fight") is immediately suspect.
    - Any photograph supposedly taken on a day when there was significant rainfall is of questionable authenticity. Soldiers' diaries and officers' after-battle reports often contain references to the weather and should be used to check against the captions of photographs (e.g., no photographs should exist of Burnside's "Mud March").

2. Forensics
    - Details of uniforms or clothing can help identify when a soldier or group of men was being photographed from different camera angles but was not captioned as such.
    - The orientation of corpses and their body positions (raised limbs, clenched fists) can also identify mislabeled photographs.

- Vegetation and clothing should also be appropriate for the season in which the photograph was reportedly taken. Dead men from the Manassas battlefield should not be wearing heavy winter clothing; both battles took place in the late summer. Other photographs exist for other summer battles, like Gettysburg, where supposedly dead men are surrounded by leafless trees.

- Dead men do not move. Except sometimes after the Battle of Corinth. And Gettysburg. If a corpse has been moved by a burial party, it will almost always be collected with other fallen soldiers, and the limbs will be positioned in such a way as to indicate the bodies had been transported (e.g., knees will show signs of having been bound together).

- Dead men are usually bloated and putrefied. If their corpses have passed through this process, their clothing will show evidence of swelling—burst trousers, torn and unbuttoned shirts.

3. Geology
   - In this respect, geological analysis becomes a subbranch of forensics, allowing the precise location on the field where a subject was photographed to be identified. Limestone outcrops at Antietam and diabase exposures at Gettysburg are excellent examples. As such, rocks can help identify staging, movement of bodies, and flat-out fabrications.

   - Rock weathering can also identify when a particular image was taken. For example, the boulders at Gettysburg were relatively pristine until the 1880s. Then, during the next two decades, soldiers returning to the battlefield and other tourists and businesses defaced the battlefield outcrops with graffiti, carved and painted. Around the turn of the century, the federal government attempted to return the diabase to its former appearance by chiseling all of these markings away, leaving turn-of-the-century photographs of the boulders of Devil's Den with unusual, unweathered surfaces. Careful examination of the large rocks and chisel marks can narrow the time frame around when a photograph from this area was taken to within a decade, distinguishing photographs created in the immediate postbellum period from those taken much later.

When combined, these three overlapping sciences provide clues about the authenticity of Civil War photographs. Next, these scientific tools will be used to analyze a number of photographs from the early 1860s to establish a hierarchy of photographic fraud.

ANALYSIS AND EVALUATION

In 1851, Alexander Gardner was owner and editor of the Scottish newspaper the *Glasgow Sentinel*. That same year he traveled to London to visit the Great Exhibition in Hyde Park, where he viewed a photography showcase featuring Mathew Brady's work. Five years later, Gardner had left the newspaper business, crossed the Atlantic, and joined Brady in his New York City gallery as a portrait photographer. Within two years of joining Brady, Gardner's talents with the camera allowed his employer to place him in charge of a second gallery in the US capital. When conflict came to the country in 1861 and army ranks swelled, business at the galleries boomed.

Mathew Brady is known to have traveled to Manassas for the first major battle of the war, although he captured no images of the actual battlefield. He did, however, develop a desire to document the war on glass negatives. To do this, Brady sent more than a dozen of his employees into the field with cameras, assistants, and mobile darkrooms. One team with particularly good access to the Army of the Potomac was led by Alexander Gardner. Thus on September 19, 1862—two days after the troops had done battle—Gardner photographed the first group of dead bodies strewn across the fields around Sharpsburg, Maryland, the first photographs of groups of American soldiers killed in action on American soil. He also mislabeled multiple captions of the photographs of the dead, placing the bodies on the wrong part of the battlefield as belonging to the wrong brigade, or even confusing Union soldiers for Rebels.

When Gardner's photographs were displayed at Brady's gallery in New York a few weeks later, they were a sensation. Viewers knew or cared little that the captions might not be historically accurate. Brady, as was his wont, placed his name on all the images—"Photographed by Brady & Co." As a result, the general public and the newspapers attributed most of Gardner's photographs to Mathew Brady, not to the actual person behind the camera lens. Brady had, after all, paid Gardner's salary and displayed the images in his own gallery. Gardner was simply a member of the "Co."

Late in 1862, Gardner decided to leave Brady's employment and start his own gallery in Washington, D.C. The motivation behind this separation was complicated. Certainly Gardner wanted more credit for his own work, but philosophical differences regarding photographic strategy also separated the two men. Gardner wished to capture the brutality of the war—as a photojournalist of sorts. Brady wanted to remain an artist, maintaining some degree of the prewar pastoral aesthetic.

When Gardner broke from Brady, he took several of his assistants, including Timothy O'Sullivan and James F. Gibson. In early 1863, they had established a gallery on the corner of Seventh and D Streets in Washington, and the photographers were in the field, following Joseph Hooker and the Army of the Potomac, hoping to re-create their Antietam death scenes on a Virginia battlefield. To do this, the photographers would need the Union to be in control of the battleground after the fighting ended, which was not a common occurrence in late 1862 and early 1863. Unfortunately for the photographers, the Battle of Chancellorsville would see the Federal Army retiring from the field yet again.

Thus it was in July 1863 that Gardner and O'Sullivan traveled to Gettysburg in the aftermath of the greatest battle of the war—and which was, importantly for them, a federal victory. Here, hoping to capture images that would best the efforts of Brady (who would arrive more than a week later), they searched for the most morbid of subject matter. It was also here that their manipulation of the photographs—and history—grew beyond simply providing misleading captions.

The Hierarchy of Manipulation

Today the ethics of photojournalism prohibits any degree of alteration to an image. Any staging, any addition of a prop, or any airbrushing or photoshopping is strictly proscribed, and even the smallest degree of modification—say, the "artistic" darkening of O. J. Simpson's complexion on the cover of *Time*—is intensely disapproved. Even the most minute manipulation renders the photograph invalid as a historical artifact.

This was not the case in the 1860s. The low-light sensitivity of the negatives and the long exposure times meant that photographs had to be posed, and *cartes de visite* of soldiers often featured multiple weapons as props. Once the photographer had left the studio, following the soldiers to the battlefield, why shouldn't an extra rifle be brought along in case a shot needed an added sense of drama and immediacy? An unarmed corpse could have died at any time, from any cause; arming one with a rifle made it look more like the soldier had *just* been cut down in combat.

Some degree of staging was necessary for any photograph from the front that depicted humans or animals, unless they were dead or asleep. As such, photographers of the day can certainly be forgiven for snapping posed camp scenes or strangely motionless men standing around artillery pieces or along a parapet.

What is more difficult to ignore, from a photojournalism perspective, is any additional crafting of the subject. The least egregious of this type of manipulation of the "historical" scene is the addition of props to a scene—usually a rifle, but occasionally an artillery shell or other battlefield detritus. This was most commonly done when the subject to be photographed was a single soldier or a pair of dead soldiers. Most images containing more than this number of corpses are bereft of small arms, perhaps because the grisly image was deemed dramatic enough without the added accoutrement. Or perhaps because the photographer only had one rifle and it would have looked suspicious had one of the soldiers, and only one, been armed while no one else had a gun.

The next level of modification was the changing of a scene for dramatic effect prior to the exposure of the negative. This included repositioning the dead. Perhaps a fallen man's face was not clearly visible, or perhaps several bodies were too far apart to reveal detail when photographed from afar. Sometimes a body, when found, wasn't in the most photogenic of locations, and another, more dramatic setting with a better story to tell was found nearby. Moving a corpse was not the most pleasant of tasks, but for the sake of art composition, and a financial payoff, sacrifices were made. On at least one occasion, a body was moved and a prop added to a photograph, truly pushing the limits of what the camera lens could objectively capture.

The final two methods of manipulation defy all pretense of photojournalism and actual and factual photography. If Mathew Brady and his colleagues were, in their own words, creating "a great and truthful medium of history," then they ought never have provided false or misleading captions for their images or—the very worst of their offenses—created new "history" in the darkroom.[9] Alexander Gardner was especially fond of the former caption fraud, photographing the dead from different angles and then describing the men as having been cut down in completely different parts of the battlefield. Later, historians would take these false captions and add details to their own descriptions, compounding the problem.

If not properly identified, the final example of photographic manipulation is also the most troublesome for historians and scholars: the wholesale fabrication of images in the darkroom through multiple exposures of the same print, using different parts of several negatives. This technique also provides the best evidence of simple financial incentives, leaving the photographer or developer no valid claim to historical contribution. If, for example, prints of General Grant were becoming especially popular toward the end of the war and a photographer were to find only a few negatives of the officer, why not make up some new images? Careful work in the darkroom can produce an amalgamation that at least appears authentic, and adding a false caption creates an all-new print that might sell very well.

This, then, leaves us with a hierarchy of alteration for Civil War photographs. Adding props changes a scene, but the scene is at least "real" in the sense that what is being photographed did occur; the corpse truthfully represents a man who was killed at this spot, the Enfield only adding slightly to the drama and implied immediacy. If anything, the staging and positioning of the rifle suggest the body had not been touched or looted, and the rifle isn't the main subject matter of the photograph anyway.

The movement of the primary subject of an image, the corpse, presents a larger problem. Now the photograph is "real" only in the sense that this man had been killed in this battle and on this portion of the battlefield, but the two do not necessarily belong together in history. This man was not killed at *this* spot, and he was not carrying *that* rifle; this photograph is more art and not entirely journalism.

The most dangerous form of modification of historical photographs might be the addition of false captions. Props and photoshopping can be easy to identify, but inaccurate captioning, whether done on purpose or not, can be difficult to detect. This process introduces new ahistorical information into the record of events, or, rather, they happened, but not necessarily at this location. The photographs are certainly real, but the false captions render them dangerous to use as an interpretive tool.

The most invidious of all photographs are the darkroom composites. These are images of events that never happened and thus are in no sense "real." These images create a false history; they don't document a real one.

William Frassanito gained recognition as the most important investigator of Civil War photographic authenticity with his publications about the negatives from Gettysburg.[10] These books, combined with his volumes about Antietam and the Overland Campaign,[11] document the extensive history of photographic fraud by Gardner, Brady, and others. In the next section of the chapter, this photographic modification is explored using many of the techniques employed by Frassanito—namely, detailed forensic and geologic examination. In doing so, the hierarchy of manipulation is quantified, starting with the addition of props at Gettysburg and ending with a fake General Grant on horseback along the fake James River. By the end of this investigation of things that never happened, the journey will travel from First Manassas to Petersburg and, in doing so, complete an evaluation of the widely established perception that Civil War photographs were the first unbiased and objective news source ever presented to the American public and, as such, are an invaluable historical resource.

The Hierarchy in Practice

The smallest degree of modification to a photographic composition involves adding or removing objects not central to the subject matter or story being told. In modern photography, this might include airbrushing or cropping a distraction out of the image. This is, of course, verboten

Figure 7.4. Timothy O'Sullivan captured a series of photographs of dead Confederate soldiers near the Spotsylvania Court House battlefield in May 1864. Note that in this photograph the soldier in the foreground has an Enfield rifle lying across his legs while the man in the background lies beside his black hat and canteen and is unarmed. (*Credit:* "Scene of Ewell's Attack, May 19, 1864, Near Spottsylvania [i.e. Spotsylvania] Court House. Dead Confederate Soldiers," Library of Congress, LC-USZ62-104043, https://www.loc.gov/pictures/collection/cwp/item/91787082/.)

in contemporary photojournalism. The degree of alteration—that is, the importance of the object being added or removed—determines how far the photograph strays from journalism toward art (or deceit).

The most common prop added to Civil War "combat" photographs is the rifle musket. The motive for adding the weapon to a scene is simple: The rifle's presence is compelling, confirming the dead man is a soldier killed in combat, conveying a sense of immediacy and realism. If a rifle is placed beside an unbloated corpse, the viewer might be led to believe that the photographer captured the image just after the man fell (figures 7.4 and 7.5).

Consider the two dead soldiers photographed near the Alsop House after the Battle of Spotsylvania (figures 7.4 and 7.5). One dead soldier lies with his back against a disassembled fence that he was presumably using as a crude breastwork. A rifle musket lies across his legs, not quite touching the split rails. The man in the background is less clear, although it appears he has fallen beside his black hat and canteen, his arms extended upward as if clenched in pain. As Timothy O'Sullivan and his assistants continue to take pictures, the Enfield rifle begins to move. First, it climbs

Figure 7.5.   These are the same two men seen in figure 7.4. The rifle of the man on the left has somehow moved such that the barrel now rests on the split rails beside him; as for the man on the right, he has now somehow become armed with, not surprisingly, an Enfield rifle. (*Credit: left:* "Dead Confederate soldier," photograph, May 19, 1864, Library of Congress, LC-DIG-ppmsca-32910, https://www.loc.gov/pictures/collection/cwp/item/2012647824/; *right:* "Dead Confederate soldier," photograph, May 19, 1864, Library of Congress, LC-DIG-ppmsca-32911, https://www.loc.gov/pictures/collection/cwp/item/2012647825/.)

onto the breastworks (figure 7.5, left), and then it jumps from body to body to lie upon the other corpse (figure 7.5, right). The viewer is left to believe that the final image captures the figure of a man who died in agony: his arm position suggest he was in a great deal of pain, and yet somehow he manages to balance a rifle musket on his chest as he passes away.

Careful examination of these three images makes clear what happened: The photographers found two unarmed dead men, but they only had one rifle to add as a prop. Wary of actually touching the corpses, the artists simply placed the rifle musket on the fallen men, adjusting it slightly for the purpose of perfecting their composition.

Analysis of photographs of the dead from many battlegrounds demonstrates how commonly rifles were used as props. When the entire collection of photographs of the dead from the Library of Congress are compared (more than fifty photographs), it is obvious that rifles were added to one particular type of image: detailed, close-up studies of one or two dead soldiers (table 7.1). When soldiers were photographed in larger groups (four or more dead in one image), they are never armed; yet when three or fewer bodies make up the composition, they have at least one rifle more than half of the time.

Table 7.1. **When fallen soldiers were photographed in small groups, they had their rifle musket more often than not; when they were photographed in larger groups, they were never found with even a single rifle**

Number of corpses	Percent armed	Number of photographs
1	59	29
2	50	6
3	50	4
1–3	56	39
4–6	0	6
7–9	0	8
10–13	0	4
14+	0	6

The only possible (nonprop) explanation for this phenomenon involves the location of the groups of soldiers on the battlefield: perhaps the larger groups were more easily found and their weapons had already been salvaged, while the smaller groups had died on more hidden part of the battlefields, their bodies not yet discovered by those tasked with collecting rifles. When the many images of the dead with rifles at Petersburg are considered, where the men lie in the open in the fortifications and trenches, this explanation becomes untenable.

This simple statistical analysis helps document a simple truth: Andrew Gardner, Timothy O'Sullivan, and T. C. Roche (an important photographer of the Petersburg dead) were carrying a rifle musket with them as if it were a standard piece of equipment from their darkroom. It would seem preposterous to add a single rifle to a group of a dozen fallen soldiers, raising questions about where the other men's weapons had disappeared to, but for a single dead soldier, it would be entirely plausible that he had died with his rifle in his hands. In the photographers' eyes, adding the rifle was likely no more of a transgression than what had taken place in their studio-photography days prior to the war, when they had often made weapons available for soldiers seeking to be photographed before they headed off to the front.

Even the most gruesome photograph from Gardner's Gettysburg battlefield series shows multiple obvious signs of staging (figure 7.6). When Gardner and his team discovered this poor disemboweled man on the Rose Farm on the southern part of the battleground, they began to imagine the story behind his demise. The damage to the torso and disarticulated arm suggested an extremely high-energy, traumatic death—something that a single minié bullet might have had a difficult time accomplishing. By the time the photograph was taken, the image conveyed the entire dramatic and devastating story of a death by direct strike from an artillery bolt. The soldier had been knocked backward off his feet by the impact of the shell, ripping open his gut and tearing off his arm.[12] His bayonetted rifle, sans ramrod, lies across his legs, its butt against his canteen. Proof of this devastating mode of death lies all around the rifle: an artillery round rests on a rock behind the barrel rings, and the man's severed hand seems to reach for the trigger.

Figure 7.6. The goriest of Gardner's images from the Rose Farm at Gettysburg. Detailed analysis of an enlargement of this image shows that this Springfield Model 1861 rifle musket is missing its ramrod. (*Credit:* "Federal Soldier Disembowelled by a Shell," detail of photograph, 1863, Library of Congress, LC-DIG-ppmsca-32915, https://www.loc.gov/pictures/item/2012647822/.)

After the visual shock of this picture has subsided, and when it is considered from afar, the manipulation of the scene seems rather absurd. Is the audience really to believe that an artillery bolt nearly bisected this man and yet his rifle came to rest, balanced, across his thighs? The bolt has the ability to sever his arm cleanly from his body but still comes to rest just behind him, and his arm, obliterated by the impact, leaves only his severed hand to fall beside him? What becomes obvious in retrospect is that Gardner positioned his tripod and camera in such a way as to maximize the viscera; the viewer immediately notices the ghastly open-cavity wound. Gardner may have added or moved the hand, or perhaps it was *in situ*, before placing the rifle and artillery round in such a manner as to complete his composition and tell his story. The eye stares at the wound, drifts down to the horror of the detached hand, and then follows the musket as it points to the cause of the carnage.

The second and third stages of manipulation involve moving the primary subject matter in the photograph and adding the appropriate props. In such death scenes, of course, the corpse would have been moved and a rifle added. Through this process, the photographer is creating the entirety of the image, leaving any "reality" far behind. The foremost example of this form of photographic fraud was best (and first) told by Frassanito in *Gettysburg: A Journey in Time.* The story in brief goes like this: Gardner and his team found a lone, dead, unarmed Confederate infantryman in the diabase boulders of Devil's Den (figure 7.7). Here they added a Springfield rifle musket (Model 1861, missing a ramrod) and took several photographs from three tripod positions. They would later add misleading captions to each image.

Some time later, around seventy yards away, the photographers found a profoundly interesting group of boulders connected by a short wall of smaller rocks—an incredibly photogenic location with perfect lighting. The perfect sniper den. Unfortunately, it lacked a dead body to add drama. Temporarily.

By adding to the scene the body and Springfield prop rifle previously owned by the disemboweled soldier (figure 7.6, above), Gardner's team created—key word *created*—the most famous photograph to emerge from the Battle of Gettysburg (figure 7.3, above).

The prop rifle in all of these pictures provides an interesting example of how critical thinking can be used to interpret "historical" images. Gardner photographed four dead soldiers (figures 7.3, 7.6, and 7.7), all of

Figure 7.7. The same dead soldier, photographed from different angles. (*Credit:* "Gettysburg, Pennsylvania. Dead Confederate Sharpshooter" and "Gettysburg, Pennsylvania. Dead Sharpshooter on the Right of the Confederate Line," Timothy H. O'Sullivan, details of photographs, July 1863, Library of Congress, LC-DIG-cwpb-00898 and LC-DIG-cwpb-00862, https://www.loc.gov/pictures/item/2018670874/ and https://www.loc.gov/pictures/item/2018670741/.)

whom were armed with the same model of Springfield rifle, the M1861. In reality, these images capture only two dead men, both Confederate. The disemboweled infantryman has a bayonetted rifle that lacks a ramrod. Gardner labels the fallen men in Devil's Den as all having been "sharpshooters," men who would never have carried a rifle with a bayonet, lest the reflection give away their position and the blade slow their loading. So when the "sharpshooters" are photographed, the bayonet is gone, but the M1861's ramrod continues to go missing from each and every one of the guns photographed next to the dead in Devil's Den. Is it really possible that Gardner found four different dead men on the battlefield who had each died carrying inoperable rifles of the same make and model?

The only scenario less plausible than this one would be found in Gardner's own description of the final sharpshooter scene (figure 7.3, above), in his *Sketch Book of the Civil War*, in which he describes returning to Devil's Den later in the year: "On the nineteenth of November, the artist attended the consecration of the Gettysburg Cemetery, and again visited the 'Sharpshooter's Home.' The musket, rusted by many storms, still leaned against the rock, and the skeleton of the soldier lay undisturbed within the mouldering uniform ..."[13] Had Gardner's fanciful tale been true, he might have encountered another of the early photographers of the Gettysburg Battlefield, P. S. Weaver, who is known to have been taking photographs in Devil's Den around this time. Weaver's photographic team was perpetrating the highest level of manipulation on the fraud hierarchy, posing living soldiers among the rocks to simulate death scenes, similar to Gardner's earlier work. Weaver attempted to mimic Gardner's compositions of dead soldiers with even more added drama—more corpses, more rifles, living doctors inspecting the dead, and bodies strewn around, on, in, and under the diabase boulders (figure 7.8).

Weaver's series of photographs veers as far away from photojournalism as is possible: the events portrayed never happened, and the subject matter is completely fictitious; only the locale is real. It seems hard to believe that the citizens on the home front, after viewing Gardner's images of bloated bodies on the fields of Antietam and Gettysburg, would have been gullible enough to accept these as candids. It seems even harder to comprehend how modern historians could still represent these photographs as

Figure 7.8. During the second week of November 1863, P. S. Weaver composed several fake shots of dead Union soldiers scattered across the boulders of Devil's Den. (*Credit:* "Dead on Little Round Top, Gettysburg," detail of photograph, Library of Congress, LC-DIG-ppmsca-32932, https://www.loc.gov/item/2012647846/.)

authentic after all the work published exposing so many of the scenes from around Devil's Den as staged and fraudulent; nevertheless, images from the series still find their way into the pages of unskeptical books, perpetuating the fraud. For example, on page 183 of *Bill O'Reilly's Legends and Lies: The Civil War* is the image found in figure 7.9.

Legends and Lies captions this picture as follows: "In the battle for Little Round Top, the Union suffered 565 casualties, including 134 killed, and the Rebels lost 1,185 men, with 279 killed. Here two doctors examine fallen men only hours after the battle."[14] So, with the inclusion of this picture and caption, *Legends and Lies* is displaying a photograph of an event that never happened and describing it as occurring on a day and time when the fake event never could have happened. How credulous does a

Figure 7.9. One of the completely believable images captured by P. S. Weaver in Devil's Den. Note the two "doctors" inspecting the fallen soldiers to see whether any might be saved. (*Credit:* "Dead at Little Round-Top, Position of Berdan's Sharpshooters," detail of photograph, November 1, 1863, Library of Congress, LC-DIG-stereo-1s03751, https://www.loc.gov/item/2004682792/.)

viewer have to be to not question how three Union soldiers could have died together, one on top of a giant boulder, one crammed into the crevasse under this boulder, and one pinched into a second, lower crack at the base of the formation? What type of defensive position had these men been assuming prior to being killed—a cheerleading pyramid? Were they struck down in close-quarters combat or during a game of hide-and-seek? Also, note that all of the soldiers retain their guns (complete with ramrods), presumably because they had just been recruited away from the dedication ceremonies for the cemetery to act as models in Weaver's compositions.

There is some question regarding whether Weaver ever intended for his photographs to be taken as authentic; after all, the same soldier can be spotted dying in several different places. Nevertheless, more than 150 years after their first printing, these images are still being presented as genuine in new works of history.

Clearly the unsuspicious caption writer for O'Reilly's book has confused this image as belonging to the series captured by the first photographers on the field, Alexander Gardner and his team (thus the doctors examining the fallen *a few hours* after they had been killed). If so, we are left with a book, published in 2017, that has mistakenly assumed this faked image belongs to a series of earlier photos that contains staged and fraudulent images, all with a caption that certainly suggests confidence in the authenticity of the photograph. Seems almost like a legendary lie.

Alexander Gardner's and P. S. Weaver's motives in taking these photographs in Devil's Den reveal their preference for putting financial interests above journalistic efforts. One name that has escaped criticism so far belongs to the most famous photographic team from the war: Brady & Co. Mathew Brady typically arrived at battlefields long after the dead had been buried, and when he did travel to the front to spend time among the soldiers in the field, he often included himself in many of his own photographs.

Brady added himself, or an assistant, to his compositions for the same reasons others added props—to make the landscape photography more interesting to the eye. No doubt he also liked to demonstrate that he, personally, had been at the battle site, documenting the fighting ground with his "eye of history."

A promotional, informal self-portrait seems relatively harmless from a photojournalistic perspective; after all, Brady actually *was* on the field, and his presence didn't change, for example, the appearance of the field where Major General John Reynolds had fallen. Nevertheless, Brady's internal businessman overwhelmed his historical senses on at least two occasions: After finding it impossible to photograph the field after First Manassas (the Rebels held the battlefield after the Union Army fled back to Washington) and arriving too late to witness the dead of Gettysburg, Brady staged a few photographs of the fallen in the field (figures 7.10 and 7.11).

Figure 7.10.   Mathew Brady labeled this image (left) as having been taken on Matthews Hill after the Battle of First Manassas. In the detail (right), it is apparent that either this image is not from First Manassas—a battle that took place in Virginia in July—or the soldiers died from heat stroke while wearing heavy winter jackets. (*Credit:* "Confederate Dead on Matthews Hill, Bull Run (i.e. Antietam)," detail of photograph, 1861, Library of Congress, LC-DIG-ppmsca-32935, https://www.loc.gov/item/2012647848/.)

The first of these faked photographs purports to show fallen soldiers on Matthews Hill after the Battle of First Manassas. Closer examination of the clothing suggests the men are in winter uniforms, which would have been completely inappropriate for a battle that had taken place in the middle of summer.[15]

The second Brady image is from Culp's Hill at Gettysburg. The "dead" man in the photograph is almost certainly one of Brady's assistants, as he can clearly be identified (alive) in several subsequent negatives taken the same day. The caption on the negative sleeve declares the image to be of "Dead soldier and battered trees, Culp's Hill, Gettysburg." One supposes this picture *might* have been authentic, assuming only that Brady's assistant had secretly enlisted in the army and Brady murdered him during their visit to Gettysburg. Perhaps the assistant had dropped one too many glass negatives?

The highest stage of photographic fraud represents complete fabrication of the subject via darkroom techniques. Neither the subject matter nor

Figure 7.11.   Unlike Brady's photograph from Matthews Hill, this photograph is actually from Culp's Hill. The problem is that the photographer didn't arrive at the hill until long after the bodies of the dead had been gathered for burial. (*Credit:* "Gettysburg, Pennsylvania. Battered Trees on Culp's Hill," detail, 1863, Library of Congress, LC-DIG-cwpb-01646, https://www.loc.gov/pictures/item/2018670705/.)

the location are real; the event is pure fiction. Two examples of this manipulation demonstrate the deception well, one accomplished by a "relatively" famous photographic developer and one perpetrated by a national newspaper.[16] The first of these was created around the turn of the nineteenth century by Mathew Brady's nephew: Levin C. Handy was apparently quite handy in the darkroom, producing an eye-catching image of "General Grant at City Point" (figure 7.12). Careful examination of the image

Figure 7.12.   Levin C. Handy's montage of "General Grant at City Point."
Handy didn't take any of the photographs used in the image—he had been
a young child during the war—but he did combine three negatives in the
darkroom to create a record of an event that never happened. (*Credit:* Ca. 1902,
Library of Congress, LC-DIG-ppmsca-15886, https://www.loc.gov/pictures/
item/2007681056/.)

provides a more accurate, if less concise, caption: "General Grant's head,
photographed across the river at Cold Harbor, sitting atop Major General
Alexander McCook's body and horse (both photographed in the western
theater of the war), while standing in front of Confederate prisoners of war
who had been captured two years earlier after the Battle of Front Royal."

Forensic and historical clues abound when viewing a magnified version of this negative. Start with the technical: Careful etching around
Grant's head and the horse's mane are visible from the multiple montage-
creating exposures in the darkroom (figure 7.13). Clues are even more
abundant from a historical perspective. At City Point, for example, Grant
rode a horse named Cincinnati, and Cincinnati did not have a sock of
white hair around his left ankle. Grant was also a general-in-chief at this
point of the war (three stars on the shoulder strap).

Figure 7.13. A magnified view of Grant's fake horse, showing the etching around the mane—indicative of darkroom manipulation of a negative or series of negatives. (*Credit:* "General Grant at City Point," Levin C. Handy, detail from photograph, c. 1902, Library of Congress, LC-DIG-ppmsca-15886, https://www .loc.gov/pictures/item/2007681056/.)

So, what we are left with, from a historical point of view, is an image that is invidious—photographic proof of an event that actually *did* happened (Grant had spent considerable time at City Point) that has actually been completely fabricated. Grant was at City Point, but this is not what he'd looked like, this is not his horse, and the background is not anything like how City Point would have appeared in the later stages of the war (figure 7.14). The composite image lies to the viewers and takes otherwise historically important documentation, in the form of three authentic photographs, and combines them into one worthless print. Perhaps it sold well.

Harper's Weekly was the most widely circulated magazine in the United States in the early 1860s, and it published extensive coverage of the war,

Figure 7.14.   The three images that Handy combined to create "Grant at City Point." (*Credit:* "Gen. U.S. Grant at His Cold Harbor, Va., Headquarters," photograph, June 1864, Library of Congress, LC-DIG-cwpb-04407, https://www .loc.gov/pictures/collection/cwp/item/2018667429/; "Washington. D.C., Vicinity. Maj. Gen. Alexander M. McCook on Horseback, Brightwood," photograph, taken between 1862 and 1865, Library of Congress, LC-DIG-cwpb-03862, https://www .loc.gov/pictures/collection/cwp/item/2018667065/; and "Confederate Prisoners Captured in the Battle of Front Royal Being Guarded in a Union Camp in the Shenandoah Valley," May 1862, Library of Congress, LC-DIG-ppmsca-15835, https://www.loc.gov/pictures/collection/cwp/item/2007684716/.)

often employing skilled artists like Winslow Homer and Alfred Waud. With the widespread availability of certifiably objective photographs now available to compete with their sketches, *Harper's* looked more and more to Alexander Gardner and Mathew Brady for illustrations. Because the technology did not exist at the time to print the photographs in the journal directly, the negatives of the "true-life" death scenes first needed to be converted to wood engravings before they could be published. This is where the artistic trouble begins.

The conversion of a glass negative to a wood carving added a step that could potentially disrupt the photojournalistic process. The carver was, presumably, someone with some artistic talent. Perhaps the final product should be called "engraving journalism" to denote another person's influence on the final product.

Soon enough, as might have been expected, images were appearing in *Harper's* of events that had never happened—or at least that had never happened at the same time. These images lacked the dramatic action presented by the competing sketch artists but promised to remove the artistic license introduced by pencil and paper. The camera lens promoted objectivity, but the developer and wood carver did not (figure 7.15).

This illustration, published two years after the Battle of Gettysburg, is captioned "The Harvest of Death, Gettysburg, July 4, 1863." The

Figure 7.15.   This plate appeared in *Harper's Weekly* on July 22, 1865 (vol. 9, no. 447, p. 452). At least five different camera exposures are recorded in this one carving. (*Credit:* Lithograph, Brooklyn Museum Libraries.)

magazine credits the photograph to "A. Gardner, Washington," making no mention that the image is a montage. In reality, the composite contains elements of at least five of Gardner's earlier-published negatives (figure 7.16).

The majority of the images in the foreground (1) were from a negative taken by Gardner assistant Timothy O'Sullivan. This original picture was incorrectly titled "Bodies of dead Federal Soldiers on the field of the first

day's battle." The closest dead soldier to the "camera" position (right, 2) is familiar; this is Gardner's dead Confederate "sharpshooter" from Devil's Den. There are several groups of dead horses in the image, taken from different negatives (3, 4, and 5). For the most distant group, the images had been cut from a print of the Trostle farm, and the white picket fence in front of the house is just visible (4). For the sake of composition, this print was broken into two parts, with the damaged caisson (5) removed from the right of the original negative and placed to the left in the carving, and the dead horses, fence, and exposed rafters moved in the opposite manner. Finally, the man on the left (6) and the corpses and man on horseback in the background (7) give the *Harper's Weekly* print its name; these images are from Gardner's photograph "A Harvest of Death."

In summary, then, we are left with a composite of images that have been rearranged with respect to geography and, according to Alexander Gardner's original captions, time. The montage is "real" only in the sense that these events did, individually, happen. Sort of ... The prop rifle of the fallen sharpshooter and the addition of cannonballs indicate a modification of the subject matter both pre- and postproduction.

Journalistic ethics and standards have certainly changed over the years, because it seems certain that any contemporary viewer of the

Figure 7.16 (facing page). These are the five photographs (top) used to compose one wood carving, with corresponding numbers indicating the locations of different aspects of the original negatives. (*Credit:* "Battlefield of Gettysburg. Bodies of Dead Federal Soldiers on the Field of the First Day's Battle," photograph, July 1863, Library of Congress, LC-DIG-ppmsca-32922, https://www.loc.gov/pictures/collection/cwp/item/2012647835/; "Gettysburg, Pennsylvania. Dead Confederate Sharpshooter in 'the Devil's Den,'" photograph, July 1863, Library of Congress, LC-DIG-cwpb-03701, https://www.loc.gov/pictures/collection/cwp/item/2018672241/; "Gettysburg, Pennsylvania. Unfit for Service. Artillery Caisson and Dead Mule," photograph, 1863, Library of Congress, LC-DIG-cwpb-00828, https://www.loc.gov/pictures/collection/cwp/item/2018670617/; "The Battle-field of Gettysburg. Dead Horses of Bigelows (9th Massachusetts) Battery," photograph, July 1863, Library of Congress, LC-DIG-ppmsca-32844, https://www.loc.gov/pictures/collection/cwp/item/2012647710/; "Incidents of the War. A harvest of Death, Gettysburg, July, 1863," photograph, Library of Congress, LC-B8184-7964-A, https://www.loc.gov/pictures/collection/cwp/item/2018667213/.)

nation's most popular magazine who had seen any of Gardner's earlier prints would have recognized elements of the altered composite image. Had this occurred today in a modern news journal, it would have immediately been recognized, leading to a scandal for the publication.

Returning to the central question to be analyzed in this chapter: Were the photographs of the Civil War the objective "lens of history" they were said to be? The answer depends on the degree of manipulation deemed allowable before objective reporting slides into the subjective art world. For the montage illustrations and the faked composites, there is no possible claim to photojournalistic objectivity or even truthfulness. Photographs containing a rifle as a prop are closer to what might today be accepted as "reporting" or "documentary photography"; yet they still do not represent the scene in an accurate manner.

If we study all the photographs from the Library of Congress's collection that include a dead soldier in the field, the degree of manipulation can be broadly assessed (table 7.2).

Table 7.2. The magnitude of manipulation in the photographs of the dead on the battlefield from the Library of Congress Civil War prints collection

Battlefield	Number of photos	Number of photos with props	Number of photos in which the corpses appear to have been moved	Number of fabrications	Percentage of photos altered in some form
Manassas	1	0	0	1	100
Antietam	18	0	0	0	0
Corinth	3	0	1	0	33
Fredericksburg	1	1 (?)	0	0	—
Gettysburg	28	7 + 1 (?)	1	2	40
Spotsylvania	6	3	0	0	50
Petersburg	17	5 + 1 (?)	0	1	41
Total	*74*	*16 + 3 (?)*	*2*	*4*	*30–34*

"(?)" indicates possible manipulation that is not definitive: "7 + 1 (?)" means there were seven photographs with clear alteration and one with possible manipulation.

There is no evidence of tampering by Alexander Gardner in his collection of photographs at Antietam. Perhaps the number of dead bodies across the fields allowed for a sufficient volume of carnage to be captured without the necessity of artificially increasing the drama. Or possibly he hadn't brought a rifle with him to the battlefield. At Gettysburg, Spotsylvania, and Petersburg, around a third to half of all the images have been "enhanced" by the artist in some manner—usually with the addition of a Springfield or Enfield.

From a historical standpoint, then, we are left with a question about the value of a collection of photographs in which approximately one-third of all the images have been changed to some degree by the photographer. Is this set of documents any more valuable than those collected by photographers who were concentrating on less dramatic landscape compositions? To take the question one step further, are the fraudulent photos of the dead any more historically accurate or relevant than the detailed sketches from war correspondents like Edwin Forbes (figure 7.17)?

Figure 7.17. Edwin Forbes was a renowned sketch artist for *Frank Leslie's Illustrated Newspaper* from 1862 to 1864. This is Forbes's sketch of "Genl. U.S. Grant at Wilderness," drawn May 7, 1864. (*Credit:* Library of Congress, LC-DIG-ppmsca-20652, https://www.loc.gov/item/2004661535/.)

In terms of objectivity, Waud's and Forbes's prints certainly surpass the composite photographs (Handy's darkroom fabrications) or *Harper's* montages, and the sketch artists could include moving subjects, an important component of an illustration for a combat correspondent. What remains less clear is a comparison between an artist's sketch and a gently modified photograph. The sketch might better document the feel of the action, but the photograph remains superior for detailing the appearance of the landscape and the clothing and condition of the fallen on the field. In the end, the photographic fraud and manipulation can at least be detected in the photographs and accounted for; the same cannot be said for the sketches and paintings, where artists' renderings have taken unknown license in interpretation.

8

The Civil War on Canvas:
Realism versus Romanticism

INTRODUCTION

DURING THE THIRD YEAR OF THE AMERICAN CIVIL WAR, A NEW THEORY
of art was introduced across the Atlantic: naturalism. This practice, when
applied to recording history, would be fresh and different, devoid of the
romanticism of the past. According to Jules-Antoine Castagnary, the
French art critic who introduced the term, "The naturalist school declares
that art is the expression of life under all phases and on all levels, and that
its sole aim is to reproduce nature by carrying it to its maximum power
and intensity: It is truth balanced with science."[1]

Naturalism is a subdiscipline of realism, and it differs from the broader
art form by specifically avoiding political or societal issues. In doing so,
naturalist paintings move into the realm of photography and, less directly,
photojournalism: a portrayal of events in an objective, unfiltered manner,
absent an artist's impressions or bias.

Both realism and naturalism attempt to represent a subject or event
in as accurate and truthful a manner as possible. Artists focusing on the
Civil War—from Edwin Forbes and Alfred Waud in the 1860s to Don
Troiani and Dale Gallon in the 1990s—have emphasized the realism
of their images and their devotion to historical accuracy. This chapter is
dedicated to evaluating this devotion, assessing Civil War artwork during
the last century and a half with respect to measurable metrics of accuracy
and historical interpretation, all from a scientific-realist perspective. In

other words, this chapter will focus on ways we can assess how accurate the illustrations of Civil War battle scenes have been through the years and which artists demonstrate the best attempts at conveying this realism to canvas.

A scientific gauge of the realism of art can be difficult to find; nevertheless, a simple assessment of how realistic a painting is can be based on basic critical thinking and instinct. Take, for example, two renderings of battle scenes that were both painted in the early 1890s. The first (figure 8.1) is *Capture of Fort Fisher*, by Louis Kurz (of Kurz and Allison); the second (figure 8.2), painted by Gilbert Gaul, illustrates a federal artillery battery in action at Cold Harbor. Both were created with an eye toward exploiting a commercial market full of aging, sentimental veterans. Gaul's painting was explicitly commissioned as a memorial portrait of the crewmembers of the Ohio Battery in his illustration.

Figure 8.1.   Kurz and Allison's chromolithograph *Capture of Fort Fisher*. Note that the fort appears undamaged and without any revetments whatsoever. Also, more than a dozen men are discharging their rifles while nary a one stops to reload. (*Credit:* January 5, 1865, Library of Congress, LC-DIG-pga-01862, https://www.loc.gov/pictures/item/91721207/.)

Figure 8.2. Gilbert Gaul's *Battery H at the Battle of Cold Harbor*. Gun smoke completely obscures 20 percent of the canvas, helping define the gun crew in the foreground. Note that only one weapon in the entire illustration is shown in the act of actually firing. (*Credit:* "Battery H," painting, 1894, Library of Congress, LC-DIG-ppmsca-59374, https://www.loc.gov/item/2018757113/.)

A quick inspection of both contemporaneous works reveals how far apart they are with respect to their presentation of Civil War combat. Kurz's image shows hundreds of men within a few yards of one another, most of whom are aiming or firing their rifles. Not a single man is in the process of reloading, which seems especially unusual for the defenders in the fort. Gaul's work is also an action scene, albeit one clouded in confusion. Gun smoke from cannons covers a large sector of the canvas, outlining the closest gun crew; the eye is naturally drawn to these men. And, unlike the soldiers fighting for Fort Fisher, Gaul's men are all wearing unique clothing, the outfits of the individual soldiers differentiated with interesting details. In a side-by-side comparison, it becomes clear which image more accurately portrayed the action from 1864 and 1865. Nevertheless, this chapter (and book) is dedicated to critically assessing Civil War subjects from a *scientific* perspective. So what is it, from a scientific point of view, that makes the presumed realism of Gaul's work superior to that of the lithograph?

The analysis herein will use scientific knowns—the volume of smoke produced by the ignition of black powder, for example, or the ratio of the duration of loading a rifle musket to the duration of firing one—to evaluate the realism of Civil War works of art. In doing so, a *measurable* feature of a battle scene, like the length of the flame that extends from a cannon muzzle, is used as a tool for determining how realistic a painting or lithograph is. With repeated tests of realism, we garner a better sense of which artists succeeded and which fell short at objectively portraying the events of the war.

It takes, for example, roughly three times longer to load a rifle musket than to aim and fire one. How realistic, then, is it that Kurz's *Capture of Fort Fisher* portrays dozens of men aiming and firing their rifles and not a single one loading or reloading? In many of Gilbert Gaul's paintings of men in combat, at least a third of the men, and often more, are operating their ramrods or fumbling with a percussion cap. In several of his more famous works, it can be argued that the focal point of the painting, or at least the first place the eye is drawn, is a vulnerable man, reloading a momentarily harmless weapon. Certainly that is a more realistic portrayal of men in combat than the illustrations showing soldiers with muzzle-loaders that never need muzzleloading.

When comparing a larger collection of the chromolithographs of Kurz and Allison to Gilbert Gaul's paintings, Gaul's attempts at realism become even more apparent. For every one man pictured reloading in the lithographs, thirty (!) are aiming or shooting. In Gaul's more histori-cally realistic work, by contrast, the ratio of firing to reloading is approxi-mately two to three. While this comparison does not fully measure how accurately Gaul's work portrays the battlefield in comparison to what an actual witness would have seen, it does give us an idea of how much more accurate Gaul's work was than Kurz's. With several additional metrics of realism, the measure of historical faithfulness can be further refined, providing insights into which artists (and artworks) came closest to the promise of objectivity and historical realism.

In summary, then, this chapter uses critical analysis of measurable subjects to evaluate Civil War artwork for placement on a continuum between romanticism and realism. In doing so, the claims by contemporary artists that their work resides on the historically accurate and "real" end of this art spectrum can be fully evaluated.

THE HISTORICAL CLAIM

In the late 1970s and early 1980s, an interesting (if coincidental) shift occurred in the understanding of Civil War photography, art, and realism. Just as several of Alexander Gardner's and Mathew Brady's iconic Civil War photographic contributions were being uncovered as manipulated or fraudulent—and hardly the conveyors of historical authenticity—realistic paintings of battle scenes from the war began to grow in popularity. This new genre of Civil War action art offered to do what the photographs could not—depict the intensity of combat as it had actually happened (and in color!). While few Civil War paintings had been produced between World War I and Vietnam, the 1980s saw a virtual explosion in new offerings by artists like Mort Künstler, Keith Rocco, Don Troiani, and Dale Gallon. Entire shops began sprouting up in historical towns like Fredericksburg and Gettysburg dedicated to selling (primarily) Civil War prints and paintings.

These modern artists of the past claimed their work was historically accurate—art, but art that was faithful to the past. Künstler's book describes his "devotion to truth and detail in history."[2] Rocco's art is described as "meticulously researched for accuracy."[3] Dale Gallon and Don Troiani's commercial websites continue the theme of accuracy and attention to detail: "Dale's art stands in a class of its own to for the collector who seeks historical accuracy," and "Today, his paintings are known for combining art and an accurate depiction of history" (Gallon)[4]; and "A traditional academic realist painter well known for his extremely accurate historical and military paintings" (Troiani).[5]

This chapter focuses on more than just claims to authenticity and attention to detail; it also analyzes realism and Civil War art through time. Has this genre of artwork always been accurate and realistic, or has it improved, or perhaps declined, through time? To accomplish this examination, we will employ critical thinking (soldiers loading rifles versus firing) and comparisons with the closest visual representations available for understanding Civil War combat: large-scale modern reenactments.

This latter form of data, gleaned from masses of reenactors pretending to march around and kill each other, is problematic.[6] Nevertheless, for the data we need—for example, the ratio of reloading to firing—an analysis of a reenactment can give us at least a first-order approximation.

Three primary criteria will be used to evaluate the realism of Civil War art, and all tend to be objective measures that lend themselves well to critical analysis: (1) the fraction of men who are discharging their weapons compared to those who are reloading their guns, (2) the length of flame emitted from the muzzle of an artillery piece, and (3) the volume of smoke present on the battlefield and in front of the men lined up in formation. The analysis *will not* focus on the quality or accuracy of unmeasurable factors—like how much the depiction of Joshua Lawrence Chamberlain looks like the real JLC. Nor will it focus on historical details from paintings—like whether Chamberlain carried an M1851 Colt or an M1860. Instead, *the evaluation will assess the historical accuracy of battle paintings and lithographs by reconstructing the combat scenes from a scientific, empirical perspective, all in an effort to discriminate romanticism from realism.*

THE SCIENCE

The Tate Gallery describes *realism* as "artwork painted in a realistic almost photographic way."[7] As such, a realist painting should provide an objective and accurate picture of what an event—or, in this case, Civil War combat—actually looked like. What were the subjects doing, and how were they behaving? How many men were actively engaged and participating in a firefight, and how many were incapacitated? What could a person present at the action have actually seen through all the haze and confusion?

Much of this book has focused on the physical sciences on the battlefield—lead hail, ballistic trajectories, spatial dimensions of the landscape. This theme continues here. Three primary physical criteria will be assessed as depicted in artwork from 1861 to the present day. First, the ratio of reloading soldiers to aiming or firing soldiers will be calculated for the men portrayed on the canvas and paper, and these values will be compared with empirical data collected from real-world experience and fake-world reenactments. Next, the depictions of artillery gunfire will be compared: How long are the actual flames extending away from the muzzle and vent on a Napoleon cannon? How long would the blast of fire really be in authentic combat? Finally, and most murkily, the expression of gun smoke from small arms and artillery on the battlefield will be critiqued and compared between reality and visual interpretation. Each of these evaluation tools has complications and limits that will be addressed, but collectively they can provide insights into which artists were most successful at portraying battlefield scenes with the greatest degree of realism and whether artwork has gotten more realistic over time.

Criteria Caveat: Small-Arms Rate of Fire

During the Civil War, a commanding officer had several choices as to how he would instruct his men to fire on the enemy. For maximum immediate devastation to the target, he might order volley fire, in which all the men fire at once. This would lead to several men firing at the same enemy soldier in some circumstances and would leave his infantry vulnerable to a counterattack during the next twenty to thirty seconds while the men reloaded. For a sustained and more consistent fire, the officer might order that the men fire by rank, where the soldiers take turns firing, moving quickly down the line. The result is a zipper-like ripping along the line as men fire in succession immediately after their neighbor, after which they promptly begin to reload. With enough men in line, the collective fire resembles a machine gun.

In reality, after the initial volley, the most popular method of firing in most combat situations was firing at will: the men could shoot and reload on their own schedule, as quickly as possible. This offered the unit the highest volume of fire and demanded the least organizational control by commanders. Firing at will also produced fewer distractions for the soldiers.

Loading a rifle musket is a tedious, time-consuming task, especially when the man holding the rifle is himself under fire. Firing one is not. Under ideal conditions, a well-trained and disciplined soldier could fire a shot every twenty seconds; in combat, reloading and selecting a target would almost certainly take longer. The time required to acquire a target could be a second or two or, on a smoke-obscured battlefield, substantially longer. Holding and aiming a rifle for more than ten or fifteen seconds becomes wearisome; rifle muskets are heavy and poorly balanced, with the majority of the gun's weight falling on the nontrigger (nondominant) arm.

This combination of loading time and shooting time means that the majority of men in a sustained firefight will be holding a ramrod, not using a gunsight. A soldier reloading as rapidly as possible in the heat of battle will take just over twenty seconds between shots (twenty to reload, two to fire: a ten-to-one reload/fire ratio). A slower soldier might take thirty seconds to reload and four to fire (a 7.5-to-one reload/fire ratio). So, in realistic artwork depicting men in combat—no volley fire, but rather portraying a sustained firefight—the theoretical number of men illustrated as reloading should be at least five times as high as those shown aiming or firing. In short, if a person were to travel back in time to witness the fighting in the Cornfield at Antietam or the Wheatfield at Gettysburg, only 20 percent of the men seen on the battlefield would actually be aiming or firing at any given time. And paintings from the realism movement should endeavor to reflect this realistic ratio.

One way to test the validity of these calculated estimates is by observing Civil War reenactments. Opinions regarding the value of these engagements, ranging from the silly to the serious, vary. The men and women participating in the staged events certainly seem to be making serious efforts to appear authentic. When videos of line-versus-line combat are observed in still-frame screen captures, the ratio of reloading to firing "soldiers" can be calculated. Table 8.1 includes data compiled from more than a hundred video still frames from nine different reenactments that occurred between 2012 and 2018.

Table 8.1.   What infantry reenactors are doing during simulated combat in Civil War "battles"

Activity	Number engaged	Percentage
Loading a rifle	412	57.7
Moving/standing	160	22.4
Aiming a rifle	114	16.0
Firing a rifle	28	3.9

Note: Soldiers counted do not include officers, cavalry, or artillery crewmembers or anyone not actively engaged in the "fighting."

A few notes about these numbers: First, no screen captures of volley fire were considered—only images of soldiers firing at will (which represents the vast majority of time spent during reenactments). Second, many soldiers appear to be standing around, simply watching the action, not really participating in the active fake shooting. Finally, with almost 60 percent of the soldiers reloading and 20 percent aiming or firing, a simple metric can be created to judge the realism of Civil War art. This is the *V/H ratio*: the number of vertical gun barrels (reloading) to horizontal (aiming/firing).[8] For reenactments, this value is approximately 2.9—that is, for every one soldier aiming and shooting, there are around three reloading.

This value should probably be slightly higher, because it is often difficult to tell through the smoke of the battle reenactments whether a soldier is reloading their rifle or simply watching the surrounding action. It is also sometimes difficult to see whether a person is placing a percussion cap on their rifle, an action less clear in observation than when a ramrod is being used. Also, reenactors aren't (usually) firing live rounds, so they can reload faster, skipping the step of ramming a minié bullet home (and they don't have to deal with fouling).

Given all of these considerations, then, it seems that a realistic painting of a Civil War battle should portray the majority of soldiers as loading their weapons instead of discharging them.[9]

Criteria Caveat: Cannon Muzzle Flash

Many Civil War paintings display the exact instant an artillery piece has fired, with flames extending from the muzzle—and, sometimes, the vent of the piece. The artist's choice to illustrate this precise moment in time is clear: The muzzle flash suggests the image has captured the height of the drama and the instantaneous millisecond of maximum energy release. That's fine. What is less acceptable is when the muzzle blast is greatly exaggerated, and any realism is lost when there is no accompanying flame or smoke from the breech vent.

As with the reloading/firing ratios, this metric can also be determined by observing modern re-creations of Civil War artillery fire. While observing Civil War reenactments to determine V/H ratios has some minor problems, the collection of muzzle-blast characteristics is more straightforward, with one large qualification: The cannon being fired must be expelling live rounds. Artillery "fired" without shells during demonstrations or reenactments behaves in a completely different manner than those firing real ordnance. For one thing, cannons firing blanks show almost no recoil; those firing live rounds jump back two full barrel lengths.[10]

Thousands of videos and still photos are available that show Civil War field artillery in action. A small fraction of these are firing live rounds.[11] Of this subset, frame captures and still photographs of the exact moment of detonation were studied to obtain data regarding the extent of vent and muzzle blast for multiple forms of Civil War field artillery. After observing dozens of live-fire events, often video frame by frame, several conclusions become clear (table 8.2).

Table 8.2. Characteristics of muzzle flash and vent flames for different varieties of Civil War field artillery

Cannon	Vent flame	Muzzle flame
	Barrel length	
12-pounder Napoleon cannon	0.50	1.00
3-inch Ordnance rifle	0.25	1.50
10-pounder Parrott rifle	0.50	1.00
Average of all observations	*0.40*	*1.30*

All measurements are in barrel lengths—the length of the barrel for the particular piece being measured. Larger-bore cannons tend to exhibit slightly longer muzzle flashes.

First, in the miniscule fraction of a second after the gunpowder is ignited, a flame will extend vertically out of the vent. At exactly the same time, a mushroom cloud of orange-red gas will emerge from the muzzle and instantly flash to smoke. From this cloud will emerge a much longer flame, roughly the same diameter as the bore, which will extend from the muzzle for approximately the same length as the barrel; this is the flame almost always depicted in artwork. The distance these horizontal and vertical flames extend away from the barrel varies, but within limits. Vertically, the vent flame consistently reaches around half the barrel length before immediately pluming into white smoke. The muzzle flash is more varied, usually extending between one and two barrel lengths before changing to smoke. The combination of vent and muzzle-blast smoke often completely obliterates target visibility for the gun crew, unless a spotter is watching from many feet to one side.

A second general observation is that smoothbore guns have a slightly smaller flame signature than rifled guns. This might be surprising, given that smoothbores like the M1857 Napoleon used more than twice as much gunpowder per charge than Parrotts or Ordnance rifles.

Before analyzing the portrayal of muzzle and vent flames in Civil War paintings and lithographs, some complications of the methodology need to be addressed. The size of the gunpowder charge influences the volume of hot gas exploding out of the gun, and more gunpowder might have been used during times of high stress, or perhaps when a double canister was being fired. The muzzle flash almost instantly turns to smoke, making determination of the exact length of the flame difficult. Thus the rather crude unit of measurements—"barrel lengths." Finally, artists should be given license for painting or drawing the cannon flame at its exact moment of maximum blast. The flame is often the most dramatic, eye-catching portion of a painting, so at least some minimal degree of freedom must be granted to the imagination of the artist.[12]

It might be tempting to measure a painting's length of flame emanating from the rifles; there would certainly be more data available for evaluation. However, the use of rifle flames as a measure of realism has a critical flaw. When dealing with the firing of rifles in paintings, many men are often illustrated in various stages of discharging their weapon, so maximum flame length may vary and cannot be used as a metric for realism. An artist could consistently paint the exactly correct (i.e., realistic) length of muzzle flash in a painting only to be criticized for having several men coincidentally firing their weapons at precisely the same time. It would be more realistic to have the men firing their guns a fraction of a second apart, but this would provide misleading data regarding the length of the flames as painted, and thus it should not be used as a tool for evaluating realism. Cannon flames, by contrast, are almost universally painted as if they are at the peak of discharge, providing less data but a more reliable metric of realism.

Criteria Caveat: Black-Powder Gun Smoke

Thirty years before the Civil War, Carl von Clausewitz introduced the concept of the "fog of war" in his posthumously published book *Vom Kriege* (*On War*).[13] While Clausewitz was referencing the lack of situational awareness soldiers have in combat and not the actual battlefield haze from the Napoleonic Wars, a quite literal supplier to this "fog" was produced in great volume by the weapons of the nineteenth century: vision-diminishing sulfurous smoke.

The chemistry that turns black powder into white smoke in such great quantities is relatively straightforward (figure 8.3).

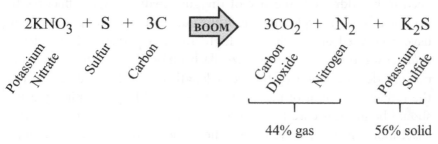

Figure 8.3. Chemistry of black-powder ignition. After igniting, the potassium sulfide, in a solid state, is divided between material left in the barrel (which causes fouling) and material that enters the local atmosphere: gun smoke.

After combustion (right side of the equation), the byproducts are split between gases and solids. The solids are divided between a small amount of residue left in the barrel, which creates fouling, and a much greater volume of airborne particulate matter—white and light gray smoke. Because of the chemistry and combustive nature of black powder, the volume of material before and after the explosion will increase by more than three hundred times.[14] This great expansion is what propels a bullet or shell down the barrel, but the resulting particles in the air also leave the muzzle so quickly and in such great density that it may be impossible for the shooter to see whether they hit their target. With several thousand soldiers firing at twenty-second intervals, large portions of the battlefield will quickly become obscured, and artillery batteries produce even more smoke: a twelve-pounder Napoleon battery of six guns in action would burn thirty pounds of black powder every minute.[15]

As a result, a realistic painting of a sustained battle in which the combatants are armed with black-powder weapons should have two characteristics, caused by all the airborne potassium sulfide: First, large portions of the illustration should be completely hidden by smoke (or at least shrouded in a translucent fog that obscures the background, especially over long distances). Second, there should be an all-encompassing haze across the field of battle—similar to what you might imagine being present downwind from a large fire, or even on a particularly humid day.

Of course, there are problems created by using gun smoke as a metric of realism in artwork. The volume of smoke and density of occurrence can change over time (more smoke and haze later in a battle) or with meteorological conditions (wind and rain both clear the air). The density of smoke also fluctuates, depending on the perspective of the viewer and their viewpoint relative to the sun. A painting showing a low, horizontal perspective would have more apparent smoke and haze, whereas one painted from an oblique view (from above, for example) might have less smoke-laden air to peer through.

With these caveats noted, we now have three measurable criteria to evaluate the realistic nature of Civil War artwork through time: (1) V/H ratios allow us to see whether the artist considered the slow rate of fire of Civil War weapons or, rather, chose a more dramatic, less realistic path—with the vast majority of men portrayed as shooting their guns. (2) Muzzle and vent flash help to determine how drama or romanticism might have been added to a scene. Finally, (3) the portrayal of black-powder smoke adds a third, if more subjective, measure of the artist's efforts at realism.

ANALYSIS AND EVALUATION

The critiquing of art in this chapter will be organized around the three previously established metrics before the overall trend in realism through time is evaluated. Analysis begins with the easiest criterion to measure—soldiers loading their rifles versus soldiers aiming and firing—before moving on to cannon flames and smoke. Combined, these three factors can provide something more than just a rudimentary test of realism.

Ready ... Aim ... Aim ... Aim ... Aim ... Aim ...

Basic critical reasoning tells us that if loading a rifle musket takes twenty to thirty seconds and aiming and firing takes two, five, or even ten seconds, then significantly more men would have a ramrod in their hand during a firefight rather than would have a finger on the trigger. Random, instantaneous screen captures of Civil War reenactments provide more empirical evidence: A V/H ratio of 2.9 suggest that almost 75 percent of men actively engaged in the fake battle will be reloading at any given time. A ratio somewhere in the vicinity of three or perhaps higher would probably also be expected on the real battlefield.

So how do artists who paint Civil War battle scenes compare? In the decades after the war ended, two forms of artwork emerged: lithographs from firms such as Currier and Ives and Kurz and Allison, and works from the school of realism, including several large and detailed dioramas. The lithographs included fabricated, composite scenes, often portraying entire battles within a single incredibly dramatized scene, with almost everyone who wasn't on horseback firing their rifle at the same moment. These illustrations are, frankly, laughable when V/H ratios are calculated. In many cases, almost everyone in the battle is aiming and firing, with perhaps one lone soldier reloading, providing acknowledgement that the artist understood that the men were operating muzzleloading weapons.

When eight of the Kurz and Allison chromolithographs were assessed, the V/H ratio extreme is apparent: 147 soldiers are illustrated in the art of firing, while only five are stopping to reload—a ratio of 0.03! In the best (most realistic?) of these popular images, the V/H ratio barely rises to 0.1 (eighteen shooting, two reloading), and the Currier and Ives illustrations are even more fanciful.[16]

Other artists of the time, working with oil and canvas, did better. When combined, the paintings of these artists, including Peter Rothermel, Théophile Poilpot, Edwin Forbes, and Gilbert Gaul, achieve a V/H ratio of 0.6—not exactly the two-plus ratio that would demonstrate a complete dedication to realism, but certainly better than the lithographs. Unfortunately for the school of realism and the general public, these paintings were, at the time, difficult to reproduce.

Of all the evaluated historic artists producing work between 1870 to 1900, one stands apart with respect to reloading ratios and realism:

Gilbert Gaul. Not only does his V/H ratio exceed 1.0 (albeit for only a few paintings, but still), but Gaul often made a soldier reloading his rifle the focal point of his work. A sense of vulnerability is cast upon the viewer as they witness an infantryman handling a ramrod, or perhaps placing a percussion cap, all while standing upright, frighteningly exposed to incoming enemy fire.

With few exceptions, the V/H ratio for Civil War artwork remained consistently around 0.1–0.6 for nearly a century after the war. For example, David Greenspan's delightful three-dimensional battle maps made for Catton's *American Heritage Picture History of the Civil War*, featuring dozens and dozens of tiny soldiers locked in battle, have a collective V/H ratio of 0.6. Similar ratios (0.5) can be found for the later popular and well-illustrated "Campaign" books produced by Osprey.

In the 1980s, the field of Civil War illustration changed forever, with the introduction of a half dozen new artists focusing on historically accurate, highly detailed combat paintings. Many of these works had a direct lineage to Gilbert Gaul's collection from a century before, and this new set of paintings included battle scenes from almost every significant fight from the war. Occasionally, there was more than one painting of a single event: for example, Chamberlain on Little Round Top, the Cornfield at Antietam, or the attacks on Marye's Heights. This new generation of artists included Mort Künstler, Don Troiani, Dale Gallon, and Keith Rocco and promised an increased dedication to historicity. The V/H numbers seem to back up their claims to realism (table 8.3).

Table 8.3. The V/H ratios of modern art are higher than those of previous generations of paintings of the Civil War

Artist	V/H ratio	Notes
Dale Gallon	1.4	Some of his most recent work has a V/H ratio at or above 2.0
Mort Künstler	1.6	The "Godfather of Pulp Fiction Illustrators"
Keith Rocco	1.2	Shoots trees to better study bullet damage
Don Troiani	1.2	Like Gaul, several of his paintings focus on soldiers reloading

An ideal score (photograph of the actual event) would be close to 3.0, but the resulting artwork might not be quite as dramatic as desired (reloading a gun isn't as exciting as firing one).

Artists, of course, have license to paint as dramatic a scene as they like, and illustration of a man shooting a rifle or pistol heightens the perceived action. To their credit, the modern school of Civil War painters consistently clusters around a 1.5 V/H (and not every single painting was analyzed—only a portion of the paintings that depicted a drawn-out firefight).

The historical trend, then, is clear: V/H ratios—and realism in Civil War artwork—have increased over time. Lithographic artwork in the late nineteenth century averaged V/H ratios that were comically low, often approaching zero. The realism that arrived from Europe around this same time period increased the ratio to 0.6, although this value indicates that almost twice as many men were shown to be shooting as opposed to reloading. It wasn't until the late twentieth century that artists began to paint, consistently, in a more realistic manner and with more men portrayed as loading rather than unloading.

To experience an actual painting from the realist school of Civil War artwork, a person must visit a museum, gallery, or personal collection. Assemblages of Civil War art are much more commonly viewed in commercially available history books. Unfortunately, the increase in realism in paintings over time did not translate into more realistic book illustrations over time—with one interesting exception. Most books published during the 1960s and 1970s, including the popular tomes by National Geographic and American Heritage, ranged between a V/H of 0.2 and one of 0.4. The battlefield guides produced by the Historical Times (and later Eastern Acorn Press) commonly sold at battlefield visitor centers had similar V/H ratios—around 0.4. In the 1980s, Time Life introduced a popular series of silver-covered hardbound books that averaged a V/H ratio of around 0.2. During the same decade, a less popular but much more realistically illustrated book was written by Paddy Griffith.[17] *Battle in the Civil War* stands apart from others published before, for Griffith trained a skeptical eye on the romantic tone given to so many other historical works; not surprisingly, the detailed black and white sketches throughout the work averaged a V/H ratio of 1.4. How refreshing—that a book written to explain how battles were actually fought was illustrated in the most realistic manner of any that had come before, with more men sketched reloading than firing.

More than two decades after Griffith's *Battle* was published, a new low was set in V/H ratios for a widely circulated text. *Bill O'Reilly's Legends and Lies: The Civil War* didn't stop at using fake photographs in its inauthentic illustrations (see chapter 7); in the entire book, 162 men are pictured as aiming and firing their weapons, while a scant twelve are reloading, a V/H ratio of below 0.1. On one lithograph, where twenty-six men are shooting and three are reloading, the caption describes the illustration as "chillingly accurate."[18]

To be completely fair, it must be acknowledged that V/H ratios are only an uncomplicated and rudimentary measure of how accurately an illustration might be when compared to reality. It would probably be more insightful to combine this metric with several others to gain a more comprehensive evaluation of realism.

Muzzle Blast

Artists are fond of painting battle scenes that include artillery in action at the exact moment a piece is igniting. A general rule is that if a cannon or four are present, then one of them must be portrayed at the precise instant a round has exited the barrel. The blast and muzzle flames add to the drama—the viewer might almost feel the concussion emanating from the canvas.

Although determining the exact magnitude of the cannon blast can be difficult, a few general conclusions can be made about flame length and duration. First, for muzzleloading pieces, a small flash of flame will emanate from the top of the breech, extending from the vent. For field artillery, including Napoleons, Ordnance rifles, and Parrotts, this flame extends vertically, perpendicular to the barrel, for a few feet before suddenly morphing into a cloud of white smoke.

At the other end of the barrel, a second, much more substantial flame will extend from the muzzle for seven to ten feet. As this flame also flashes to smoke, the fieldpiece kicks backward a dozen feet or so. When viewed in slow motion, this flash and recoil seems to resemble a horizontal rocket launch, with the flames pushing the barrel like an elongated jet of fire.

Because these flames can be measured, they add a second tool for evaluating the realism of art. If a Civil War Parrott is painted with a muzzle flash that is twice the length of the barrel, the artist has slightly abused artistic license—at least from a physics perspective.

For a lithograph, sketch, or painting to accurately portray cannon fire, the flames from the vent should be around half the length of the barrel, and the muzzle blast should extend around 1.3 times the length of the barrel—with room obviously left on the margins for variations, depending on the timing of the blast and the type of cannon. For a realistic illustration, though, flames really should not extend much beyond 1.5 barrel lengths.

With respect to the depiction of cannon flames, artists working during the late 1800s show as much variability as do those painting during the late 1900s. Table 8.4 summarizes this admittedly limited data set.

Table 8.4. The length of vent and muzzle flames, measured in barrel lengths, from lithographs and paintings from 1865 to 2010

Artist	Vent flame	Muzzle flame (average)	Muzzle flame (maximum)
		Barrel length	
Kurz and Allison	Nonexistent	0.8	2.0
Edwin Forbes	Nonexistent	0.5	0.5
Paul Philippoteaux	Nonexistent	1.5	1.5
Gilbert Gaul	Undetermined	1.0	1.0
Dale Gallon	0.5	0.6	1.0
Mort Künstler	Undetermined	2.2	2.5

From this, again, restricted data set, it is possible to conclude that early artists largely ignored vent flashing, while contemporary artists like Dale Gallon reliably included this realistic detail. Gallon also painted realistic muzzle flashes, while Künstler somewhat dramatized how far the fire would extend across a few of his canvases.

Gun Smoke

The final measure of realism is also the most difficult to quantify: the distribution and density of black-powder smoke across the battlefield. The reason for this complication is the nature of the smoke itself—its inconsistent rate of dispersion and dissipation and its tendency to change visibility depending on the viewpoint of an observer. Smoke obscures much more of an observer's line of sight when looking across a battlefield than it will if the viewer's perspective is above a fight; the amount of airborne particulate matter may be the same, but much less of the battlefield will be visible to a person standing on the ground compared with one who is above the action.

Observations of Civil War reenactments offer a few insights into the appearance of black-powder smoke across battlegrounds. Smoke from an individual muzzle of a just-fired rifle musket usually appears to dissolve into a second, larger, less dense cloud within a second, adding to the general haze across the pretend battlefield. Viewed from a greater distance, the gun-smoke haze is distinctly denser near the line of men in battle. Depending on the volume of fire, how stagnant the air is, and ambient lighting conditions, the field of view in front of a soldier is often reduced to just a few yards.

For this critique of artwork, the same types of paintings that were used in the previous analysis will be compared to lithographs and paintings of drawn-out battle scenes (no illustrations of combat that had just commenced or volley fire). The illustration of smoke on a battle scene will be divided into four constituents:

1. Smoke that obscures a small sector of the combat—in front of the *muzzle* of a single rifle or perhaps the smoke in front of several men who are proficiently shooting.

2. Smoke that obscures a slightly larger portion of the combat, such as smoke in front of a *line* of men in a firefight.

3. Smoke that obscures a *large sector* of the battle or landscape, where entire areas are completely covered in dense smoke. These areas are especially common around actively engaged artillery.

4. Smoke that is less dense but more widespread and evenly distributed—battlefield *haze*.

Each category of smoke can rapidly disappear or transform into another category entirely. And the degree of obscuring cover and density of the smoke is dependent on the duration of the fight and the strength of the wind. Because of these factors, this point will be the most subjective of the "realism" criteria found in this chapter.

Early Civil War artists were somewhat inconsistent in their inclusion of gun smoke in battle scenes (table 8.5). Many illustrations contain much more smoke because every single man in the painting is firing at the same time—not a particularly good representation of reality. Kurz and Allison lithographs and William Delaney Travis, the worst artist of the Civil War, are guilty of this unrealistic romanticism of the intensity of battle.

Table 8.5. The depiction of smoke on a battlefield varies by artist

Artist	Muzzle	Line	Large sector	Haze
Edwin Forbes	x	x	x	xx
William D. Travis	xx	x		x
Peter Rothermel		x		x
Gilbert Gaul		x	xx	xx
Paul Philippoteaux	x	x	x	xx
Kurz and Allison	xx	xx	x	x
William B. T. Trego	xx	xx	xx	xx
Mort Künstler	xx	xx	xx	xx
Keith Rocco	xx	xx	xx	x
Don Troiani	xx	xx	xx	xx
Dale Gallon	xx	xx	xx	xx

Here the illustrations are broken down by the four categories described in the text, from smallest scale (smoke from a single gunshot) to the largest (battlefield-obscuring haze). One x signifies that an artist sometimes includes this type of smoke; two (xx) designate that an artist consistently portrays this type of smoke.

Gilbert Gaul often used dense smoke to backlight his figures in combat, placing the viewer in the same position as the intended target of his shooting soldiers. William B. T. Trego painted with a magnificent combination of all four categories of battlefield smoke and haze. Contemporary artists are as good as Trego when illustrating smoke. All combine variations of transparent to opaque smoke across the canvas with a battlefield covered in a muted haze. Don Troiani's work frequently includes smoke and haze that appears to come and go in a highly realistic manner. Dale Gallon often uses smoke to obscure the otherwise-distracting backgrounds of his studies of small groups of men. White smoke frequently covers more than 20 percent of his paintings, and when smoke is notably absent, his notes about the illustration will include references to address the lack of airborne particulate: for example, he will refer to a brigade "preparing to fire its first volley." Clearly all of these artists have given careful consideration to how black-powder smoke might influence what would and would not be visible during a firefight.

Mort Künstler would have to be considered the most romantic painter of this group of contemporary artists. He often uses flame and smoke in a highly dramatic manner, backlighting or outlining the primary subject of his work—frequently a celebrated general. This characteristic of his work is not especially noticeable at first viewing, but when several of his paintings are viewed together in a collection, the fact that Robert E. Lee's head is constantly surrounded and backlit by either flame or white smoke suggests that the artwork has begun to tilt toward impressionism over realism.

After consideration of these three measures of realism, then, it is safe to say that modern paintings are generally more realistic than those from the postbellum decades. Recently several books have been published investigating what Civil War combat was really like, seeking new insights into traditional thinking about how the war was actually fought. Noted historian Earl Hess's *Rifle Musket in Civil War Combat: Reality and Myth* is one such tome, and it is interesting that the cover chosen for this work contains a detail from a painting by Don Troiani, with a Confederate infantryman, surrounded by gun smoke, prominently reloading his rifle at the center of the image.[19] Gallon, Rocco, and Troiani have done well following this realist school of Civil War art, which was earlier advanced by Gilbert Gaul and William Trego, and not a single painting can be found from the last fifty years that contains lead precipitation or bodies distributed such that one might cross a field while never setting foot on the earth.

9

Conclusion

Historical Skepticism

A SKEPTIC IS A PERSON WHO QUESTIONS THE IDEAS AND FACTS THAT have already been widely accepted by society. Any serious scholar of the Civil War should be a skeptic to some degree. After all, the flowery and romantic language contained in the letters of the day would, if read too literally, lead one to conclude that there was an amazing number of "obedient servants" spread among the ranks of commanding officers.

The exaggerations, grandiose analogies, and hyperbole found in so much of this wartime writing is a product of the era as well as an indication that the authors were struggling to properly express the impact or horror of what they had experienced or witnessed. These embellished accounts mark the birth of myths that would later be magnified into the tropes discussed in this book.

Historical skepticism is important. Authors and interpreters often regale their audiences with tall tales from the Civil War without even a suggestion that the descriptions might be a bit exaggerated. Contemporary authors sometimes recognize this fact. Sometimes they don't. Popular websites including Eyewitnesstohistory.com, Historynet.com, and Harvardmagazine.com have all relayed Grant's oft-quoted remark about the density of dead in one particular field after the Battle of Shiloh without a hint of doubt about its plausibility.[1]

Contrast that, however, with Battlefields.org (website of the American Battlefield Trust), commenting on the "myths" revolving around the same battle: "Buffs and even some historians who are not very knowledgeable about Shiloh's history have perpetuated rumors and stories that are not actually based on fact. It is regrettable that over the years the truth about the battle has become distorted. Fortunately, however, today's historians are looking at the battle from a different perspective. Hopefully, as more research is published, the oft-repeated campfire stories will be phased out and replaced by the reality of Shiloh, which in itself is much grander and more honorable than any of the myths that have grown up about the battle." The author adds, concisely, "The most boring fact is better than the most glamorous myth."[2]

Analyzing the degree of reality surrounding these "campfire stories" is at the core of this book, and it is now possible to summarize these findings and document the truth of the tropes. Of all the analogies and exaggerated comparisons presented in the chapters of this book, several stand out as particularly specious.

It certainly seems plausible—but is not—that the bodies on the Miller Cornfield at Antietam or Rose Wheatfield at Gettysburg were distributed in such a manner that they lay as a thick carpet of corpses. A much more realistic scenario is that soldiers' reminiscences of the density of death in the Sunken Road were eventually spatially transferred to a different, nearby location that suffered an equal degree of carnage. It could also be that the eyewitnesses were so shocked by the slaughter around the Wheatfield that they simply had no adequate words to describe what they'd seen. Nevertheless, it is surprising that so many witnesses to these scenes, from battlefields across the country, would select the same trope for their recounting.

Similarly, the claims of bullets falling with the intensity of hail might be possible for the briefest of seconds but certainly not in the manner the soldiers were describing. Otherwise, how would anyone have survived to report the cacophonous bombardment of lead?

Also falling into the "specious" category is the myth of the Civil War sniper. The key here is not to confuse the cause of death of an officer killed by semi-random, extreme-range "area fire" with the cause of death of those killed by directly targeted, expertly executed, long-range sniping. Many senior officers were killed by what could only be classified as lucky shots at many hundreds of yards. It is highly improbable, given the low muzzle velocity and the rainbow trajectory of the rifles of the era, that any directly targeted kills (or multiple successive kills) were accomplished at more than a quarter mile's distance.

Other chapters in this book investigated subjects that were not so much specious as they were "fallacious." These are the claims, passed down through the years, that are based on mistaken beliefs or whose very foundation is mistaken. The rifle musket was an improvement on the smoothbore, but it certainly was not a "game-changing" weapon that revolutionized warfare. The metallic cartridge and the repeating action of later rifles was the improvement that proved to be a greater leap forward when compared with the contribution of a hollow-based bullet and rifling. Put simply, during the nineteenth century very few soldiers would choose the benefit of a few hundred extra yards of range for their rifle over a tenfold increase in the effective rate of fire, especially given the short range over which most firefights occurred.[3]

Also (perhaps) falling into the fallacious category of tropes is the explanation as to why so many of the rifle muskets found at Gettysburg were misloaded with five, ten, or even twenty or more miniés rammed down their barrels. The traditional explanation points to evidence of panic and inexperience on the part of the soldiers. Yet properly loaded, multiply loaded, or unloaded rifle muskets are extremely difficult to differentiate, and the theory that a soldier picked up a discarded weapon and mistakenly loaded a misfired gun is just as sensible and reasonable as any other. Given the rate of misfires for these weapons, it is probably also the most plausible explanation. Not as good of a story, though.

Two subjects discussed in the book presented themselves as surprisingly—and disappointingly—contrived and factitious. The authenticity of Civil War photographs, with almost a third of the compositions of the dead having been manipulated in some manner, leaves open the question of whether their creators should be classified as artists or journalists. The addition of false or mislabeled captions to the images seems to suggest artistry, with any discussion of whether these negatives represent early photojournalism rendered a bit premature. Additionally, and in the same general theme, while modern paintings and artwork were demonstrated to be more historically realistic than the paintings and lithographs from the past, current illustrated books continue to include the fanciful litho-graphs and canvases that drift so far from reality.

One young gentleman who would not be skeptical of any of these photographs or illustrations is seen at the center of figure 9.1.

The reason for his probable incredulity is very simple: It is hard to be skeptical at the same time that you are dead. History tells us that at the time this photograph was taken, the young man had been deceased for several days. He was killed earlier in the week in the trenches at

Figure 9.1.   A particularly unskeptical man, photographed in front of a damaged house in Petersburg, April 1865. (*Credit:* "Petersburg, Virginia. View in Rear of Dunlop's House, Bolling Brook Street," detail, Library of Congress, LC-DIG-cwpb-02651, https://www.loc.gov/pictures/item/2018671096/.)

Petersburg. There is photographic evidence to corroborate this claim (figure 9.2): that's him in the background—same dark vest, same checkered pants.[4]

He was killed alongside a Confederate artilleryman, as evidenced by the broken cannon brush. The caption tells us that this South Carolinian was mortally wounded by a shell fragment to the head, easily identifiable by the flow of blood across his face, emanating from his mouth and nose.

Perhaps not. There is no evidence that the man was an artilleryman (figure 9.3) or from South Carolina. And his colleague wasn't killed (or even in combat).

Figure 9.2.   The unskeptical young man, in the background. This photograph was taken several days before the photograph presented as figure 9.1 was shot. (*Credit:* "Confederate and Union Dead Side by Side in the Trenches at Fort Mahone," detail, April 3, 1865, Library of Congress, LC-DIG-cwpb-02551, https://www.loc.gov/pictures/item/2018666707/.)

Figure 9.3. The same "artilleryman" from South Carolina (previous image), taken from a different angle. Now the cannon brush, and presumably the skeptical young man, have gone missing. (*Credit:* "Petersburg, Virginia. Dead Confederate Soldier in Trenches before Petersburg," detail of photograph, April 3, 1865, Library of Congress, LC-DIG-cwpb-02568, https://www.loc.gov/pictures/collection/cwp/item/2018671069/.)

The story here is one we have heard before: Corpse found and photographed, prop added and another photograph taken, scene still deemed insufficiently interesting, so fake dead soldier added along with the prop, and third negative recorded.[5] Three photographs, zero authenticity. And apparently the photographer, T. C. Roche, forgot to include a prop musket for the "dead" man.

There are other tropes that might have been included in this book. During the Civil War, when the bullets started raining like hail the results were remarkably consistent (and agricultural): the men under fire fell as if they had been cut down like wheat or corn before a scythe or sickle or knife. The volume of fire needed to create this scenario would be relatively straightforward to estimate: calculate the number of 0.58-inch objects flying at great speed that would be required to create a swath of strikes for the appropriate distance across a farm field. Stated another way, how many bullets would need to be fired to cover every half-inch of space for a long path across the battlefield that is less than a foot off the ground? Note that you will need to assume that all crop damage was caused by gunfire and not the boots of thousands of men on the move, the hooves of cavalry, or the wheels of artillery pieces or wagons.

Another factual error and misconception that has been repeated over the years is the confusion of the terms *casualties* (meaning killed, wounded, and missing or captured) and *combat deaths*. During promotion of his film *Gettysburg* (1993), Ted Turner stated that more men were killed on these south-central Pennsylvania fields than during the entirety of the Vietnam War.[6] More than fifty-eight thousand US soldiers died in Southeast Asia, while at Gettysburg around eight thousand men died (with around fifty-eight thousand killed, wounded, captured, missing, or deserted). This mistake was repeated nearly twenty years later in the promotional material for the A&E Network's television program about the same battle, *Gettysburg* (2011): History promised to put "viewers inside the three-day conflict where over fifty thousand men paid the ultimate price."[7]

This numerical category of errors could also be expanded to include mistakes about the number of men killed during the one-day battle of Antietam: the bloodiest day in America's *military* history but not in the history of the country.[8]

A final trope that might have been included in this text deals with the rivers and streams that were flowing across the war-torn landscape of so many battlefields. At Plum Run at Gettysburg, there were so many dead and wounded bleeding on the drainage basin that the little creek "literally ran red with blood."[9] Of course, after this phenomenon occurred, the stream was given a second, more popular name: Bloody Run. Second only to Gettysburg in terms of casualties was the Battle of Chickamauga, and naturally its namesake has a bloody connection: Chickamauga Creek has a "legendary translation" as the "River of Blood."[10] The second- and third-bloodiest battles in the western theater were fought at Stones River and Shiloh. The former "ran red at McFadden's Ford," while the latter had a small pond that is today a major battlefield landmark, Bloody Pond.[11] The entire battle of Cold Harbor was a bloodbath, and the battlefield is naturally bisected by Bloody Run.

Testing and evaluating this claim would be fairly direct. Two factors would need to be compared: the discharge of the stream or river (velocity of flow multiplied by the volume of water[12]) and the potential volume of blood from the wounded, dying, or dead. Both of these can be objectively quantified. One subjective complication would need to be predetermined: How much blood is added to water until it *appears* to turn red? What is the exact ratio where water is considered to "run red"? For a small creek or stream like Plum Run, with a very low discharge, running red seems possible but unlikely for very long or over a long stretch of the channel. For a river (or fast-flowing stream), it would be impossible; there is simply too much water and too much mixing for the blood to not be diluted beyond visual recognition.

In the end, the need to quantify the degree of exaggeration and speciousness found in these Civil War tropes is necessary to prevent an expansion of the false historical narrative in the future. Famous philosopher George Santayana, who was born in 1863, is best known for his aphorism "Those who cannot remember the past are condemned to repeat it."[13] But what if the history one is hoping to learn from is full of fallacies and fraud? In the worst-case scenario, this is already happening: fake history based on terrible tropes.

A new golf course opened in 2009 on an island in the Potomac River several miles upstream from the US capital. Between the fourteenth hole and the fifteenth tee there was a fine view of the river, and a flagpole was erected with a stone base. The face of this rocky monument provided a backdrop for a plaque, commemorating the view and giving the river a new designation:

The River of Blood

Many great American soldiers, both of the North and South, died at this spot, "The Rapids," on the Potomac River. The casualties were so great that the water would turn red and thus became known as "The River of Blood."

There are only three small problems with this designation of the "The Rapids" as bloody. First, from a geological perspective, this location doesn't mark the rapids of the Potomac; those would be found around ten miles downriver where the Piedmont meets the Atlantic Coastal Plain at the Fall Zone (thus Great Falls Park).

Second, the trope itself: the Potomac along this stretch of the river has an average discharge of more than ten thousand cubic feet per second. There probably wasn't enough blood spilled in all of Virginia and Maryland during the entire war to turn red a river flowing with this volume, let alone during a single battle.

Finally, the battle: there was no battle, of any size, on or near this island or along this stretch of the river during the Civil War. The closest battle was probably at Ball's Bluff, a dozen miles upstream, and it was hardly a bloodbath (approximately one thousand casualties, almost half of whom were missing and probably not bleeding).

When questioned about why historians said there was no fighting anywhere near the location of the plaque, the owner of the golf resort pushed back: "How would they know that? Were they there?"[14] And he is correct: the historians were not present along this stretch of river in the 1860s to prove that something that didn't happen didn't happen. However, that points to the motivation for this book: historians can't prove there wasn't a battle, but we can prove the damn river did not turn red. In reality, the monument to the "River of Blood" uses a completely implausible analogy to commemorate a battle that never existed. Fake historical news indeed.

APPENDIX A

Evaluating "Knockdown Power" or "Striking Power" of Military Rifles

To be an effective battle weapon, a rifle must be capable of inflicting a disabling wound that would prevent the enemy combatant from continuing on as a threat. This degree of energy, or *knockdown power*, is a gray area with many variables. For example, a lethal bullet at fifty yards may lose enough velocity and corresponding energy at four hundred yards such that it inflicts only a slight wound. A smaller-caliber full-metal-jacket bullet with a sharp point may not do an adequate job transferring energy to the target; it may simply pass through the body, retaining much of its potential energy with it as it continues on in flight.

The calculation of muzzle energy is the simplest way to estimate the hitting power of a rifle. This metric uses the square of the muzzle velocity and the mass of the bullet, neglecting bullet shape or type or jacketing. As a result, the knockdown power of the .58 minié bullet is underestimated compared with later, faster-moving rounds. The minié has a large diameter and is constructed entirely of lead, so it does a better job of transferring its energy to a human target, compared to a .223 or .30-06 full-metal-jacketed spitzer bullet. Nevertheless, the hitting power of the .58 is not as impressive when compared with the metallic cartridge that replaced it in US service, the .45-70 Government. The .45-70 also fired a solid-lead bullet, but at a significantly higher muzzle velocity.

There are several other ways to calculate the terminal ballistics of bullets. The most widely used is the Hornady Index of Terminal Standards—or HITS—a measure more impartial to the Civil War bullet than simply using muzzle energy, because it increases the importance of the bullet weight (and includes a factor for the projectile's diameter).[1] HITS is calculated by squaring the weight of the bullet (in grains) and multiplying by the muzzle velocity. This number is then divided by the square of the bullet diameter multiplied by seven hundred thousand. Interestingly, the HITS values for the M1855 rifle musket, the M1873 "Trapdoor," and the M1906 and M1 Garand all fall within 5 percent of each other—nearly identical hitting power. This metric also indicates that the two most dissimilar service weapons, the smoothbore musket of .69 caliber and the .223 M4, have the lowest knockdown power, with the smoothbore having only half the energy of the other later guns and the tiny .223 full-metal jacket being the weakest of all. This is a large reason why hunting cartridges, whether in .223 or .30-06, will use soft-point or hollow-point bullets to alter the terminal ballistics in such a way that more energy can be transferred to the target by an expanding or fragmenting bullet. These types of bullets, of course, were banned in warfare by the Hague Conventions of 1899 and 1907.

APPENDIX B

Effectiveness of Civil War Revolvers in Combat

BETWEEN JANUARY 1861 AND JUNE 1866, THE FEDERAL GOVERNMENT purchased almost three hundred thousand revolvers from Colt and Remington.[1] Despite this acquisition, it is the Confederate cavalryman who is most associated with the use of the pistol. Many of Mosby's Raiders carried four or more revolvers on raids, magnifying their firepower during brief engagements.

The Civil War rifle musket and its effectiveness in battle are the subjects of entire books, yet no such discussion has taken place regarding the second-most-common firearm on Civil War battlefields. How good was the Civil War revolver as a fighting tool? After all, discussions took place during the war regarding the role of the pistol alongside the saber. Muddying the debate, somewhat, was the fact that the most likely soldier to be issued a Colt or Remington was also the same man who would be handed a breechloader or repeater—the Union cavalryman. As a result, the revolver was often carried by a soldier who needed it the least. Meanwhile, in the South many horsemen rode into combat with muzzleloaders or shotguns. And those Rebels on horseback who could get a pistol would obtain as many as they could carry. This was especially true in irregular units.

The primary benefits of the black-powder revolver involve its ability to deliver rapid, short-range firepower in a weapon that is relatively easy to operate with one hand. The pistol handles well, especially for a man on a horse. There were severe drawbacks to the gun, however. Most important, it was incredibly slow to reload. With a rifle musket (or muzzleloading pistol, the precursor to the Colt revolver), a soldier would fire once and take twenty or so seconds to reload. With the revolver, a soldier fired five or six times and then spent several *minutes* reloading. Even if a second, previously loaded cylinder was carried, reloading required multiple steps (and extra cylinders were very hard to find). Other drawbacks of the weapon included the tendency for the percussion caps to fall off (occasionally causing a misfire) or the less-than-occasional chain fire—when one percussion cap causes all the chambers to fire at once. Nothing inspires confidence in a handheld weapon more than the thought that it might blow your hand apart.

Let us start our brief evaluation of the black-powder revolver in a manner similar to our assessment of the rifle musket: years in use as a service weapon (figure B.1).

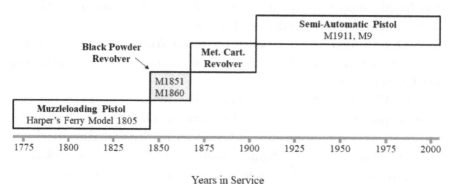

Figure B.1.   Before the introduction of metallic cartridges, the black-powder revolver lasted about a decade in service with the US military.

The black-powder revolver was certainly an improvement on the muzzleloading pistols it replaced, but it only lasted in service for around ten years before being replaced by guns firing metallic cartridges. The reason for this is simple: the time it takes to reload an M1860 Colt (an eternity) versus an M1873 Colt Single Action Army. If duration in service is any indicator of the impact and improvement of a new pistol, the M1873 Peacemaker takes a backseat to only one other Colt product, the venerable M1911 semiautomatic. In other words, the M1860 lasted around six years in service, and the M1911 lasted more than six decades.

Nevertheless, the Colt and Remington pistols of the Civil War could deliver five or six shots in rapid succession—an important attribute in a firefight or skirmish at close range. What about hitting power? This question is difficult to answer precisely because of the nature of Civil War guns: the amount of black powder loaded into the weapon determined the muzzle velocity. Without a standardized metallic cartridge, the amount of powder and resulting energy could vary slightly. A "standard" military load for the Colt 1851 Navy Revolver would propel a .36-caliber 130-grain conoidal bullet at approximately 950 feet per second. This would produce a muzzle energy of around 260 foot-pounds. For the larger-bore .44-caliber M1860 Colt Army, a 140-grain bullet is propelled at nine hundred feet per second, producing a similar muzzle energy to the gun's older brother. Both guns could be loaded to fire with more velocity and energy, but this was a dangerous proposition. For example, one of the guns the Civil War Colts were replacing, the M1847 Walker pistol, fired a 140-grain bullet at 1,100 feet per second, but it also had a proclivity to occasionally explode.

This means that the Colt and Remington pistols of the Civil War era had a striking power, with a standard military load, comparable to a modern .38 Special revolver or a .380 automatic pistol. This would equate to a gun that has a cartridge with a muzzle energy of about 75 percent of a Colt M1911 or Beretta M9. Interestingly, when other metrics of knockdown power are calculated, the two Civil War Colts rate identically with the nine-millimeter M9 and fall short of the hitting power of the lower-velocity, bigger-bullet .45 M1911.

This is not to suggest the M1851 and M1860 were similar to the Beretta in combat. A soldier carrying an M9 and a few additional loaded fifteen-round magazines could fire enough bullets in a minute (or so) to wipe out an entire company of Civil War cavalry. With the guns of the Civil War period, you had essentially six shots per gun, and then you were done. This is why so many men carried more than one gun into combat. Rebel guerrillas in Missouri often carried as many as six handguns; when "Bloody Bill" Anderson's gang was ambushed and six members were killed, the federals recovered thirty total pistols from the men.[2] Mosby's famous raiders often carried two six-guns in their belts and another two on their saddles. Given this quantity of guns, a Civil War cavalryman could, at least temporarily, mimic the firepower of a Berretta, albeit a single-action Berretta.

APPENDIX C

The Faults with Fake Fighting

BATTLE REENACTMENTS DATE BACK TO THE FIRST YEAR OF THE CIVIL War. These "shams" were especially popular in the North during holidays, where the pretend battles were used to prepare new recruits and, at the same time, entertain the common folk. Reenactments continued to take place somewhat regularly into the 1880s, with the fake battles often portraying fictional events. The heyday of battle re-creations came on the centennial of the war, with the largest reenactment to date occurring at Manassas over July 21 and 22, 1961. The 125th and 135th anniversaries of the war also drew huge gatherings: the former was a Manassas event of six thousand soldiers that seemed to bring new enthusiasm into modern reenacting, and the latter event, which took place on the farm fields near Gettysburg, was almost certainly the largest reenactment in history. The hobby lost some popularity at the turn of the century before making a comeback of sorts during the 150th anniversary of the war.

Civil War reenactors and living-history participants divide themselves into three categories depending on their self-professed dedication to authenticity: "Farbs," or "polyester soldiers," are the most casual, concerning themselves little with obtaining historically accurate clothing or weapons or other accoutrement. "Mainstream" reenactors are the most common variety, and they make a committed effort to appear authentic to the 1860s and behave in a period-appropriate manner. Reenactors who categorize themselves as "Progressives" ~~are insane~~ are the most immersive, often setting up camp away from the other, less dedicated participants, where they live and eat in a manner deemed most similar to what a soldier from this time period would have experienced.

Most large-scale battle reenactments are scripted and based on actual historical battles. In many instances, these re-creations take place near the original battlefield—or at least on similar terrain. Nevertheless, it is often impossible to match the authentic landscape; there is, after all, only one Little Round Top or Devil's Den.

While most reenactors go to great lengths to appear as accurate as possible in appearance and at camp, some degree of realism is lost when the invisible miniés start flying. After watching hours of videos of large-scale reenactments and witnessing live (but smaller) skirmishes, several silly aspects of these simulations became apparent.

The first assault on authenticity is one that I, as a rather large man, am hesitant to bring up: the soldiers from both armies in these battles appear to be rather well fed. Although I have never studied the physical appearance of soldiers from the era, it is probably safe to say that most of the infantrymen and officers did not approach fifteen stones in weight. Most of these modern soldiers would not have fared very well in Jackson's Foot Cavalry. At one reenactment, the Confederate officer corps shared more in common with the offensive line of a typical National Football League team than it did with Lee, Longstreet, Ewell, and Hill.

Speaking of commanding officers, why are there so many of them, especially in smaller reenactments? On more than a few occasions, a company of ten men will have three or four officers standing behind them, complete with sword, pistol, and seemingly never-ending commands.

Closer inspection reveals more inauthenticities, especially with the portrayal of rifle fire. Without live ammunition (hopefully), the rifle muskets and cannon do not kick. And, for safety reasons, the soldiers are clearly shooting in the air, aiming many feet over their intended targets. Nary a single horizontal rifle can be found along the lines. When hand-to-hand combat is required by history, like at the culmination of Pickett's Charge, the sequence of events gets comical: Yanks and Rebs grapple, showing all the coordination of middle school children at a first dance.

When reenactors are used in films, like *Glory* or *Gettysburg*, the authenticity is usually greatly improved. That is, right up until the point when Ted Turner, saber in hand, takes a bullet to the chest on the fields below Cemetery Ridge. At least he's skinny.

APPENDIX D

Isaac Newton Would Have Hated Civil War Films

As originally planned, this book would have included a third chapter dedicated to analyzing the realism of Civil War artistry, but unlike chapters discussing paintings and photography, this third chapter would have concentrated on the depiction of combat in Civil War films and television shows. The metrics intended to evaluate this realism would be different—V/H ratios and muzzle flashes don't really work with movies—but the basic idea would have remained the same: From a measurable perspective, which shows and films are the most realistic, and have motion pictures gotten more realistic through time?

Here's why there is not a complete chapter on this subject: The movies and shows are universally terrible in this respect. They fail nearly every test of realism. And what were the tests? Simply put, they were measurable and quantifiable evaluation tools designed with the help of Sir Isaac Newton. They involve his Third Law of Motion: For every force there is an equal and opposite force. This concept can be applied to the analysis of the depiction of combat in two separate ways, both dealing with basic ballistics. The first of these involves *internal* ballistics—the magnitude of recoil of a rifle or cannon. The second involves *terminal* ballistics—what happens when a bullet strikes a human body.

Newton's Third Law is directly related to the concept of conservation of momentum, and, for firearms and artillery, it can be expressed as

$$mv = MV$$

where m is the mass of a bullet (or shell) and v is its velocity. On the other side of the simple equation is M, the mass of the rifle musket (or cannon), and V is the recoil velocity.

According to this relationship, a large-caliber, high-velocity rifle will produce more recoil than one firing a smaller bullet or firing with a lower velocity. This is part of the reason why big-game guns are so heavy; otherwise their recoil would make them extremely unpleasant to shoot. A small-caliber bullet fired at a high speed (a .223, or a varmint rifle) or a larger-caliber gun firing a slower bullet will have similar kicks. Civil War rifle muskets had a low muzzle velocity, but they fired a very heavy bullet, so they would produce a fair amount of recoil, despite the heavy weight of the gun. For most rifle muskets, the energy of the recoil would fall between that of a varmint rifle and a rifle intended for larger game, like deer. In other words, a Springfield or Enfield rifle musket kicks about as much as a .243 rifle, or perhaps a .30-30—enough that the shooter definitely feels the impact on the shoulder but not enough to be particularly nasty.[1] Until you fire a hundred shots, that is. And soldiers' diaries make reference to this kick. Sam Watkins mentioned it when describing his experiences at the Battle of Kennesaw Mountain:

> *After we had abandoned the line, and on coming to a little stream of water, I undressed for the purposes of bathing, and after undressing found my arm all battered and bruised and bloodshot from my wrist to my shoulder, and as sore as a blister. I had shot one hundred and twenty times that day. My gun became so hot that frequently the powder would flash before I could ram home the ball, and I had frequently to exchange my gun for that of a dead comrade. After I reloaded I found that the dead fellow had already loaded this gun twenty-two times.[2]*

Pistols, and rifles to a smaller degree, also produce recoil that causes the muzzle to rise. This is because the force of the recoil pushes the barrel horizontally back toward the shooter in the opposite direction that the bullet is traveling, but the arm and wrist holding the weapon act as a lever, creating torque. This torque causes the muzzle of the gun to jump upward. The combat in Civil War movies and television shows, almost without exception, ignore these basic tenets of physics and have recoilless and torque-free guns.

While recoil is consistently ignored on the big screen, the illustration of terminal ballistics, in the form of bullet meeting flesh, is generally preposterously presented. According to movies and television shows, a soldier who catches a minié in the torso will either (1) clutch his stomach and chest, grimacing, and collapse forward or (2) be blown off his feet backward into the air, hitting the ground several feet behind where he had been standing. Many soldiers grab their wound, showing no effect from the striking of the bullet or the transfer of energy, and then look down at the spot of the impact before slumping to the ground. Others stumble backward with their arms flailing around as if they were attempting to simultaneously cast two fly-fishing lines at the same time. One new trend is to have a stream of blood and bloody mist explode from the point of impact with flesh—usually in slow motion—even though the man's body shows no sign of being impacted and any hint of body recoil or convulsion is absent.

The broad diameter of a .54- or .58- or even .69-caliber bullet allows it to transfer much of its kinetic energy to a victim. A faster, smaller caliber, like a .223 or .30-06 full-metal-jacketed bullet, may pass completely through a body, so the higher-velocity projectile transfers less energy and momentum (and is more dangerous to those standing behind the person who was shot). So, despite its low muzzle velocity, the rifle musket is hard-hitting. Perhaps not enough to satisfy Hollywood, however, as soldiers are often sent airborne when hit by rifle fire. This fictionalization is summarized well by ballistics expert Mark Denny, who points out that if a gun were powerful enough to knock a victim completely off his feet, the recoil of the gun would also flatten the shooter.[3]

Returning to the earlier equation, relating bullet mass and velocity to gun weight and recoil: In movies and on television, the bullet energy is increased by a factor of ten, while the recoil energy is reduced to zero. Newton would not be pleased with recoilless rifles sending men airborne.

Direct comparisons between bullet-impact energy and other common (or more imaginable) phenomena are useful. Denny provided a few useful comparisons between bullet forces and the resulting impacts felt by the person being shot: A .45 Colt round (similar ballistics to Civil War pistols) strikes a person with the energy of a ninety-mile-per-hour fastball to the chest.[4] When a ballplayer—hopefully a Yankee—is struck in the chest by a pitch, they will typically react by flinching backward and perhaps falling to the ground, but the impacting ball will not propel them any distance backward in the air. As the ball strikes, the player's muscles and nerves will react to the strike by flinching backward as well; a strike to the front of the rib cage will usually result in the back arching away from the site of the impact and the head being pulled down and the shoulders being thrust slightly forward.

Denny also pointed out that a nine-millimeter-handgun bullet strikes with the same energy as a one-pound weight falling from a height of six feet.[5] With a bit of extrapolation from these examples, then, it is clear that a rifle musket minié would hit with the force of a few pounds falling from the same height, with the results feeling something like being hit by a baseball bat to the chest.

Imagine a soldier, armed only with a pistol, down to his last bullet and facing two oncoming enemy soldiers. He fires the pistol into the chest of one and then throws his gun as hard as he can at the other, striking him in the chest as well. Science tells us that the physical reaction by both stricken men should be similar. But imagine how this scene would play out on the big screen . . .

With all of this being said (and calculated), here are some general rules for bullet-impact realism in movies and on television:

1. When a soldier is moving forward and is struck by a bullet to the center of mass, the impact produced will stop their momentum, causing them to fall in place or slightly to the front or rear of their current position, depending on their size, the distance of the shot, and the incoming angle of the bullet. *The soldier will not be thrown off their feet and backward through the air.*

2. When struck from the front in the torso or head, a soldier will not fall many feet forward. A soldier shot while standing behind a stone wall *will never be thrown forward over the wall.*

3. When struck on the periphery (arms, legs—the majority of strikes in real Civil War combat), a soldier may rotate but not be elevated so as to leave the ground *or travel horizontally through the air.*

4. When shot from above, a soldier will fall down, not suddenly leave the ground. If the bullet was fired from above, the momentum of impact will force the victim *downward*, never upward.

5. When shot from below, a soldier will only rise a small amount, if at all. *A falling soldier who is shot will continue to fall.* Also, the magnitude of uplift is dependent on the angle of bullet impact. Soldiers are rarely standing directly above the person who is shooting them. Imagine striking a person who was falling over with a baseball bat—a mighty uppercut to the stomach. Even a Yankee on performance enhancers would not be able to lift his victim several feet off the ground.

6. Artillery rounds rarely explode directly under a soldier, and when they do it is even more infrequent that the flying shrapnel lifts the poor soul more than a dozen feet in the air.

7. Civil War weapons were not capable of causing a human to vaporize.[6]

What follows is a brief survey of Civil War movies and television programs from the last seventy-five years, with, for the most part, a few selections from each decade. Included is a commentary about the depiction of internal and terminal ballistics and how they relate to the realism of the movies through time. Civil War art may be getting more realistic through time, but the same cannot be said for motion pictures.

- *The Red Badge of Courage* (1951). This MGM war film was directed by John Huston and was based, of course, on the 1895 novel of the same name by Stephen Crane. Huston's two-hour movie was apparently cut to a mere seventy sanitized minutes by the studio before release, and most of the combat included in the film is rather comical. No rifles show any hint of recoil, and running men who are shot in the chest appear to have been tripped rather than gunshot.

- *The Red Badge of Courage* (1974). Similarities with the earlier Huston film: Lasts less than seventy-five minutes, because it was made for television. Differences from original movie: Huston's film stars Audie Murphy, a decorated World War II veteran; this one has John-Boy from *The Waltons*. Other, sillier similarities: No one, seemingly, could locate enough rifle muskets for the filming of either movie. In the 1951 film, soldiers can be seen carrying M1903 bolt-action Springfields. In the 1974 show, Richard Thomas muzzleloads an M1873 Trapdoor Springfield.

  The recoil of artillery in the later movie is inconsistent. Cannons usually appear to not move at all upon firing, but occasionally there is a slight, if delayed, rollback of a few feet. Rifle recoil is nonexistent—perhaps a byproduct of muzzleloading a breechloader? The portrayal of gunshot victims is actually worse in the 1974 television show than in the earlier movie, with men taking minié ball strikes to the gut and head without so much as wincing before clutching the wound and dramatically collapsing.

- *The Blue and the Gray* (1982) and *North and South* (mid-1980s). *The Red Badge of Courage* had given us John-Boy in the Army of the Potomac; *The Blue and the Gray* gives us his younger brother, Jim-Bob (David W. Harper), joining Union ranks. This pair of television miniseries introduced a new level of creativity when dealing with the physics of war, and both are riddled with many of the tropes discussed in this book.

  The impact of a pistol bullet is apparently much greater than that of a minié ball in both shows. In *North and South*, men consistently fall forward from rifle shots, but when Parker Stevenson leaps on top of a parapet at Petersburg, he dispatches two Rebels with consecutive pistol shots, sending them both backward into the air. This is especially impressive physics considering his pistol clearly misfires on the second shot.

  Recoil is also inconsistent. In one scene, the 1st US Sharpshooters are firing their new Sharps rifles during target practice. The camera focuses on the rifles, with the first gun kicking in a highly realistic manner, followed by several discharges from other guns on the line that show not even a hint of recoil. Perhaps the army only had one single bullet for target practice that day.

Any hint of recoil is absent from *The Blue and the Gray* for small arms and artillery alike. However, and not surprisingly, a river does run red with blood, and accurate rifle fire, from a soldier on the run, is possible at hundreds of yards. Probably the most dramatic sequence in either miniseries, the battle for the Geysers' homestead in *The Blue and the Gray*, is also the most comically unrealistic.

The home sits atop a strategically critical hill in war-torn central Virginia. Union cavalry have decided to take the hill from a company of fifteen Confederate horsemen, who are dismounted and positioned behind a low stone wall. The small band of Rebels will have a few extra guns on their side, because 2.5 Geysers decide to join them, protecting their home, women, and God-given way of life from the marauding Yankee criminals.

As the history books tell us, the Yankee cavalry follow the standard military doctrine for attack: They dismount two hundred yards away, across the other side of a perfectly flat, wide-open farm field, and proceed to walk in a straight line toward the Confederate position. At least they have superior numbers; there are at least twenty of them. This is shaping up to be Marye's Heights all over again: Rebels behind a stone wall, Union infantry attacking sans cover, only with one–one hundredth the number of men engaged.

When the gunfire opens, far beyond 150 yards, carbine bullets bring down men on both sides. Two Rebels are struck and actually fly forward, over the wall, defying all possible physics for a human hit in the chest. Eventually, the federals—all fifteen of them now—fall back, regroup, and charge a second time. By the end of this charge, they are down to less than ten men, but these remaining soldiers are extraordinarily gifted when it comes to shooting skills. For example, as they begin to retreat a second time, a single federal carbine is fired . . . and three Rebels instantly fall dead.

At this point, the Confederate cavalry—all ten of them—begin the world's tiniest counterattack, led by a Geyser brother who naturally and symbolically grabs the Colors. One of the six remaining federal cavalrymen then completes the greatest feat of marksmanship from the Civil War or any war, and he accomplishes this with a carbine: While running in retreat, he spins, fires, and hits the brother in the lower abdomen, center of mass, dropping him with a mortal wound. The other brother and father rush to the brother's side, only to find the wound has now migrated twelve inches up his chest to his collarbone. Apparently the director was inconsistent when calculating bullet drop for the carbine bullet? Anyway, total outcome of this skirmish: Confederate victory on Virginia soil, Union cavalry suffer casualty rate of over 75 percent. Note that this extremely high casualty rate was the result of breechloading carbines and Spencers and not the war-revolutionizing rifle musket.

• A few years after these miniseries debuted, two other big-budget films appeared that promised an intensified attempt at realism. *Glory* (1989) and *Gettysburg* (1993) were released around the 125th anniversary of the Civil War, and both featured battles that took place within a month of each other during the summer of 1863.

In terms of the physics of combat, both movies are similar, with no observable recoil shown for pistols, rifles, or cannon. Even the coastal artillery in Battery Wagner are recoilless guns. The depiction of bullet strikes is inconsistent during both films as well. Ted Turner, who owned the production company that made *Gettysburg*, makes a cameo as Colonel Waller T. Patton, and he suffers a shockingly gentle gut strike during Pickett's Charge. On Little Round Top, men are shot from above, and yet their torsos fly upward from the impact of the bullet (perhaps a ricochet off the rock they are crossing?). In *Glory*, men are shot convincingly, falling backward into the dunes, before artillery explosions throw other soldiers dozens of feet in the air. Apparently, gravity works differently on Morris Island.

• Surprisingly, *Gods and Generals* (2003), the inferior follow-up to *Gettysburg*, is actually better about both terminal and internal ballistics, although the recoil of cannons is apparently completely controlled by which battle is being fought. *Gods and Generals* often has long clips of men reloading their rifles, so it scores well on the action version of the V/H rating. And when the gunfire starts crashing, like during the Battle of Antietam, the director includes footage of stalks of corn being cut down.

Gettysburg also makes reference to the tropes. John Reynolds is killed by a Rebel sniper who is armed with a scoped target rifle. When a member of his color guard bends down to aid the fallen general, a squib (blood packet) is clearly visible in the left hand. It is only when this bag is ruptured that his aides realize that Reynolds has been critically injured.

- Speaking of squibs, these are the main feature of 2011's *Gettysburg* film, which was a History Channel production released to commemorate the 150th anniversary of the war and was executive produced by Ridley and Tony Scott. The promotional material for the two-hour film promised a "visceral new perspective" that would be "stripping away the romanticized veneer of past treatments."[7]

When watching this film with a critical eye toward physics and realism, one is left with one overriding thought: they must not have had filmed enough combat footage. The same scene of soldiers being killed is shown multiple times, occasionally from slightly different perspectives, but often not. In one scene of the Confederate artillery fuselage that precedes Pickett's Charge, we see a series of cannon firing. The first explodes with no recoil, followed by a second gun that jumps back several feet, followed by two more recoilless guns. Within a minute, we see four more guns fire in succession in the opposite direction: no recoil, recoil, no recoil, no recoil—and everyone tending these guns is now left-handed.

This film should have been subtitled *Blood in the Air*. The director and props coordinator have an unusual fascination with blood spurting from wounds in slow motion. Does this qualify as a "visceral new perspective" or a new perspective of viscera?

The film opens with Lieutenant Colonel Rufus Dawes leading a portion of the Iron Brigade toward the famous Railroad Cut. "For Dawes, retreat is not an option," so he orders a charge. Through the thick smoke, the audience is told, his Colors will be the only way possible to command his men forward. "But flags are a magnet for enemy fire," Sam Rockwell, the narrator, tells the viewer.

What follows is a description of the next sequence of the film that shows, in slow motion (depicting perhaps a half-dozen seconds in real time), what this magnet can attract:

- Flag bearer is shot twice; blood spurts from his wounds.
- Before the flag falls to the ground, it is seized by another soldier, who is immediately shot, with his blood actually hitting and pooling on the camera lens.
- A third soldier instantaneously grabs the flag, which is still vertical, and he is shot.
- As the third soldier falls (twice?), the still-upright flag is taken by a fourth private, who is hit by *four* bullets within the next half second.
- As his bullet-riddled body falls backward, the flag nearly falls to the ground, but it is again clutched by a fifth man, who is shot in the upper back as he reaches for the staff.
- The next man to grab the flag—which is upright again; the flag never touches the ground in this sequence—receives the most confusing wound possible. Blood spurts from his back, but as he turns around, blood, and a small plastic bag, spring away from a wound on his chest.
- As this sixth gunshot victim falls, another man, who was apparently helping to hold the flag upright, is struck in the chest and collapses.
- And then another.
- And perhaps another, although this dying soldier really looks like the unfortunate fellow that was shot four times only four seconds ago.

So, for a quick recap of the Confederate marksmanship accomplished through the thick smoke: More than ten gunshots—all to the chest—during far less than ten seconds. And this sequence is, of course, repeated during the last minute of the film, as we hear Lincoln's Gettysburg Address. *Four seconds and seven dead flag-bearers ago . . .*

For this scene to represent a realistic depiction of the actual events around the Railroad Cut, nearly every Confederate infantryman on that sector of the battlefield would have needed to focus exclusively on whoever was currently holding this flag for the 6th Wisconsin. Everyone in the entire 2nd Mississippi would be aiming at, and hitting, the same target, ignoring Dawes and the rest of his regiment. And with that volume of fire—more than two bullet strikes to the chest per second per man—well, the bullets would have been falling like hail.

Notes

Chapter 1

1. Michael Shaara, *The Killer Angels: A Novel about the Four Days of Gettysburg* (New York: McKay, 1974); Ronald F. Maxwell, writer, dir., *Gettysburg*, prod. Turner Pictures, Esparza/Katz Productions, TriStar Television, and New Line Cinema ([Burbank, CA]: New Line Cinema, 1993).

2. See chapter 22, "History Thrice Removed: Joshua Chamberlain and Gettysburg," in Crompton Burton, *Memory and Myth: The Civil War in Fiction and Film, from "Uncle Tom's Cabin" to "Cold Mountain"*, ed. David B. Sachsman, S. Kittrell Rushing, and Roy Morris Jr. (West LaFayette, IN: Purdue University Press, 2007).

3. Quoted from William C. Oates and Frank A. Haskell, *Gettysburg: Lt. Frank A. Haskell, U.S.A., and Col. William C. Oates, C.S.A.*, ed. and intro. Glenn W. LaFantasie, ed. Paul Andrew Hutton (New York: Bantam Books, 1992), 2.

4. Both quotations from Thomas A. Desjardin, *These Honored Dead: How The Story Of Gettysburg Shaped American Memory* (Cambridge, MA: Hachette Books, 2008), 20. Desjardin's book is one of the best discussions of the history of Gettysburg, full of investigative insights and explanations of how the understanding of the great battle changed over time.

Chapter 2

1. In late June 1863, many Northern newspapers were reporting that a great battle was developing at the crossroads of Shippensburg, misinterpreting the location where Lee's dispersed divisions would eventually congregate.

2. Gary E. Adelman and Timothy H. Smith include an even more fanciful tale from the seventy-fifth-anniversary edition of the *Gettysburg Times* (1938), including twelve total shots and the soldiers meeting for the first time on a postbattle tour of the battlefield. *Devil's Den: A History and Guide* (Gettysburg, PA: Thomas Publishers, 1997), 71–72.

3. There is a great deal of confusion in the literature about the origin of the term *sharpshooter*. Did it refer to the fine marksmanship of the soldier or the Sharps Model 1859 breechloading rifle the men carried? I've reviewed twenty texts on sharpshooting, and there is an equal split between camps. Personally, I think it would be a rather huge coincidence if the sharpshooters were shooting Sharps and the name had nothing to do with the gun.

4. Martin Pelger, *Sniper: A History of the US Marksman* (Oxford and New York: Osprey, 2009), 127.

5. Mark Weaver, "Whitworth Rifle," January 22, 2019, *American Civil War Story*, http://www.americancivilwarstory.com/whitworth-rifle.html; Andy Dougan, *Through the Crosshairs: A History of Snipers* (New York: Carroll & Graf, 2004), 140.

6. Charles Stronge, *Kill Shot: The Deadliest Snipers of All Time* (Berkeley, CA: Ulysses Press, 2011), 16; Leigh Neville, *Modern Sniper* (Oxford: Osprey, 2016), 18; Pelger, *Sniper*, 217; Pat Farey and Mark Spicer, *Sniping: An Illustrated History* (Grand Rapids, MI: Zenith Press, 2009), 84; Americanrifleman.org, accessed January 21, 2019; History net.com, accessed January 24, 2019; Garry James, "I Have This Old Gun: Whitworth Rifle," *American Rifleman*, December 8, 2015, https://www.americanrifleman.org/articles/2015/12/8/i-have-this-old-gun-whitworth-rifle; Fred L. Ray, "The Killing of Uncle John," *Historynet.com*, January 24, 2019, https://www.historynet.com/the-killing-of-uncle-john.htm.

7. Bruce Catton, *Glory Road: The Bloody Route from Fredericksburg to Gettysburg* (Garden City, NY: Doubleday and Company, 1952), 274; Glenn Tucker, *High Tide at Gettysburg: The Campaign in Pennsylvania* (Indianapolis: Bobbs-Merrill, 1958), 110. The official blog of the Gettysburg National Military Park has an interesting three-part discussion of these accounts, amusingly titled "Who Shot J. R.?" As a person who watched a lot of bad television in the early 1980s, I wish I'd have thought of that. See https://npsgnmp.wordpress.com/2011/12/21/romances-of-gettysburg-who-shot-j-r/, https://npsgnmp.wordpress.com/2012/01/05/romances-of-gettysburg-who-shot-j-r-part-two/, and https://npsgnmp.wordpress.com/2012/01/20/who-shot-j-r-part-three/.

8. John L. Plaster, *Sharpshooting in the American Civil War* (Boulder, CO: Paladin Press, 2009), 123.

9. Farey and Spicer, *Sniping*, 84.

10. Martin Pelger, *Sharpshooting Rifles of the Civil War: Colt, Sharps, Spencer and Whitworth*, illus. Johnny Shumate and Alan Gilliland (London: Osprey, 2017), 59.

11. Pelger, *Sharpshooting Rifles*, 59.

12. While on horseback Brigadier General William Haines Lytle was shot in the head by a sniper using a Whitworth rifle during the Battle of Chickamauga.

13. Brent Nosworthy, *The Bloody Crucible of Courage: Fighting Methods and Combat Experience of the Civil War* (New York: Carroll & Graf, 2003), 585.

14. As Mark Denny explains, "Bullet drop means that sight setting works only over a limited-range swath. The extent of this range swath increases as the square of muzzle speed." *Their Arrows Will Darken the Sun: The Evolution and Science of Ballistics* (Baltimore: Johns Hopkins University Press, 2011), 84.

15. Fred Ray, *Shock Troops of the Confederacy: The Sharpshooter Battalions of the Army of Northern Virginia* (Asheville, NC: CFS Press, 2006), 275.

16. Philip R. N. Katcher, *Sharpshooters of the American Civil War, 1861–65*, illus. Stephen Walsh (Oxford: Osprey, 2002), 51.

17. Marksmen were required to produce a string of ten shots at a distance of two hundred yards that did not exceed fifty inches.

18. John Plaster attributes this widening of the MOA to wind drift or the quality of the riflescope. *Sharpshooting in the Civil War*, 54.

19. Martin Pelger, *Sharpshooting Rifles*, 71.

20. There are a few estimates from Civil War soldiers that fall outside this range.
21. Pelger, *Sharpshooting Rifles*, 59.
22. Plaster, *Sharpshooting in the Civil War*, 123.
23. Historian William Frassanito demonstrated in the 1970s that this photograph belonged to a series of images that were mislabeled and staged. The Springfield rifle was added as a prop, as it appears in multiple other images of fallen soldiers. In reality, Gardner and his team of photographers were taking photographs of the same dead soldier from different angles and adding misleading captions before eventually carrying the corpse seen in figure 2.6 to the famous "Rocks Could Not Save Him" location (note the blanket under the soldier used for transport).
24. Interestingly, this was once an actual concern. On September 10, 1978, President Jimmy Carter took Israeli Prime Minister Menachem Begin and Egyptian President Anwar Sadat on a tour of Gettysburg Battlefield prior to the signing of the Camp David Accords. The United States Secret Service was especially concerned about potential sniper fire when the visit made its way to Little Round Top.
25. Now Gettysburg College.
26. Sarah Kay Bierle, "Cloudy with a Chance of Battle," *Gazette665*, January 12, 2016, https://gazette665.com/2016/01/12/cloudy-with-a-chance-of-battle/.
27. Ray, *Shock Troops of the Confederacy*, 277.
28. Dougan, *Through the Crosshairs*, 141.
29. Plaster, *Sharpshooting in the Civil War*, 123.
30. Edward Nichols, *Towards Gettysburg: A Biography of General John F. Reynolds* ([Philadelphia]: Pennsylvania State University Press, 1958), note 881.
31. Mark Adkin, *The Gettysburg Companion: A Guide to the Most Famous Battle* (Mechanicsburg, PA: Stackpole Books, 2008), 270.
32. Allen C. Guelzo, *The Last Great Invasion* (New York: Vintage, 2014), 147.
33. Stephen W. Sears, *Gettysburg* (Boston: Houghton Mifflin, 2003), 170.
34. Colonel Patrick O'Rourke (also spelled O'Rorke) was also shot and killed on Little Round Top. It is claimed that the Confederate who shot him was brought down by fire from Companies A and G of the 16th Michigan regiment, and the dead soldier was later found with seventeen bullet wounds. Glenn W. LaFantasie, *Twilight at Little Round Top: July 2, 1863; The Tide Turns at Gettysburg* (Hoboken: Wiley, 2005), 154.
35. Whitworth rifles were more accurate but also slower to load, making consecutive shots at two officers at the same location equally difficult, if not more so. Historians generally agree that the "snipers" in Devil's Den were armed with Enfields or with the slightly less accurate Springfield rifle muskets.
36. Neville, *Modern Sniper*, 18.

Chapter 3

1. Chapter 25 of Ulysses S. Grant, *Personal Memoirs of U. S. Grant*, vol. 1 of 2 (New York: Charles L. Webster and Company, 1885–1886).
2. Desjardin, *These Honored Dead*, 180–81; parenthetical original.
3. Washington had taken home the Oscar for Best Supporting Actor in 1990 for his work in *Glory*, the story of the 54th Massachusetts Volunteer Infantry (Edward Zwick,

dir., Freddie Fields Productions [Burbank, CA: TriStar Pictures, 1989]). See appendix D for a breakdown of this and other movies with respect to realism (and physics).

4. Martin Pengelly, "My Guilty Pleasure: *Gettysburg*," *The Guardian*, March 21, 2014, https://www.theguardian.com/film/filmblog/2014/mar/21/my-guilty-pleasure-gettysburg-jeff-daniels-civil-war; Marc Hoover, "Haunted Gettysburg: The Ghost of Seminary Ridge," Opinion, *Clermont Sun*, March 26, 2018, https://www.clermontsun.com/2018/03/26/marc-hoover-haunted-gettysburg-the-ghost-of-seminary-ridge; "The Ghosts of Gettysburg," Travel Channel, accessed April 5, 2021, https://www.travelchannel.com/interests/history/articles/ghosts-of-gettysburg; "A Local Describes Gettysburg after the Battle," *The History Engine*, accessed April 5, 2021, https://historyengine.richmond.edu/episodes/view/5807; Stephen Smith, "Battle of Gettysburg Day 3: A 'Do-or-Die Moment,'" CBS News, July 3, 2013, https://www.cbsnews.com/news/battle-of-gettysburg-day-3-a-do-or-die-moment/; "Gettysburg: A Battle that Changed the Course of History," *Intercross* (blog of the International Committee of the Red Cross), July 2, 2014, https://intercrossblog.icrc.org/blog/gettysburg-%E2%80%93-a-battle-that-changed-the-course-of-history.

5. Drew Faust, "'. . . In My Mind I Am Perplexed': Civil War and the Invention of Modern Death," *Harvard Magazine*, January/February 2008, 46–47, https://harvardmagazine.com/2008/01/in-my-mind-i-am-perplexe.html.

6. Mark Swank and Dreama J. Swank, *Maryland in the Civil War* (Chicago: Arcadia, 2013), 41.

7. Robert McNamara, "The Battle of Antietam," *ThoughtCo*, updated April 1, 2019, https://www.thoughtco.com/the-battle-of-antietam-1773739.

8. Frederick Tilberg, *Antietam National Battlefield Site, Maryland*, US National Park Service Historical Handbook Series, vol. 31 (Washington, DC: [US Government Printing Office], 1961), 36.

9. Tom Huntingdon, *Searching for George Gordon Meade: The Forgotten Victor of Gettysburg* (Mechanicsburg, PA: Stackpole Books, 2013), 99.

10. Peter Carlson, "And the Slain Lay in Bloody Rows," part 1 of 2, *Washington Post*, July 30, 1995, https://www.washingtonpost.com/archive/lifestyle/magazine/1995/07/30/and-the-slain-lay-in-rows/dc755bc7-f701-474e-81a9-4b93496d98ef/.

11. Michael Sanders, *More Strange Tales of the Civil War* (Shippensburg, PA: Burd Street Press, 2000), 88.

12. Codie Eash, "We Will Make Our Stand on These Hills: An Essay on the Battle of Antietam," *Codie Eash—Writer and Historian*, September 2013, https://www.codieeashwrites.com/we-will-make-our-stand-on-these-hills-an-essay-on-the-battle-of-antietam.html.

13. Charles W. Mitchell, *Travels through American History in the Mid-Atlantic: A Guide for All Ages*, maps by Elizabeth Church Mitchell (Baltimore: Johns Hopkins University Press, 2014), 126.

14. James McPherson, *Crossroads of Freedom: Antietam* (New York: Oxford University Press, 2002), 122.

15. Norman K. Risjord, *The Civil War Generation* (Lanham, MD: Rowman & Littlefield, 2002), 103.

16. Richard E. Clem, "Antietam Samaritan No Longer Unknown," *Washington Times*, February 8, 2003, https://www.washingtontimes.com/news/2003/feb/8/20030208-010906-5839r/.

17. Terry Kroenung, *Gentle Rain: A Civil War Drama* (Lincoln: iUniverse, 2001), 44.

18. Nicholas Peel, *The Lost Story: The Civil War Diaries of a Country Gentleman* (New York, Lincoln, and Shanghai: Writers Club Press/iUniverse, 2001), 172.

19. Stephen Sears, *Landscape Turned Red: The Battle of Antietam* (New Haven, CT: Ticknor and Fields, 1983), 225.

20. McPherson, *Crossroads of Freedom*, 117; parenthetical original.

21. "Carnage at Antietam, 1862," *EyeWitness to History*, 1997, http://www.eyewitnessto history.com/antiet.htm.

22. theGelf, December 28, 2008, comment on Linda Wheeler, "Union Soldier's Remains Found at Antietam," *A House Divided* (blog), December 28, 2008, http://voices .washingtonpost.com/house-divided/2008/12/a_union_soldier_found_buried_a.html.

23. George F. Sprenger, *Concise History of the Camp and Field Life of the 122d Regiment, Penn'a Volunteers: Compiled from Notes, Sketches, Facts and Incidents* (Lancaster, PA: New Era Steam Book Print, 1885), 368.

24. Gene Smith, "The Destruction of Fighting Joe Hooker," *American Heritage* 44, no. 6 (October 1993), https://www.americanheritage.com/destruction-fighting-joe-hooker-0.

25. Chris Heisey, "'We Should Grow Too Fond of It,'" *Catholic Witness*, February 5, 2016, p. 8, https://www.hbgdiocese.org/wp-content/uploads/downloads/2016/02/FEBRUARY-5.pdf.

26. Garry W. Rable, *The Fredericksburg Campaign: Decision on the Rappahannock* (Chapel Hill: University of North Carolina Press, 2008), 55.

27. Steven Foster, "The Battle of Gettysburg: Hallowed Ground that Shaped the Civil War," *Medium: @StevenLFoster22*, July 15, 2015, https://medium.com/@stevenlfoster22/the-battle-of-gettysburg-b83d0ba2b0c7.

28. Bradley M. Gottfried, *Brigades of Gettysburg: The Union and Confederate Brigades at the Battle of Gettysburg* (La Vergne, TN: Skyhorse, 2012), 260.

29. James M. McPherson, *Hallowed Ground: A Walk at Gettysburg* (New York: Crown, 2003), 91; parenthetical original.

30. Kevin Carroll, *1862: The Confederates Strike Back* (N.p.: iUniverse, 2015), 408.

31. Marc Wortman, *The Bonfire: The Siege and Burning of Atlanta* (New York: PublicAffairs, 2009), 232.

32. Michael Thomas, *The 1864 Franklin-Nashville Campaign: The Finishing Stroke* (Santa Barbara, CA: Praeger, 2014), 85.

33. W[illiam] A[llen] Keesy, *War as Viewed from the Ranks: Personal Recollections of the War of the Rebellion, by a Private Soldier* (Norwalk, OH: Experiment and News Company, 1898), 111.

34. H[ardin] P[erkins] Figuers, "A Boy's Impression of the Battle of Franklin," *Confederate Veteran* 23, no. 1 (January 1915): 6, archived at https://archive.org/details/confederateveter23conf/page/n19/mode/2up?q=Figuers. 4–7.

35. Jackie Sheckler Finch, *Insiders' Guide to Nashville* (Guilford, CT: Morris Book Publishing, 2009), 165.

36. Sally Walker Davies, *Tennessee: An Explorer's Guide* (Woodstock, VT: Countryman Press, 2011), 193.

37. Carole Robinson, "Battle of Franklin: The Death of an Army," *Williamson Herald*, November 29, 2016, http://www.williamsonherald.com/news/battle-of-franklin---the-death-of-an-army/article_a567f6ef-9c85-5580-bc32-1c3e172bbe8e.html.

38. Brian Craig Miller, "The Dead at Franklin," *New York Times*, December 1, 2014, https://opinionator.blogs.nytimes.com/2014/12/01/the-dead-at-franklin/.

39. Robert Hicks, *The Widow of the South* (New York: Grand Central Publishing, 2006), chapter 17.

40. Nina Cardona, "After the Battle of Franklin: A Town Overwhelmed by 10,000 Casualties," *WPLN News*, updated December 2, 2014, https://wpln.org/post/800-residents-emerge-hiding-find-10000-dead-battle-franklin/.

41. For most major engagements, approximately 15–20 percent of casualties were fatalities. Obvious outliers include battles with high numbers of captured soldiers (e.g., Vicksburg). At Gettysburg, 17 percent of casualties were fatalities; at Antietam, 16 percent of the casualties were killed in action; values for Spotsylvania, Chickamauga, Shiloh, and the Wilderness are 13 percent, 11 percent, 15 percent, and 13 percent, respectively.

42. Size estimates for the Cornfield range from seventeen to thirty acres; the Wheatfield estimates vary between nineteen to twenty-six acres.

43. In this manner, the analysis will follow the precedent established in the "Civil War sniper" chapter: The choice of values will always tilt toward the side of the historical accounts being accurate. That way, if the analysis proves otherwise, there is less room for debate concerning the methodology of determination.

44. McPherson, *Crossroads of Freedom*, 118.

45. William A. Frassanito, *Antietam: The Photographic Legacy of America's Bloodiest Day* (New York: Scribner, 1978), 206.

46. Charles D. Broomhall, letter dated June 29, 1891, reproduced by Thomas G. Clemens in "Antietam Remembered," *Civil War Times* (October 2010), archived at *HistoryNet* .com, https://webcache.googleusercontent.com/search?q=cache:KnIlqNKQ-GgJ:https://articles.historynet.com/antietam-remembered.htm+&cd=1&hl=en&ct=clnk&gl=us&client=safari.

47. Jay Jurgensen, *Gettysburg's Bloody Wheatfield* (Shippensburg, PA: White Mane Books, 2002), 136–42.

48. There were 7,108 killed in action at Gettysburg, and 16,522 would be needed to complete a "carpet of death" across the Wheatfield; had every man killed in the battle been brought to the Wheatfield, the would have been 116 square feet per corpse—more than twice the fifty-square-foot surface area each fallen soldier could cover.

49. Perhaps it is not coincidental that John Hood's men were fighting in, or near, every single one of the "carpet of death" locations analyzed in this chapter.

50. While technically this statement isn't true—if dead soldiers were found covering the roofs of these buildings, then the square footage of the grounds would have remained the same—there were no dead soldiers on the roofs of any buildings.

51. James R. Knight, *Hood's Tennessee Campaign: The Desperate Venture of a Desperate Man* (Charleston: The History Press, 2014), 181.

52. Jack H. Lepa, *Breaking the Confederacy: The Georgia and Tennessee Campaigns of 1864* (Jefferson, NC: McFarland, 2011), 190.

53. Desjardin, *These Honored Dead*, 87.

54. Perhaps it is time for historians to follow Desjardin's example of providing contemporary skeptical criticism along with historical accounts.

55. Josiah Strong, "The Teacher: Studies in the Gospel of the Kingdom; The Perils of Peace," *The Homiletic Review* 58 (July–December 1909): 211.

56. With approximately 205,000 battle deaths during the Civil War, each fallen soldier would have almost eighty square feet were they all laid across the farm fields between Seminary and Cemetery Ridges; the number of killed in action would need to have been doubled to achieve the "carpet of death" after Pickett's Charge.

Chapter 4

1. Corporal Samuel J. English, Company D, 2nd Rhode Island Volunteers, as quoted at "The First Battle of Bull Run, 1861," *EyeWitness to History*, 2004, http://www.eye witnesstohistory.com/bullrun.htm.

2. John Dooley of the First Virginia, from the diary entry dated September 17, 1862, in *John Dooley, Confederate Soldier: His War Journal*, ed. Joseph T. Durkin ([Washington, DC]: Georgetown University Press, 1945).

3. Confederate general John Bell Hood, as recorded at "Tour Stop 4—The Cornfield," Antietam, National Park Service, last updated September 15, 2020, https://www.nps .gov/anti/learn/photosmultimedia/tour-stop-4.htm.

4. "Carnage at Antietam, 1862," *EyeWitness to History*, 1997, http://www.eyewitnessto history.com/antiet.htm.

5. Howard Preble Cotton, *We Three: A Tale of the Erie Canal* (Boston: C. M. Clark Publishing Company, 1910), 274.

6. James Longstreet, *From Manassas to Appomattox: Memoirs of the Civil War in America* (Philadelphia: J. B. Lippincott, 1896), 46.

7. Lieutenant Colonel J. J. Scales, 13th Mississippi Infantry, in A. M. Crary, *A. M. Crary Memoirs and Memoranda* (Herington, KS: Herington Times Printers, 1915), 76.

8. Bruce Catton, *Mr. Lincoln's Army* (New York: Doubleday and Company, 1951), 162.

9. William R. Kiefer, *History of the One Hundred and Fifty Third Regiment Pennsylvania Volunteer Infantry* (Easton: Chemical Publishing Co., 1909), 213.

10. Harry W. Pfanz, *Gettysburg: The First Day* (Chapel Hill: University of North Carolina Press, 2011), 85.

11. Patriotic Daughters of Lancaster, *Hospital Scenes after the Battle of Gettysburg, July, 1863* ([Lancaster, PA]: Daily Inquirer Steam Job Print, 1864), 30.

12. David Silkerat, *Raising the White Flag: How Surrender Defined America* (Chapel Hill: University of North Carolina Press, 2019), 113.

13. John W. Stevens, *Reminiscences of the Civil War* (Hillsboro: Hillsboro Mirror Print, 1902), 114.

14. William Worthington Goldsborough, *The Maryland Line in the Confederate States Army* (Baltimore: Kelly, Piet, and Company, 1869), 153; John W. Lokey, "Wounded at Gettysburg," *The Confederate Veteran* 22 (January 1914), 400.

15. Longstreet, *From Manassas to Appomattox*, 46.

16. From the *New York Herald* as recounted in chapter 15 of Ronald C. White, *American Ulysses: A Life of Ulysses S. Grant* (New York: Random House, 2017).

17. William Simmers and Paul Bachschmid, *Ten Months with the 153rd Pennsylvania Volunteers* (Easton: D. H. Neiman, 1863), 29.

18. Samuel M. Smucker, *The History of the Civil War in the United States* (Philadelphia: Jones Brothers, 1865), "hail-storm of balls," 252; "fiery and destructive hail ladened the air," 462; "leaden hail of musketry," 727; "hailstorm of shot," 167, 288, 344, and 418; "torn by the iron hail," 617; "thick falling leaden hail," 657; "tempest of iron hail," 487; "the air seemed filled with sulphurous hail," 217; and "contemptuous hail-storm of shot and shell," 94.

19. Kathryn S. Meier, "'No Place for the Sick': Nature's War on Civil War Soldier Mental and Physical Health in the 1862 Peninsula and Shenandoah Valley Campaigns," *Journal of the Civil War Era* 1, no. 2 (2011): 176.

20. Technically a swath is composed of two or more hail streaks—the continuous area of stones produced by the hail from a single moving cloud.

21. Stanley A. Changnon, David Changnon, and Steven D. Hilberg, Illinois State Weather Service, *Hailstones Across the Nation: An Atlas about Hail and Its Damages*, Illinois State Water Survey, contract report no. 2009-12 (Champagne: Midwestern Regional Climate Center, 2009), https://www.isws.illinois.edu/pubdoc/CR/ISWSCR2009-12.pdf.

22. Cavodonga Palencia, Amaya Castro, Dario Giaiotti, Fulvio Stel, Freddy Vinet, and Roberto Fraile, "Hailpad-Based Research: A Bibliometric Review," *Atmospheric Research* 93, nos. 1–3 (2009): 664–670.

23. Calculations found via G. Georgiev's Body Surface Area Calculator, at https://www.gigacalculator.com/calculators/bsa-calculator.php (accessed March 14, 2020). This number is for twenty-first century humans; men during the Civil War would certainly have had slightly less surface area.

24. Five strikes per square foot per minute equals ten strikes per two square feet per minute, which equals one strike per two square feet per every approximately six seconds.

25. A formation fifty feet long and around twenty-five feet deep.

This semester I have a class of fifty-eight students in my environmental geology class; the seating area in our classroom is approximately 1,300 square feet. The spacing between seated students and soldiers in combat seems reasonable, even if the comparison is a bit strange.

26. And half of the Army of Northern Virginia would have run out of ammunition after about a half hour.

Chapter 5

1. As quoted in John Watson Morton, *The Artillery of Nathan Bedford Forrest's Cavalry* (Nashville: Pub. House of the M. E. Church South, 1909), 181.

2. Dave Grossman, *On Killing: The Psychological Cost of Learning to Kill in War and Society* (New York: Back Bay, 2009), section 1, chapter 1.

3. T. T. S. Laidley, "Breech-Loading Musket," *United States Service Magazine* 1 (January 1865): 69.

4. Mike Wright, *What They Didn't Teach You about the Civil War* (Novato, CA: Presidio Press, 1996), 2.

5. Jonathan M. Steplyk, *Fighting Means Killing: Civil War Soldiers and the Nature of Combat* (Lawrence: University Press of Kansas, 2018), 60.

6. Charles Edward Chapel, *Guns of the Old West: An Illustrated Reference Guide to Antique Firearms* (Mineola, NY: Dover, 2013), 90–91.

7. Ian Harvey, "Why the Guns at Gettysburg Were Found Loaded," *The Vintage News*, August 30, 2016, https://www.thevintagenews.com/2016/08/30/guns-gettysburg -found-loaded/.

8. Grossman, *On Killing*, 23–28; parenthetical original.

9. Steplyk, *Fighting Means Killing*, 61.

10. Grossman, *On Killing*, 23–28.

11. Although nearly thirty thousand guns were recovered by the Confederates after the Battle of Chancellorsville, the Army of Northern Virginia's chief of ordnance, Lieutenant Colonel Briscoe Baldwin, estimated that only 19,500 of these had been dropped by Yankees.

12. Earl J. Hess, *The Rifle Musket in Civil War Combat: Reality and Myth* ([Lawrence]: University Press of Kansas, 2016), 47–52.

13. Denny, *Their Arrows Will Darken the Sun*, 29–30 and 56.

14. One variety of Enfield rifle was particularly prone to fouling to the point of being inoperable. According to Joseph Bilby, Enfields were delivered in two bore sizes: .577 British (twenty-eight gauge) and .58 caliber (to match the American Springfields— twenty-five gauge). When .58 ammunition was used in the .577 guns, the slightly oversized bullets and fouling led to difficulty loading very quickly. Bilby noted that this was a problem reported by Confederates after the Battle of Chickamauga, which had occurred less than three months after Gettysburg and had involved many of the same units. See Joseph G. Bilby, *Small Arms at Gettysburg: Infantry and Cavalry Weapons in America's Greatest Battle* (Yardley, PA: Westholme Publishing, 2008), 92–98.

15. Samuel R. Watkins, *"Co. Aytch": Maury Grays, First Tennessee Regiment; or, A Side Show of the Big Show* (Chattanooga, TN: Times Printing Company, 1900), 138.

16. Paddy Griffith, *Battle Tactics of the Civil War* (Ramsbury: Crowood Press, 2014), 86.

17. Jeffrey C. Hall, *The Stand: The US Army at Gettysburg* (Bloomington: Indiana University Press, 2003), 329.

18. Joseph G. Bilby discusses these in more detail in *Small Arms at Gettysburg*.

19. Steplyk, *Fighting Means Killing*, 62.

20. See appendix A for a more thorough discussion of the firepower available with military weapons through the years.

Chapter 6

1. Bruce Catton, *The American Heritage Picture History of the Civil War*, ed. Richard M. Ketchum (New York: American Heritage Publishing, 1960).

2. Catton, *The American Heritage Picture History*, 147.

3. Judy Ehlen and R. C. Whisonant, "Military Geology of Antietam Battlefield, Maryland, USA: Geology, Terrain, and Casualties," *Geology Today* 24, no. 1 (January/February 2008): 20–27.

4. These included the Army of the Potomac Trilogy—*Mr. Lincoln's Army* (1951), *Glory Road* (1952), and *A Stillness at Appomattox* (Garden City, NY: Doubleday and Company, 1953)—and the Centennial History of the Civil War Trilogy—*The Coming Fury* (Garden City, NY: Doubleday and Company, 1961), *Terrible Swift Sword* (Garden City, NY: Doubleday and Company, 1963), and *Never Call Retreat* (Garden City, NY: Doubleday and Company, 1965).

5. Catton, *Mr. Lincoln's Army*, 112.

6. Catton, *A Stillness at Appomattox*, 154.

7. Catton, *The American Heritage Picture History*, 356.

8. Bruce Catton, *Reflections on the Civil War* (New York: Berkley Books, 1982), part 4, "The First Modern War."

9. John Keegan, *The American Civil War: A Military History* (New York: Knopf Doubleday, 2009), 338.

10. James M. McPherson, *Battle Cry of Freedom: The Civil War Era* (New York: Oxford University Press, 2003), 475.

11. Stephen W. Sears, "The American Civil War and the Origins of Modern Warfare," *American Heritage* 41, no. 2 (March 1990), https://www.americanheritage.com/american-civil-war-and-origins-modern-warfare.

12. Pat Leonard, "The Bullet that Changed History," *New York Times*, August 31, 2012, https://opinionator.blogs.nytimes.com/2012/08/31/the-bullet-that-changed-history/. Brett Gibbons wrote an entire book dedicated to demonstrating the battle-changing effectiveness of the rifle musket: *The Destroying Angel: The Rifle-Musket as the First Modern Infantry Weapon* (N.p.: Independently published, 2018).

13. William Hallahan devotes a chapter of his interesting book to the decision to choose the Springfield rifle musket over a breechloading rifle in the 1850s and 1860s. See William H. Hallahan, *Misfire: The History of How America's Small Arms Have Failed Our Military* (New York: Scribner's, 1994).

14. Slowing the rate of fire is not always a deficit: Consider, for example, more modern weapons like the M14. When introduced, the primary advantage of the M14 over its predecessor, the Garand, was that the newer gun could be fired on full automatic from a removable magazine. It was soon determined that this was a relatively useless feature in battle because the power and recoil of the .308 round made controlling the gun extremely difficult when fired in this manner. Later, US service rifles offered the ability to fire three-round bursts, a compromise between the "ammunition-wasting" full-automatic fire and the slower, more controllable and conservative semiautomatic mode.

15. There are other ways to calculate striking power—or knockdown power. See appendix A for a more thorough discussion of these other metrics.

16. To calculate muzzle energy, you square the muzzle velocity and multiply this by the bullet weight (in grains). This value is then divided by 450,435 to give energy in foot-pounds.

17. The "Myth of the Civil War Sniper" chapter opened with a discussion of groundhog hunting using rifles firing different velocity cartridges. With a .222 Remington rifle, a groundhog that is 250 yards away will still be hit if the shooter misjudges the range by fifty *yards*. With a .22 rimfire rifle (or a rifle musket with a similar muzzle velocity), the range will need to be estimated to within fifty *feet*. Hitting a small target at range is very difficult with any gun that fires a low-velocity bullet.

18. An Enfield rifle was inherently both precise and accurate; it could consistently print relatively small groups if accurately aimed. However, if the range of the target is poorly estimated, it will become inaccurate, despite remaining precise.

19. The geology of the Antietam Battlefield, and how it influenced the fighting and tactics, is discussed in detail in these three publications: Ehlen and Whisonant, "Military Geology of Antietam Battlefield"; Scott Hippensteel, "Carbonate Rocks and American Civil War Infantry Tactics," *Geosphere* 12, no. 2 (2016): 234–365; and Scott Hippensteel, *Rocks and Rifles: The Influence of Geology on Combat and Tactics during the American Civil War* (Cham, Switzerland: Springer International, 2019), chapter 8.

20. A. Hunter, "A High Privates Sketch of Sharpsburg," *Southern Historical Society Papers* 11 (1883): 18.

21. Both the M1873 carbine and the M16 had serious issues with their ammunition early in their service time that resulted in rifles jamming and needing to be cleared in combat. For the Springfield, the problem was the soft copper cartridges, which oxidized and became jammed in the single-shot guns. For the M16, the problem was the choice of gunpowder. See Hallahan, *Misfire*, for a thorough breakdown of these breakdowns.

22. Catton, *The American Heritage Picture History*, 356.

23. Leonard, "The Bullet that Changed History."

24. Gibbons, *The Destroying Angel*, book cover and pp. 3–8.

25. Paddy Griffith, "The Infantry Firefight," in Michael Barton and Gary M. Logue, *The Civil War Soldier: A Historical Reader* (New York: New York University Press), 210.

26. Earl Hess, *The Rifle Musket*, 5.

27. Guelzo, *Gettysburg*, 37; parenthetical original.

28. David A. Ward, *The 96th Pennsylvania Volunteers in the Civil War*, fore. Edwin C. Bearss (Jefferson, NC: McFarland 2018), 277–80.

29. And remember that Major T. T. S. Laidley's report to the Ordnance Department about the thousands of misloaded rifles collected from the Gettysburg Battlefield (previous chapter) was intended to argue exactly this point: the muzzleloading rifle's time had passed.

30. Appendix B provides a brief analysis of the effectiveness of Civil War revolvers.

Chapter 7

1. "Brady's Photographs; Pictures of the Dead at Antietam," *New York Times*, October 20, 1862, https://www.nytimes.com/1862/10/20/archives/bradys-photographs-pictures-of-the-dead-at-antietam.html.

2. William A. Frassanito, *Gettysburg: A Journey in Time* (New York: Scribner, 1975), 29.

3. Estimate of the quantity of photographs including dead soldiers is from Earl J. Hess's chapter, "Andrew J. Russell and the Stone Wall at Fredericksburg," in *Lens of War: Exploring Iconic Photographs of the Civil War* (ed. James Matthew Gallman and Gary W. Gallagher [Athens: University of Georgia Press, 2015]), 163.

4. Quoted in "Faces of Great Men: An Endeavor to Establish a Gallery of Portraits in This City," *Washington Post*, December 18, 1889.

5. "Photographs of War Scenes," *Humphrey's Journal* 13, no. 9 (September 1, 1861): 133.

6. Alexander Gardner, *Gardner's Photographic Sketch Book of the War* (Washington, DC: Philp & Solomons, 1866), 39.

7. James I. Robertson Jr., *The Untold Civil War: Exploring the Human Side of War*, ed. Neil Kagan (Washington, DC: National Geographic, 2011), 230.

8. "Photography and the Civil War: Bringing the Battlefield to the Homefront," *Battlefields.org*, website of the American Battlefield Trust, https://www.battlefields.org/learn/articles/photography-and-civil-war, accessed May 21, 2020.

9. As quoted in "Faces of Great Men: An Endeavor to Establish a Gallery of Prints in this City," *Washington Post*, December 18, 1889.

10. Frassanito's two most important texts about this battle were published twenty years apart: *Gettysburg: A Journey in Time* (1975) and *Early Photography at Gettysburg* (Gettysburg, PA: Thomas Publications, 1995).

11. Including Frassanito, *Antietam: The Photographic Legacy of America's Bloodiest Day*; see also William Frassanito, *Grant and Lee: The Virginia Campaigns, 1864–1865* (New York: Macmillan, 1983).

12. Frassanito makes a compelling argument in his two volumes about the photography at Gettysburg that this man's wounds were enlarged by the feeding of wild pigs. The historian found contemporaneous records of soldiers describing feral pigs feeding on the dead on the battlefield, and he noted the precise nature of the wound to the torso—no entrails are present, as if cleanly trimmed by an animal rather than an artillery bolt.

13. Alexander Gardner, *Gardner's Photographic Sketch Book of the War* (Washington, DC: Philp & Solomons, 1866), 40.

14. David Fisher, *Bill O'Reilly's Legends and Lies: The Civil War*, intro. Bill O'Reilly ([New York]: Henry Holt and Company, 2017), 183.

15. In *Antietam: The Photographic Legacy of America's Bloodiest Day* (1978), William Frassanito also demonstrates the unlikelihood that this photograph is authentic. During his research, Frassanito came across the Matthews Hill image in two forms—the first pictured here. In the second, all the soldiers are alive and in "combat," firing their rifles and pistols at an imaginary enemy. Frassanito pointed out the absurdity that Brady would have photographed the men in combat and then witnessed them all being slain in identical positions before he took a second shot.

16. A more detailed account of how this latter fraud was revealed can be found at the Library of Congress's website: "Civil War Glass Negatives and Related Prints," 2008, http://www.loc.gov/pictures/collection/cwp/mystery.html.

Chapter 8

1. Albert Ten Eyck Gardner, *Winslow Homer: A Retrospective Exhibition* (Boston: Museum of Fine Art, 1959), 77.

2. Mort Künstler, *The Civil War Art of Mort Künstler* (Seymour, CT: Greenwich Workshop Press, 2004), xi.

3. Robert I. Girardi, *The Civil War Art of Keith Rocco* (Forest Park, IL: Crimson Books, 2010), 5.

4. "About Gallon: Dale Gallon . . . The Artist That Brings You the History," The Gallon Gallery (website), https://www.gallon.com/about-gallon/, accessed June 6, 2020.

5. "The Art of Don Troiani," W. Britain (website), https://www.wbritain.com/the-art-of-don-troiani, accessed June 4, 2020.

6. Appendix C includes a discussion of the realism of reenactments.

7. "Realism," Tate (website), https://www.tate.org.uk/art/art-terms/r/realism, accessed June 22, 2020.

8. Soldiers holding their rifles such that where they are placing a percussion cap on the gun are also considered to be in the act of loading their gun, even though the barrel of the rifle may no longer be as vertical as it was when the ramrod was being used.

9. This criterion, of course, deals only with sustained firefights (which can be judged by the amount of smoke present in the illustration). No circumstances in which soldiers might be holding their fire or conducting volley fire should be considered with respect to V/H ratios—no "whites of their eyes" circumstances.

10. The use of actual round shot or bolts requires more powder, and the force exerted on the round will push the barrel in the opposite direction. See appendix D for more discussion of artillery recoil.

11. Firing live ammunition is obviously more dangerous, especially downrange. An exploding barrel can be a real problem for a gun crew using real, deadly ammunition; those firing blanks face much less of a threat.

12. I surveyed Dale Gallon, Don Troiani, and Keith Rocco about whether they took some of the "metrics" used in this chapter into consideration for their artwork. Don Troiani seemed to be the most interested in the idea of including empirical data to capture realism when crafting his fine paintings. He, for example, has participated in reenactments in the past and has been known to shoot trees with rifle muskets to gain insight into what a forest landscape might have looked like during or after combat.

13. Carl von Clausewitz, *Vom Kriege* (*On War*) (Berlin: Dümmlers Verlag, 1832).

14. Denny, *Their Arrows Will Darken the Sun*, 30.

15. Six guns firing two shots per minute, with each gun charge weighing 2.5 pounds.

16. An analysis of five prints revealed thirty soldiers shooting, none reloading.

17. Paddy Griffith, *Battle in the Civil War: Generalship and Tactics in America, 1861–65*, illus. Peter Dennis (Mansfield, Nottinghamshire, Eng.: Fieldbooks, 1986).

18. Fisher, *Bill O'Reilly's Legends and Lies*, 75.

19. Troiani's work is titled *The Gray Wall*, and it has a V/H ratio of 1.3.

Chapter 9

1. "The Battle of Shiloh, 1862," *EyeWitness to History*, 2004, http://www.eyewitnessto history.com/shiloh.htm; Drew Lindsay, "Rest in Peace? Bringing Home U.S. War Dead," History.com, 2013, https://www.historynet.com/rest-in-peace-bringing-home-u-s-war-dead.htm; Faust, "'. . . In My Mind I Am Perplexed.'" In his *Personal Memoirs*, Grant wrote, "I saw an open field so covered with dead that it would have been possible to walk across the clearing, in any direction, stepping on dead bodies, without a foot touching the ground" (vol. 1, ch. 9, p. 211). It is important to note that Grant did not specify the size of the clearing, only implying it was a large enough area that the carnage of the battle was truly stupefying.

2. "Battle of Shiloh: Shattering Myths," American Battlefield Trust, https://www .battlefields.org/learn/articles/battle-shiloh-shattering-myths, accessed July 8, 2020.

3. Even the private purchase of repeaters by soldiers underscores this conclusion.

4. This reincarnation was presented in David Lowe and Philip Shiman, "Substitute for a Corpse," *Civil War Times* 49, no. 6 (December 2010): 40–41, archived at https://web-cache.googleusercontent.com/search?q=cache:_YronMqcGF0J:https://www.historynet .com/substitute-for-a-corpse.htm+&cd=1&hl=en&ct=clnk&gl=us&client=safari.

5. On an insidious note, the staged photograph containing both men has been cited as proof that many African Americans were to be found among the Confederate ranks.

6. Desjardin, *These Honored Dead*, 58.

7. *Gettysburg*, directed by Richard Bedser and Ed Fields, *History Channel*, 85 minutes, May 30, 2011.

8. Consider, for example, the Galveston Hurricane of 1900, where some estimates say as many as eight thousand were killed. At Antietam, by comparison, a combined 3,650 Rebel and Union soldiers died ("Casualties of Battle," National Park Service, last updated December 30, 2015, https://www.nps.gov/anti/learn/historyculture/casualties .htm).

9. Jennifer Jones, "The Ghosts of Devil's Den," *The Dead History*, August 14, 2016, https://www.thedeadhistory.com/ghosts-devils-den/.

10. "The Bloodbath: Confusion in Command at Chickamauga Creek," American Battlefield Trust, https://www.battlefields.org/learn/articles/bloodbath, accessed April 1, 2021.

11. Stones River reference from Mike West, "Stones River: A Bitter Night Ends Walk to Gates of Hell," *Murfeesboro Post*, March 9, 2008, available at http://rutherfordtn history.org/stones-river-a-bitter-night-ends-walk-to-gates-of-hell/. There is also an entire book called *Stones River Ran Red* by Richard J. Reid (Owensboro, KY: Commercial Print Co., 1992). It probably contains at least one reference to this trope. The Shiloh myth is described in the American Battlefield Trust's feature, "Battle of Shiloh: Shattering Myths."

12. *Discharge* is the measure of how much water is flowing by a particular spot along a stream or river per unit of time. This measurement is usually given in units, like cubic feet per second or cubic meters per second.

13. George Santayana, *Reason in Common Sense*, vol. 1 in *The Life of Reason: Or, The Phases of Human Progress* (London: Constable, 1905), 284.

14. Nicholas Fandos, "In Renovation of Golf Club, Donald Trump Also Dressed Up History," *New York Times*, November 24, 2015, https://www.nytimes.com/2015/11/25/us/politics/in-renovation-of-golf-club-donald-trump-also-dressed-up-history.html.

Appendix A

1. Another metric used to estimate hitting power is the Taylor Knock-Out Index—or TKO. John Taylor, an experienced big-game hunter, developed this estimate to give hunters an idea of how effective a particular round might be for dropping large animals. This index is heavily biased in favor of big-bore guns because it places equal value on muzzle velocity, bullet weight, and bullet diameter. Low- and medium-velocity rounds that fire a huge bullet rank much higher than higher-velocity rounds firing comparably smaller bullets. As a result, the smoothbore and rifle musket both earn a TKO in the forties, while the .45-70 cartridge falls into the thirties, and the .30-06 only scores seventeen. The .223 may not be a good choice when hunting elk or elephants, but its score of six on the TKO scale vastly underestimates what the bullet would do when striking human flesh.

Appendix B

1. Adkin, *Gettysburg Companion*, 196.
2. Joseph G. Bilby, *Civil War Firearms: Their Historical Background and Tactical Use and Modern Collecting and Shooting* (Cambridge, MA: DaCapo Press, 1997), 169.

Appendix D

1. Black powder burns in a different manner than modern smokeless powder, and, as a result, rifle muskets have is less of a sudden kick and more of a quick push; the recoil force is similar, but the black-powder kick seems more spread out or slightly delayed.
2. Watkins, *"Co. Aytch"*, 138. Of course, Watkins did not actually write that final line.
3. Denny, *Their Arrows Will Darken the Sun*, 163.
4. Denny, *Their Arrows Will Darken the Sun*, 163.
5. Denny, *Their Arrows Will Darken the Sun*, 163.
6. There are actual Civil War weapons "experts" on the History Channel who claim that field artillery was capable of vaporizing a human body, apparently removing any evidence that a soldier or his uniform existed.
7. The promotional material was from the iTunes description included under "About the Show."

Bibliography

Adelman, Gary E., and Timothy H. Smith. *Devil's Den: A History and Guide*. Gettysburg, PA: Thomas Publishers, 1997.

Adkin, Mark. *The Gettysburg Companion: A Guide to the Most Famous Battle*. Mechanicsburg, PA: Stackpole Books, 2008.

American Battlefield Trust. "Battle of Shiloh: Shattering Myths." https://www.battlefields.org/learn/articles/battle-shiloh-shattering-myths, accessed July 8, 2020.

———. "The Bloodbath: Confusion in Command at Chickamauga Creek." https://www.battlefields.org/learn/articles/bloodbath, accessed April 1, 2021.

———. "Photography and the Civil War: Bringing the Battlefield to the Homefront." *Battlefield.org* (website). https://www.battlefields .org/learn/articles/photography-and-civil-war, accessed May 21, 2020.

Bailey, Ronald H. *The Bloodiest Day: The Battle of Antietam*. Alexandria, VA: Time-Life Books, 1984.

Bedser, Richard, and Ed Fields, dir. *Gettysburg. History Channel*. 85 minutes. May 30, 2011.

Bierle, Sarah Kay. "Cloudy with a Chance of Battle." *Gazette665*, January 12, 2016. https://gazette665.com/2016/01/12/cloudy-with-a-chance-of-battle/.

Bilby, Joseph G. *Civil War Firearms: Their Historical Background and Tactical Use and Modern Collecting and Shooting*. Cambridge, MA: DaCapo Press, 1997.

———. *Small Arms at Gettysburg: Infantry and Cavalry Weapons in America's Greatest Battle*. Yardley, PA: Westholme Publishing, 2008.

Brown, Andrew. *Geology and the Gettysburg Campaign.* Educational series, Bureau of Topographic and Geologic Survey, Pennsylvania, 5. Illustrations by Albert E. Van Olden. Harrisonburg: Pennsylvania Geological Survey, 1962.

Burton, Crompton. *Memory and Myth: The Civil War in Fiction and Film, from "Uncle Tom's Cabin" to "Cold Mountain".* Edited by David B. Sachsman, S. Kittrell Rushing, and Roy Morris Jr. West LaFayette, IN: Purdue University Press, 2007.

Cardona, Nina. "After the Battle of Franklin: A Town Overwhelmed by 10,000 Casualties." *WPLN News,* updated December 2, 2014. https://wpln.org/post/800-residents-emerge-hiding-find-10000-dead-battle-franklin/.

Carlson, Peter. "And the Slain Lay in Bloody Rows." Part 1 of 2. *Washington Post,* July 30, 1995. https://www.washingtonpost.com/archive/lifestyle/magazine/1995/07/30/and-the-slain-lay-in-rows/dc755bc7-f701-474e-81a9-4b93496d98ef/.

Carroll, Kevin. *1862: The Confederates Strike Back.* N.p.: iUniverse, 2015.

Catton, Bruce. *The American Heritage Picture History of the Civil War.* Edited by Richard M. Ketchum. New York: American Heritage Publishing, 1960.

———. *The Coming Fury.* Garden City, NY: Doubleday and Company, 1961.

———. *Glory Road: The Bloody Route from Fredericksburg to Gettysburg.* Garden City, NY: Doubleday and Company, 1952.

———. *Grant Moves South.* Boston: Little, Brown and Company, 1960.

———. *Mr. Lincoln's Army.* New York: Doubleday and Company, 1951.

———. *Never Call Retreat.* Garden City, NY: Doubleday and Company, 1965.

———. *Reflections on the Civil War.* New York: Berkley Books, 1982.

———. *A Stillness at Appomattox.* Garden City, NY: Doubleday and Company, 1953.

———. *Terrible Swift Sword.* Garden City, NY: Doubleday and Company, 1963.

Changnon, Stanley A., David Changnon, and Steven D. Hilberg. *Hailstones Across the Nation: An Atlas about Hail and Its Damages.* Illinois

State Water Survey, contract report no. 2009-12. Champagne: Midwestern Regional Climate Center, 2009. https://www.isws.illinois.edu/pubdoc/CR/ISWSCR2009-12.pdf.

Chapel, Charles Edward. *Guns of the Old West: An Illustrated Reference Guide to Antique Firearms.* Mineola, NY: Dover, 2013.

Clem, Richard E. "Antietam Samaritan No Longer Unknown." *Washington Times,* February 8, 2003. https://www.washingtontimes.com/news/2003/feb/8/20030208-010906-5839r/.

Clemens, Thomas G. "Antietam Remembered." *Civil War Times* (October 2010). Archived at *HistoryNet.com,* https://webcache.google-usercontent.com/search?q=cache:KnIlqNKQ-GgJ:https://articles.historynet.com/antietam-remembered.htm+&cd=1&hl=en&ct=clnk&gl=us&client=safari.

Cotton, Howard Preble. *We Three: A Tale of the Erie Canal.* Boston: C. M. Clark Publishing Company, 1910.

Crary, A. M. *A. M. Crary Memoirs and Memoranda.* Herington, KS: Herington Times Printers, 1915.

Denny, Mark. *Their Arrows Will Darken the Sun: The Evolution and Science of Ballistics.* Baltimore: Johns Hopkins University Press, 2011.

Desjardin, Thomas A. *These Honored Dead: How The Story Of Gettysburg Shaped American Memory.* Cambridge, MA: Hachette Books, 2008.

Dooley, John. *John Dooley, Confederate Soldier: His War Journal.* Edited by Joseph T. Durkin. [Washington, DC]: Georgetown University Press, 1945.

Dougan, Andy. *Through the Crosshairs: A History of Snipers.* New York: Carroll & Graf, 2004.

Eash, Codie. "We Will Make Our Stand on These Hills: An Essay on the Battle of Antietam." *Codie Eash—Writer and Historian,* September 2013. https://www.codieeashwrites.com/we-will-make-our-stand-on-these-hills-an-essay-on-the-battle-of-antietam.html.

Ehlen, Judy, and R. C. Whisonant. "Military Geology of Antietam Battlefield, Maryland, USA: Geology, Terrain, and Casualties." *Geology Today* 24, no. 1 (January/February 2008): 20–27.

EyeWitness to History. "The Battle of Shiloh, 1862." 2004. http://www.eyewitnesstohistory.com/shiloh.htm.

———. "Carnage at Antietam, 1862." 1997. http://www.eyewitnessto
history.com/antiet.htm.

———. "The First Battle of Bull Run, 1861." 2004. http://www.eye
witnesstohistory.com/bullrun.htm.

Fandos, Nicholas. "In Renovation of Golf Club, Donald Trump Also
Dressed Up History." *New York Times*, November 24, 2015. https://
www.nytimes.com/2015/11/25/us/politics/in-renovation-of-golf-
club-donald-trump-also-dressed-up-history.html.

Farey, Pat, and Mark Spicer. *Sniping: An Illustrated History*. Grand Rapids, MI: Zenith Press, 2009.

Faust, Drew. "'. . . In My Mind I Am Perplexed': Civil War and the
Invention of Modern Death." *Harvard Magazine*, January/February
2008, 44–50. https://harvardmagazine.com/2008/01/in-my-mind-i-
am-perplexe.html.

Figuers, H[ardin] P[erkins]. "A Boy's Impression of the Battle of Franklin." *Confederate Veteran* 23, no. 1 (January 1915): 4–7. Archived
at https://archive.org/details/confederateveter23conf/page/n17/
mode/2up?q=Figuers.

Fisher, David. *Bill O'Reilly's Legends and Lies: The Civil War*. Introduction
by Bill O'Reilly. [New York]: Henry Holt and Company, 2017.

Foster, Steven. "The Battle of Gettysburg: Hallowed Ground that
Shaped the Civil War." *Medium: @StevenLFoster22*, July 15,
2015. https://medium.com/@stevenlfoster22/the-battle-of
-gettysburg-b83d0ba2b0c7.

Frassanito, William A. *Antietam: The Photographic Legacy of America's
Bloodiest Day*. New York: Scribner, 1978.

———. *Early Photography at Gettysburg*. Gettysburg, PA: Thomas Publications, 1995.

———. *Gettysburg: A Journey in Time*. New York: Scribner, 1975.

———. *Grant and Lee: The Virginia Campaigns, 1864–1865*. New York:
Macmillan, 1983.

The Gallon Gallery (website). "About Gallon: Dale Gallon . . . The Artist That Brings You the History." Accessed June 6, 2020. https://
www.gallon.com/about-gallon/.

Gardner, Alexander. *Gardner's Photographic Sketch Book of the War.* Washington, DC: Philp & Solomons, 1866.

Gibbons, Brett. *The Destroying Angel: The Rifle-Musket as the First Modern Infantry Weapon.* N.p.: Independently published, 2018.

Girardi, Robert I. *The Civil War Art of Keith Rocco.* Forest Park, IL: Bloomsburg, 2010.

Goldsborough, William Worthington. *The Maryland Line in the Confederate States Army.* Baltimore: Kelly, Piet, and Company, 1869.

Gottfried, Bradley M. *Brigades of Gettysburg: The Union and Confederate Brigades at the Battle of Gettysburg.* La Vergne, TN: Skyhorse, 2012.

Grant, Ulysses S. *Personal Memoirs of U. S. Grant,* vol. 1 of 2. New York: Charles L. Webster and Company, 1885–1886.

Griffith, Paddy. *Battle in the Civil War: Generalship and Tactics in America, 1861–65.* Illustrated by Peter Dennis. Mansfield, Nottinghamshire, Eng.: Fieldbooks, 1986.

———. *Battle Tactics of the Civil War.* Ramsbury: Crowood Press, 2014.

———. "The Infantry Firefight." In *The Civil War Soldier: A Historical Reader,* edited by Michael Barton and Gary M. Logue, 199–227. New York: New York University Press.

Grossman, Dave. *On Killing: The Psychological Cost of Learning to Kill in War and Society.* New York: Back Bay, 2009.

Guelzo, Allen C. *Gettysburg: The Last Invasion.* New York: Vintage, 2014.

Hall, Jeffrey C. *The Stand: The US Army at Gettysburg.* Bloomington: Indiana University Press, 2003.

Hallahan, William H. *Misfire: The History of how America's Small Arms Have Failed Our Military.* New York: Scribner's, 1994.

Harvey, Ian. "Why the Guns at Gettysburg Were Found Loaded." *The Vintage News,* August 30, 2016. https://www.thevintagenews .com/2016/08/30/guns-gettysburg-found-loaded/.

Heisey, Chris. "We Should Grow Too Fond of It.'" *Catholic Witness,* February 5, 2016, 8. https://www.hbgdiocese.org/wp-content/uploads/ downloads/2016/02/FEBRUARY-5.pdf.

Hess, Earl J. "Andrew J. Russell and the Stone Wall at Fredericksburg." In *Lens of War: Exploring Iconic Photographs of the Civil War,* edited by James Matthew Gallman and Gary W. Gallagher, 159–66. Athens: University of Georgia Press, 2015.

———. *Field Armies and Fortifications in the Civil War: The Eastern Campaigns, 1861–1864.* Chapel Hill: University of North Carolina Press, 2005.

———. *The Rifle Musket in Civil War Combat: Reality and Myth.* [Lawrence]: University Press of Kansas, 2016.

———. *The Trenches at Petersburg: Field Fortifications and Confederate Defeat.* Chapel Hill: University of North Carolina Press, 2009.

Hicks, Robert. *The Widow of the South.* New York: Grand Central Publishing, 2006.

Hippensteel, Scott P. "Carbonate Rocks and American Civil War Infantry Tactics." *Geosphere* 12, no. 2 (2016): 234–365.

———. *Rocks and Rifles: The Influence of Geology on Combat and Tactics during the American Civil War.* Cham, Switzerland: Springer International, 2019.

The History Engine. "A Local Describes Gettysburg after the Battle." Accessed April 5, 2021. https://historyengine.richmond.edu/episodes/view/5807.

Hook, Philip. *The Ultimate Trophy: How Impressionist Painting Conquered the World.* Munich: Prestel Verlag, 2012.

Hoover, Marc. "Haunted Gettysburg: The Ghost of Seminary Ridge." Opinion. *Clermont Sun,* March 26, 2018. https://www.clermontsun.com/2018/03/26/marc-hoover-haunted-gettysburg-the-ghost-of-seminary-ridge.

Hunter, A. "A High Privates Sketch of Sharpsburg." *Southern Historical Society Papers* 11 (1883): 18.

Huntingdon, Tom. *Searching for George Gordon Meade: The Forgotten Victor of Gettysburg.* Mechanicsburg, PA: Stackpole Books, 2013.

Intercross. "Gettysburg: A Battle that Changed the Course of History." Blog of the International Committee of the Red Cross. July 2, 2014. https://intercrossblog.icrc.org/blog/gettysburg-%E2%80%93-a-battle-that-changed-the-course-of-history.

James, Garry. "I Have This Old Gun: Whitworth Rifle." *American Rifleman*, December 8, 2015. https://www.americanrifleman.org/articles/2015/12/8/i-have-this-old-gun-whitworth-rifle.

Jones, Jennifer. "The Ghosts of Devil's Den." *The Dead History*, August 14, 2016. https://www.thedeadhistory.com/ghosts-devils-den/.

Jurgensen, Jay. *Gettysburg's Bloody Wheatfield*. Shippensburg, PA: White Mane Books, 2002.

Katcher, Philip R. N. *Sharpshooters of the American Civil War, 1861–65*. Illustrated by Stephen Walsh. Oxford: Osprey, 2002.

Keegan, John. *The American Civil War: A Military History*. New York: Knopf Doubleday, 2009.

Keesy, W[illiam]. A[llen]. *War as Viewed from the Ranks: Personal Recollections of the War of the Rebellion, by a Private Soldier*. Norwalk, OH: Experiment and News Company, 1898.

Knight, James R. *Hood's Tennessee Campaign: The Desperate Venture of a Desperate Man*. Charleston: The History Press, 2014.

Kroenung, Terry. *Gentle Rain: A Civil War Drama*. Lincoln: iUniverse, 2001.

Künstler, Mort. *The Civil War Art of Mort Künstler*. Seymour, CT: Greenwich Workshop Press, 2004.

LaFantasie, Glenn W. *Twilight at Little Round Top: July 2, 1863; The Tide Turns at Gettysburg*. Hoboken: Wiley, 2005.

Laidley, T. T. S. "Breech-Loading Musket." *United States Service Magazine* 1 (January 1865): 67–70.

Leonard, Pat. "The Bullet that Changed History." *New York Times*, August 31, 2012. https://opinionator.blogs.nytimes.com/2012/08/31/the-bullet-that-changed-history/.

Lepa, Jack H. *Breaking the Confederacy: The Georgia and Tennessee Campaigns of 1864*. Jefferson, NC: McFarland, 2011.

Library of Congress. "Civil War Glass Negatives and Related Prints." 2008. http://www.loc.gov/pictures/collection/cwp/mystery.html.

Lindsay, Drew. "Rest in Peace? Bringing Home U.S. War Dead." History.com, 2013. https://www.historynet.com/rest-in-peace-bringing-home-u-s-war-dead.htm.

Lokey, John W. "Wounded at Gettysburg." *The Confederate Veteran* 22 (January 1914): 400.

Longstreet, James. *From Manassas to Appomattox: Memoirs of the Civil War in America.* Philadelphia: J. B. Lippincott, 1896.

Lowe, David, and Philip Shiman. "Substitute for a Corpse." *Civil War Times* 49, no. 6 (December 2010): 40–41. Archived at https://webcache.googleusercontent.com/search?q=cache:_YronMqcGF0J:https://www.historynet.com/substitute-for-a-corpse .htm+&cd=1&hl=en&ct=clnk&gl=us&client=safari.

Maxwell, Ronald F., writer, dir. *Gettysburg.* Produced by Turner Pictures, Esparza/Katz Productions, TriStar Television, and New Line Cinema. [Burbank, CA]: New Line Cinema, 1993.

McNamara, Robert. "The Battle of Antietam." *ThoughtCo,* updated April 1, 2019. https://www.thoughtco.com/the-battle-of -antietam-1773739.

McPherson, James M. *Battle Cry of Freedom: The Civil War Era.* New York: Oxford University Press, 2003.

———. *Crossroads of Freedom: Antietam.* New York: Oxford University Press, 2002.

———. *Hallowed Ground: A Walk at Gettysburg.* New York: Crown, 2003.

Meier, Kathryn S. "'No Place for the Sick': Nature's War on Civil War Soldier Mental and Physical Health in the 1862 Peninsula and Shenandoah Valley Campaigns." *Journal of the Civil War Era* 1, no. 2 (2011): 176–206.

Miller, Brian Craig. "The Dead at Franklin." *New York Times,* December 1, 2014. https://opinionator.blogs.nytimes.com/2014/12/01/ the-dead-at-franklin/.

Mitchell, Charles W. *Travels through American History in the Mid-Atlantic: A Guide for All Ages.* Maps by Elizabeth Church Mitchell. Baltimore: Johns Hopkins University Press, 2014.

Morton, John Watson. *The Artillery of Nathan Bedford Forrest's Cavalry.* Nashville: Pub. House of the M. E. Church South, 1909.

National Park Service. "Casualties of Battle." Last updated December 30, 2015. https://www.nps.gov/anti/learn/historyculture/casualties .htm.

———. "Tour Stop 4—The Cornfield." Antietam. National Park Service, last updated September 15, 2020. https://www.nps.gov/anti/ learn/photosmultimedia/tour-stop-4.htm.

Neville, Leigh. *Modern Sniper*. Oxford: Osprey, 2016.

New York Times. "Brady's Photographs; Pictures of the Dead at Antietam." October 20, 1862. https://www.nytimes.com/1862/10/20/ archives/bradys-photographs-pictures-of-the-dead-at-antietam .html.

Nichols, Edward J. *Towards Gettysburg: A Biography of General John F. Reynolds*. [Philadelphia]: Pennsylvania State University Press, 1958.

Nosworthy, Brent. *The Bloody Crucible of Courage: Fighting Methods and Combat Experience of the Civil War*. New York: Carroll & Graf, 2003.

Oates, William C., and Frank A. Haskell. *Gettysburg: Lt. Frank A. Haskell, U.S.A., and Col. William C. Oates, C.S.A.* Edited and introduction by Glenn W. LaFantasie, edited by Paul Andrew Hutton. New York: Bantam Books, 1992.

O'Reilly, Francis Augustín. *The Fredericksburg Campaign: Winter War on the Rappahannock*. Baton Rouge: Louisiana State University Press, 2003.

Palencia, Cavodonga, Amaya Castro, Dario Giaiotti, Fulvio Stel, Freddy Vinet, and Roberto Fraile. "Hailpad-Based Research: A Bibliometric Review." *Atmospheric Research* 93, nos. 1–3 (2009): 664–670.

Patriotic Daughters of Lancaster. *Hospital Scenes after the Battle of Gettysburg, July, 1863*. [Lancaster, PA]: Daily Inquirer Steam Job Print, 1864.

Peel, Nicholas. *The Lost Story: The Civil War Diaries of a Country Gentleman*. New York, Lincoln, and Shanghai: Writers Club Press/iUniverse, 2001.

Pelger, Martin. *Sharpshooting Rifles of the American Civil War: Colt, Sharps, Spencer and Whitworth*. Illustrated by Johnny Shumate and Alan Gilliland. London: Osprey, 2017.

———. *Sniper: A History of the US Marksman*. Oxford and New York: Osprey, 2009.

Pengelly, Martin. "My Guilty Pleasure: *Gettysburg*." *The Guardian*, March 21, 2014. https://www.theguardian.com/film/filmblog/2014/mar/21/my-guilty-pleasure-gettysburg-jeff-daniels-civil-war.

Pfanz, Harry W. *Gettysburg: The First Day*. Chapel Hill: University of North Carolina Press, 2011.

Plaster, John L. *Sharpshooting in the American Civil War*. Boulder, CO: Paladin Press, 2009.

Rable, Garry W. *The Fredericksburg Campaign: Decision on the Rappahannock*. Chapel Hill: University of North Carolina Press, 2008.

Ray, Fred L. "The Killing of Uncle John." *Historynet.com*, January 24, 2019. https://www.historynet.com/the-killing-of-uncle-john.htm.

———. *Shock Troops of the Confederacy: The Sharpshooter Battalions of the Army of Northern Virginia*. Asheville, NC: CFS Press, 2006.

Reid, Richard J. *Stones River Ran Red*. Owensboro, KY: Commercial Print Co., 1992.

Risjord, Norman K. *The Civil War Generation*. Lanham, MD: Rowman & Littlefield, 2002.

Robertson, James I., Jr. *The Untold Civil War: Exploring the Human Side of War*. Edited by Neil Kagan. Washington, DC: National Geographic, 2011.

Robinson, Carole. "Battle of Franklin: The Death of an Army." *Williamson Herald*, November 29, 2016. http://www.williamsonherald.com/news/battle-of-franklin---the-death-of-an-army/article_a567f6ef-9c85-5580-bc32-1c3e172bbe8e.html.

Sanders, Michael. *More Strange Tales of the Civil War*. Shippensburg, PA: Burd Street Press, 2000.

Santayana, George. *Reason in Common Sense*. Vol. 1 in The *Life of Reason: Or, The Phases of Human Progress*. London: Constable, 1905.

Sears, Stephen W. "The American Civil War and the Origins of Modern Warfare." *American Heritage* 41, no. 2 (March 1990). https://www.americanheritage.com/american-civil-war-and-origins-modern-warfare.

———. *Gettysburg*. Boston: Houghton Mifflin, 2003.

———. *Landscape Turned Red: The Battle of Antietam*. New Haven, CT: Ticknor and Fields, 1983.

Shaara, Michael. *The Killer Angels: A Novel about the Four Days of Gettysburg*. New York: McKay, 1974.

Sheckler Finch, Jackie. *Insiders' Guide to Nashville*. Guilford, CT: Morris Book Publishing, 2009.

Simmers, William, and Paul Bachschmid. *Ten Months with the 153rd Pennsylvania Volunteers*. Easton: D. H. Neiman, 1863.

Smith, Gene. "The Destruction of Fighting Joe Hooker." *American Heritage* 44, no. 6 (October 1993). https://www.americanheritage.com/destruction-fighting-joe-hooker-0.

Smith, Michael Thomas. *The 1864 Franklin-Nashville Campaign: The Finishing Stroke*. Santa Barbara, CA: Praeger, 2014.

Smith, Stephen. "Battle of Gettysburg Day 3: A 'Do-or-Die Moment.'" CBS News, July 3, 2013. https://www.cbsnews.com/news/battle-of-gettysburg-day-3-a-do-or-die-moment/.

Smucker, Samuel M. *The History of the Civil War in the United States*. Philadelphia: Jones Brothers, 1865.

Sprenger, George F. *Concise History of the Camp and Field Life of the 122d Regiment, Penn'a Volunteers: Compiled from Notes, Sketches, Facts and Incidents*. Lancaster, PA: New Era Steam Book Print, 1885.

Steplyk, Jonathan M. *Fighting Means Killing: Civil War Soldiers and the Nature of Combat*. Lawrence: University Press of Kansas, 2018.

Stevens, John W. *Reminiscences of the Civil War*. Hillsboro: Hillsboro Mirror Print, 1902.

Strong, Josiah. "The Teacher: Studies in the Gospel of the Kingdom; The Perils of Peace." *The Homiletic Review* 58 (July–December 1909): 211–18.

Stronge, Charles. *Kill Shot: The Deadliest Snipers of All Time*. Berkeley, CA: Ulysses Press, 2011.

Swank, Mark, and Dreama J. Swank. *Maryland in the Civil War*. Chicago: Arcadia, 2013.

Tate (website). "Realism." Accessed June 22, 2020. https://www.tate.org.uk/art/art-terms/r/realism.

Tilberg, Frederick. *Antietam National Battlefield Site, Maryland.* US National Park Service Historical Handbook Series, vol. 31. Washington, DC: [US Government Printing Office], 1961.

Travel Channel. "The Ghosts of Gettysburg." Accessed April 5, 2021. https://www.travelchannel.com/interests/history/articles/ghosts-of-gettysburg.

Tucker, Glenn. *High Tide at Gettysburg: The Campaign in Pennsylvania.* Indianapolis: Bobbs-Merrill, 1958.

von Clausewitz, Carl. *Vom Kriege* (*On War*). Berlin: Dümmlers Verlag, 1832.

W. Britain (website). "The Art of Don Troiani." Accessed June 4, 2020. https://www.wbritain.com/the-art-of-don-troiani.

Ward, David A. *The 96th Pennsylvania Volunteers in the Civil War.* Foreword by Edwin C. Bearss. Jefferson, NC: McFarland, 2018.

Washington Post. "Faces of Great Men: An Endeavor to Establish a Gallery of Prints in this City." December 18, 1889.

Watkins, Samuel R. *"Co. Aytch": Maury Grays, First Tennessee Regiment; or, A Side Show of the Big Show.* Chattanooga, TN: Times Printing Company, 1900.

Weaver, Mark. "Whitworth Rifle." January 22, 2019. *American Civil War Story.* http://www.americancivilwarstory.com/whitworth-rifle.html.

West, Mike. "Stones River: A Bitter Night Ends Walk to Gates of Hell." *Murfeesboro Post*, March 9, 2008. Available at http://rutherfordtn history.org/stones-river-a-bitter-night-ends-walk-to-gates-of-hell/.

Wheeler, Linda. "Union Soldier's Remains Found at Antietam." *A House Divided* (blog), December 28, 2008. http://voices.washingtonpost .com/house-divided/2008/12/a_union_soldier_found_buried_a .html.

White, Ronald C. *American Ulysses: A Life of Ulysses S. Grant.* New York: Random House, 2017.

Wortman, Marc. *The Bonfire: The Siege and Burning of Atlanta.* New York: PublicAffairs, 2009.

Wright, Mike. *What They Didn't Teach You about the Civil War.* Novato, CA: Presidio Press, 1996.

Zen, E-an, and Alta Sharon Walker. *Rocks and War: Geology and the Civil War Campaign of Second Manassas*. Shippensburg, PA: White Mane Books, 2000.

Zwick, Edward, dir. *Glory*. Produced by Freddie Fields Productions. Burbank, CA: TriStar Pictures, 1989.

Index

About the Author

Scott Hippensteel is associate professor of earth sciences at the University of North Carolina at Charlotte, where he focuses on coastal geology, geoarchaeology, and environmental micropaleontology. His early research involved the *H. L. Hunley*, the famous Confederate submarine, and used microfossils to interpret that great historical artifact. His previous work includes *Rocks and Rifles: The Influence of Geology on Combat and Tactics during the American Civil War* (2018) and more than thirty peer-reviewed journal publications. A native of Mechanicsburg, Pennsylvania, Hippensteel holds graduate degrees from the University of Delaware. He lives in Charlotte, North Carolina.